VILLAGE DEVELOPMENT IN NORTH-EAST INDIA

About the Editor

Komol Singha (1972) is a faculty in Economics. St. Joseph's College, Jakhama, Nagaland. He is specialized in Development Economics, and at present actively involved in the development of Hill Tribal Village Economy.

His research interests include the study of Human Resource Development and Social System in Economic Development. He has published a good number of research papers in journals of repute. Also, he has participated in many National and International seminars.

Village Development In North-East India

(New Approaches)

Edited by
Komol Singha

CONCEPT PUBLISHING COMPANY, NEW DELHI-110059

Cataloging in Publication Data—DK
Courtesy: D.K. Agencies (P) Ltd. <docinfo@dkagencies.com>

National Seminar on Development of Hill Tribal Villages in North-east India (2007 : Jakhama, India)
Village development in North-east India : new approaches / edited by Komol Singha.
p. cm.
Papers presented at the National Seminar on Development of Hill Tribal Villages in North-east India, held at Jakhama during 14-15 September 2007.
Includes bibliographical references.
Includes index.
ISBN 13: 9788180695919
ISBN 10: 8180695913

1. Rural development—India, Northeastern—Congresses. 2. Tribes—India, Northeastern—Economic conditions—Congresses. 3. Education—India, Northeastern—Congresses. 4. Infrastructure (Economics)—India, Northeastern-Congresses. 5. Microfinance—India, Northeastern—Congresses. 6. Agriculture—Economic aspects—India, Northeastern—Congresses. I. Singha, Komol, 1972- II. Title.

DDC 307.141 209 541 22

ISBN-13: 978-81-8069-591-9
ISBN-10: 81-8069-591-3

First Published 2009

Published and Printed by
Ashok Kumar Mittal
Concept Publishing Company
A/15-16, Commercial Block, Mohan Garden
New Delhi-110059 (INDIA)

Phones : 25351460, 25351794
Fax : 091-11-25357109
Email : publishing@conceptpub.com

FOREWORD

I am very happy to write the foreword on the compendium on "Village Development in North East India (New Approaches)" by Shri Komol Singha, Lecturer, St. Joseph's College, Jakhama, Nagaland, an affiliated college of Nagaland University.

I had the privilege to inaugurate the National Seminar on "Development of Hill Tribal Villages in North East India" held on 14th–15th September 2007 at St. Joseph's College, Jakhama. The St. Joseph's College is one of our premier affiliated institutions which has been accredited by NAAC. I always admired the great efforts put by Faculty and Principal of St. Joseph's College, Jakhama to enlighten the students in order to make them a very good human being.

The topic chosen is very relevant as the whole of North East has a very interesting history where the unit of development has been the village. Interestingly, the villages though large in number but evolved independently in the true sense of word of sustainable development and sustainable life styles. The model has been so successful that even today we are seeing tremendous agricultural growth of more than 10 per cent unlike the rest of India which is only 2 per cent. When the rest of India abandoned the agricultural sector and moved into industrial age and now ICT age leaving behind nearly 70 per cent of the farmers not having the benefit of even normal livelihood, the North East has shown the model to the country. It is in this context that this book assumes greater importance so that others can re-look into this model and appreciate and compare organic farming *versus* green revolution. I am sure; anybody who will read through this book will appreciate the importance of village as a fundamental unit of life for human beings capable of independent existence just like a cell being the unit of life. It should further be emphasized that in the state of Nagaland the concept of Village Development Council and Communitization is bringing out a model of growth unlike the rest of India. One has to be appreciative of the reality that there is no begging in the state of Nagaland, thanks to the Village Council as well as each tribe and village maintaining its brand identity.

I have no doubt that anybody who will have the opportunity to lay hands on this book will immensely benefit not only intellectually but appreciate that our fore-fathers had wisdom whereas today we have only information which we are not able to convert into knowledge and wisdom.

Prof. K. Kannan

Kohima

Vice-Chancellor
Nagaland University

PREFACE

India's North-eastern Region consists of eight states and it is a 'mixed bag' of several ethnic groups. 200 out of the 635 tribal groups in the country most of the mongoloid stock are found here. It covers an area of approximately 262500 sq. km., i.e., 8 per cent of the total area of the country. Its population is about 39 million, i.e., 3.9 per cent of the country's total population. Around three-fourth of the North-East is covered by hilly terrain and majority of the people (around 85 per cent) live in villages, in poverty in the midst of abundant resources.

So, the development of villages has become the need of the hour, especially the hill villages in North-East India. This volume tries to explore ways and means which directly or indirectly can help in remodelling the hill village economy. However, it goes beyond the conventional development models; it focuses also on social, political, and other aspects of development.

Most of the essays in this volume were presented at a National Seminar on "Development of Hill Tribal Villages in North-East India" held on 14–15 September 2007 at St. Joseph's College, Jakhama, Nagaland with financial assistance from the ICSSR, New Delhi. A few papers were contributed by other scholars in the field. I am grateful to all the contributors.

I am grateful to the Indian Council of Social Science Research (ICSSR), New Delhi especially Mrs. Ramesh Madan (Asstt. Director, ICSSR, New Delhi) for the financial assistance in organizing this National Seminar. A few financial help was also extended by the Nagaland University and State Bank of India, Jakhama Branch. For which, I would like to thank Prof. K. Kannan, the Vice Chancellor, Nagaland University and Mr. Besi Sol Chalai, Branch Manager, SBI, Jakhama Branch respectively. My special thanks go to Isaac Padinjarekuttu, the Principal of St. Joseph's College and the

Management and the Department of Economics for their help in organizing the Seminar and in bringing out this volume. Lastly, but not the least, I would like to thank Mr. Ashok Kumar Mittal of Concept Publishing Company, New Delhi for taking keen interest in bringing out this volume.

March 3, 2008 **Komol Singha**

CONTENTS

SECTION III

INFRASTRUCTURE AND BIO-RESOURCE CONSERVATION

SECTION IV

MICRO FINANCE AND RURAL DEVELOPMENT

SECTION V

FOOD AND AGRICULTURE

LIST OF CONTRIBUTORS

Bhaduri, Saradindu, Asstt. Professor (Economics), Centre for Studies in Science Policy, Jawaharlal Nehru University, New Delhi.

Basantia, T.K., Faculty Member, Department of Education, Assam University, Silchar.

Chandrasekhar, K., Environmental Consultant, OK International, Bangalore.

Chhuanawma, L.H., Sr. Lecturer, Department of Political Science Pachhunga University College *(A Constituent College of Mizoram University),* Aizawl, Mizoram.

Deka, P.K., Reader and Head, Department of Commerce, Nagaland University, Kohima, Nagaland.

Dutta, P.C., Head and Sr. Lecturer, Department of Statistics, S. S. College, Hailakandi, Assam.

Debnath, A., Faculty Member, Department of Economics, S. S. College, Hailakandi, Assam.

Dutta, Subhendu, Sr. Lecturer, Department of Economics, Public College of Commerce, Dimapur, Nagaland.

Debnath, Chandan, Faculty Member, Department of Commerce Dimapur Government College, Dimapur, Nagaland.

Jamir, B.K., Reader, Department of Economics, Nagaland University, Nagaland.

Kabra, K.C., Sr. Lecturer, Department of Commerce, North Eastern Hill University, Shillong, Meghalaya.

Kikhi, Kedilezo, Faculty Member, Department of Sociology, Tezpur University, Assam.

Mitra, Amitava, Prof. and Head, Department of Economics, Rajiv Gandhi University, Rono Hills, Arunachal Pradesh.

Mandal, R.K., Faculty Member, Department of Economics, D.N. Government College, Itanagar, Arunachal Pradesh.

Mathew, Saju, Head, Department of Economics, St. Joseph's College, Jakhama, Nagaland.

Patikar, Gautam, Faculty Member, Department of Commerce, Nagaland University, Kohima, Nagaland.

Sahoo, U.K., Faculty Member, Department of Forestry, Mizoram University, Aizawl.

Singh, Bhartendu, Faculty Member, Department of Commerce, Pachhunga University College, *(A Constituent College of Mizoram University),* Aizawl, Mizoram.

Singh, A.I., Sr. Lecturer, Department of Economics, D.N. Government College, Itanagar, Arunachal Pradesh.

Singh, A.R., Associate Prof. Department of Commerce, Manipur University, Imphal.

Singh, W.C., Reader, Department of MIMS, Manipur University, Imphal, Manipur.

Singha, Komol, Sr. Lecturer, Department of Economics. St. Joseph's College, Jakhama, Nagaland.

Singha, R.K.P.G., Head, Department of Commerce, Pachhunga University College *(A Constituent College of Mizoram University),* Aizawl, Mizoram.

Thangjam, Robert, Faculty Member, Department of Biotechnology, Mizoram University, Aizawl.

INTRODUCTION

KOMOL SINGHA

"I would say that if the village perishes India will perish too. India will be no more India. Her own mission in the world will get lost. The revival of the village is possible only when it is no more exploited. Industrialization on a mass scale will necessarily lead to passive or active exploitation of the villagers as the problems of competition and marketing come in. Therefore we have to concentrate on the village being self-contained, manufacturing mainly for use. Provided this character of the village industry is maintained, there would be no objection to villagers using even the modern machines and tools that they can make and can afford to use. Only they should not be used as a means of exploitation of others."

—Mahatma Gandhi

Majority of the world's poor live in villages. Basic necessities of life of these people are much lower than that of the people living in the town or city. Generally, they are isolated from the mainstream and are identified as an independent economic unit. For example (Taylor and Adelman, 1996: 1), their production and consumption activities take place within small units, usually households. There are some difficulties in defining a village. The village in England or even in Lebanon and the village in the India-Pakistan-Bangladesh sub-continent must mean different things in terms of physical, economic and social structure (Haq, 1973: 2). Definitely, a hill village is different from the village in the valley. So, the tribal hill village, particularly in the North-East is quite different from other villages in the country. They have some uniqueness in their structure, socially, culturally, and economically. At the same time villages have something in common too.

There are some common characteristics of a village:

1. Remoteness.
2. Settled together in a particular area.
3. Settled by people of the same origin or indigenous people.
4. Their main occupation is agriculture or related primary activities.
5. Low rate of literacy.
6. Prevalence of traditional culture, belief, orthodoxy and conservatism.
7. Backwardness of infrastructure.
8. Mainly consisting of only one caste/community.
9. Commonality of some economic behaviours.

Thus there are a few fundamental features common to all villages. Though they have settled in different places, they have some common features primarily in economic structure, basic physical infrastructure, and more importantly village norms. Keeping this in mind, this volume is a modest attempt to explore the problems and prospects in developing the village economy.

Village Social Structure

A village or a *gaon* (UP), *Basti* (Assam, Meghalaya, Nagaland), *gram* (Tripura, Bengal), *Khung-gang* (Manipur), is not just a physical space or a settlement of a group of people. Social life here is organized along definite ritual and secular principles, such as those of caste, kinship, economy, politics, and religion. The physical character of the village is influenced by its dynamic interaction with these principles and patterns of settlement (Madan, 2004: 13). A village could be clustered or dispersed in its settlement pattern. Every village has a definite pattern of social relations based on traditional principles of kinship and marriage, such as those of village exogamy. These relations extend the interactive network and social space of a village well beyond its boundaries into neighbouring regions (As quoted by Madan 2004: 17). The bond of kinship (real or fictive) and marriage govern not only intra-familial interaction but also that between larger kin groups, often across village boundaries. The typical rural family in rural India is the patriarchal (or it is a matrilineal in the case of

Meghalaya) joint family the members of which, even when divided into number of households, live together in the village and own property in common (community land especially in the hill villages in NE). More importantly, unlike in other parts of India predominantly ruled by orthodox Hindu caste system or hierarchy in the hill villages of NE region, community land plays a vital role in shaping their economy. The economic system of these communities revolves around their social structure. It is the village law or social norm which binds the people of a village. Traditional norms and beliefs deeply rooted in people's minds are more difficult to change than formal laws so that they are likely to become more fetters on modern economic development (see North, 1994, as quoted by Singha in this volume). Trust is the social capital, which can reduce social transaction cost. community institutions and organizations are inflexible and fail to adjust to changing economic needs. Traditional norms and conventions in communities have been formed slowly over many, many years (Hayami and Godo, 2006: 346).

Approximately 70 per cent of the people in the NE live in hill villages, and economically they are far behind the national level. So, the development of the villages has become the need of the hour. Therefore, while framing development policies for the villages, only conventional approaches cannot break the vicious circle of poverty, we have to incorporate alternative views (Long, 1996: Sillitoe, 2002 as is quoted by Singha later in this volume) too. Any development policy or programme is to be tuned to the local environment without much disturbing traditional system, and it should be need-based (Beardsley, R.K. *et al.,* 1959).

Development Policy

The term 'Development' is generally used in connection with the poor or underdeveloped regions. Development differs from economic growth in that it pays attention to the conditions of production, for example, the environments affected by economic activity, and to the social consequences, for example, income distribution and human welfare. Stemming from Enlightenment notions of the use of the modern, scientific mind for improving existence, development entails human emancipation in two senses: liberation from the vicissitudes of nature through advanced technology and self-emancipation, that is, control over social relations, conscious control over the conditions under which human nature is formed. In both senses, development entails economic, social, and cultural progress, including, in the latter sense, finer ethical ideals and higher moral values. Development means improvement in a complex of linked natural, economic, social, cultural, and political conditions. Developmentalism is the belief in the viability and desirability of this kind of economic progress (Peet *et al.*, 2005: 1). A resource-rich region can be developed only when it is exploited efficiently in right direction. The NE region especially the hill areas are poor in the midst of abundant resources due to non-exploitation, under-exploitation or non-utilization of resources.

For rural development to succeed in a global environment, three things are essential: human capital, physical infrastructure, and adequate financing. For (Rainey, D.V. *et al.*, 2003), human capital and infrastructure (public capital) are critical components of sustainable community development. However, they feel that the third element should be social capital. Communities that have thriving social networks and institutions and good human capital will have adequate financing as well. Another component, which is very much talked about today is social capital. Importance of infrastructure in the development of village economy is accepted by everyone, but the equally important factor which is not noticed by everyone is the social norms.

As for improvement of social capital, T.W. Schultz's research suggests that economic growth is largely the result of investment in the human capital. He further argues that increase in the capital income-ratio is largely due to human capital development, not material capital (i.e., reproducible, non-human capital), which was originally thought to account for all increases in income and subsequent economic growth. Investment in human knowledge and skill is the critical determinant of economic growth and is necessary if regions lacking human capabilities ever expect to attract and fully benefit from infusions of new capital. No matter how powerful the computer hardware or how user-friendly the software, most functions provided by computers still require hands-on human contact to be productive*.

---

* As quoted by Komol Singha later in this volume.

Chapter Scheme

The primary objective of this volume is to provide readers with case studies and empirical insights into the structure of village economy. This volume is broadly divided into five sections and contains seventeen essays on various aspects of development in the village economy especially hill villages in North-East India.

Section I of the volume concentrates on social systems and the role of the community in the transition of rigid village economy. This section contains four essays concerning people's/community's role in sustainable hill village development. This section is titled as "Social Norms, Institutions, and Participation".

Chandrasekhar and Bhaduri try to analyze the ongoing process of economic transformation in the region of Indian Trans-Himalaya. By using the theories of Social Cognitive Learning (mindset of the people/beliefs and values, beyond the conventional factors like investment) used in evolutionary economic research, they throw light on the direction and speed of socio-economic transformation, and thereby help in developing an effective policy framework in the Indian Trans-Himalayan region. The penetration of individualistic economic profit-centric behaviour (changing from cattle grazing to road construction job) in two hill villages under Spiti district of Himachal Pradesh, breaks the vicious circle of poverty in the community. Their involvement in economic profit generating activities (dis-embedded from social needs) helped in legitimizing such activities in the community, and encouraged common people to participate in developmental projects in large number without fearing social sanction and opposition.

Debnath and Singha in their essays "*People's Participation...*" and "*The Role of Social Capital...*" respectively focus on community's/people's role in the development of rigid traditional tribal society. Debnath highlights that development is not a one-way traffic. Only government intervention without people's participation cannot bring about development in the collectivist society like that of the Nagas. Singha tries to highlight the importance of Social Capital in the process of economic development in a strongly locked-in tribal community. He further suggests that quality education takes care of negative social capital (social systems which do not suit to bring about economic development).

The essay of Singh and Mitra "*Complexities of Commons and Rural Livelihoods....... in Arunachal Pradesh*" highlights the urgent need of formation of policy for sustainable management of Common Property Resources (CPRs) particularly forest by strengthening the age-old traditional village system headed by the village Chief. Like Singha's paper above, this paper also focuses on the role of village norms for effective management of CPRs. They suggest that if common resources are not managed properly through a regulation by the village institution in time, it will be trapped in the 'Tragedy of Commons' very shortly.

Section II of the volume concentrates mainly on education and it is categorized as 'Human Resource Development'. This section contains three essays on education in the context of the Northeastern region.

T.K. Basantia's and R.K.P.G. Singha's joint paper '*Education and Development of NE Tribal Region.....*' identifies the role of education in the development of the region. They say that the root cause of underdevelopment of the North-East particularly in the hill regions does not lie only with its socio-cultural and geographical features alone, but also with its level of education. The light of education has not reached properly in the hill areas of the North-East where thousands of tribal people live. They suggest that if these regions want to develop, there is a need for properly trained, skilful and proficient man power. On the other hand, the human resource or man power efficiency can be developed with the help of a good and well developed educational system. So, they say that the relationship between the two (education and development) is a "Seed-corn' relation. More emphasis should be given to higher and technical education and a triangular relationship ought to be established among governments, the general public and the educational system in an effective manner.

Kedilezo Kikhi's essay "*Educated Youth in Nagaland: Aspirations vis-à-vis Employment Opportunities*" highlights the demand and supply of job opportunities in the state. There is a great discrepancy between the occupational preferences and the occupational expectations. Most educated job seekers do not like the hard work, but they want sedentary jobs, and are inclined towards office work. Their first preference is relatively for white-collar jobs. This is the gloomy picture of job seekers in Nagaland at present.

Subhendu Dutta in his essay "Human Development in Nagaland: An Inter-District Analysis" tries to analyse the human development level among the districts in Nagaland. With the help of 'Deprivation method' he finds that, though Dimapur emerged top in HDI value in the state, no district has developed as per HDI criteria.

Section III of the volume concentrates on physical infrastructure and technology, which are prerequisites for any development activities especially, village economy. This section is titled as "Infrastructure and Bio-resource Conservation". This section contains three essays, two essays on physical infrastructure and the third one is on Bio-resource respectively. Poor infrastructure is also one of the common difficulties faced by the village community.

The first essay of this section, '*Infrastructure Development in NEI with Special Reference to Mizoram*' jointly contributed by R.K.P.G. Singha and K.C. Kabra tries to highlight the importance of physical infrastructure in the development of NE region particularly Mizoram. It further tries to depict the problems confronting in the development of infrastructure in the state. Mizoram is the most developed state in the North-East but on the other hand, it is the poorest in terms of physical infrastructure particularly road transport. There is only one National Highway No. 54, which is the lifeline of the state. Further they analyse that if the road transport develops, it could be one of the most developed states in the country.

In the second essay contributed jointly by Gautam Patikar and P.K. Deka entitled '*Existing Scenario of Infrastructure in NEI*" basically depicts the present status of physical infrastructure, which is again the key factor in the economic development in the region. The present scenario of infrastructure in North East India is unsatisfactory excepting the level of education. There are several problems that retard infrastructure development. The problems are social, economic or political in nature. The geographical location is also a hurdle for development of infrastructure. On the other hand, the region is rich in natural resources, ideal for the growth of industries. As a result, there is imperative need for basic infrastructure on a more liberal scale so as to ensure smooth and sustained industrial growth. As a measure to come out of this bottleneck, toll free roads and express highways, called the 'Malayasian Model' is suggested.

Robert and Sahoo in their essay entitled '*Application of biotechnological tools for the conservation...bio-resources in the*

Indo-Burma biodiversity hotspot' speak about the importance of conservation of bio-resources. According to their findings, the Indo-Burma hotspot was one of the first places where humans developed agriculture, and has a long history of using fire to clear land for agriculture and other needs. The richness of plant and animal diversity in developing countries is a major asset in agricultural development and, therefore, the conservation of such resources is fundamental to the progress of biotechnology.

Section IV of this volume contains three essays on Micro Finance and Rural Development. Two essays focus on the role of small credit in rural development and the third essay tries to depict the socio-economic condition of rural area in Assam. This section is categorized as 'Micro Finance and Rural Development'.

Rajmani Singh in his essay '*Micro Finance and its Impact on Rural Development of Manipur*' shows the benefits of Micro Finance in the rural areas of Manipur. To uplift the rural poor, the Rural Development Organization (RDO), Manipur has initiated a Bangladesh Grameen Bank model institution called *Loyalam Bank Project* (LBP) with financial assistance from NABARD under a Revolving Fund Assistance (RFA) since 1992 in Manipur with the support from Grameen Trust, Bangladesh, NABARD and Rashtriya Mahila Kosh. He tries to replicate the LBP model to other parts of the hill villages. As a result the International Fund for Agricultural Development (IFAD) has started the North Eastern Region Community Resource Management Project (NERCRMP) in the Ukhrul district of Manipur. Altogether 83 project villages were covered out of the 230 villages in the district. Further the 83 project villages were managed and controlled by fewer than 128 Natural Resource Management Groups (NaRM-G) and 502 SHGs with financial assistance from the IFAD. The same project was also started simultaneously in the Senapati district covering 108 project villages with 427 SHGs and 148 Natural Resource Management Groups with financial assistance from the IFAD. Construction of roads, community halls, safe drinking water facilities, agro processing units, plantation of banana, orange, pineapple, passion fruit, piggery, fishery , etc. are some of the important activities undertaken by the SHGs and NaRM-G with financial assistance from the IFAD.

Similarly, W.C. Singh in his essay "Micro Finance and Economic Backwardness" also tries to highlight the role of micro finance, micro enterprises and self help groups in bringing up the poor communities in the country. He tries to replicate the experience of micro credit system in Manipur especially in the hill villages. Though micro finance plays a significant role in rural development, he shows apprehension about the sustainability in the region. It is still in a nascent stage. The SHG-Bank linkage programme and RGVN's Credit Support Programme failed to stimulate growth of micro finance activities in Manipur as compared to other parts of the country.

The third essay "Socio-Economic Development in Rural Assam: Problems and Prospects" contributed jointly by P.C. Dutta and A. Debnath depicts the Socio-Economic conditions of Assam's village areas. Assam is broadly divided into valleys, namely Brahmaputra and Barak valleys. Apart from insurgency related difficulties, the region is being handicapped in the growth process by two forces. They are regular and prolonged flood over three months every year on the one hand, and influx of Bangladeshis on the other. This essay concentrates more on the problems faced by the villagers in the Barak valley bordering to Bangladesh.

Section V concentrates on Food and Agriculture, which are primary activities in the region. Agriculture is the main occupation of the village community. The study of village economy without agriculture is incomplete and irrelevant.

Kilangla Jamir in her essay 'Agricultural Development in Nagaland......' tries to highlight the pressures to adopt more intensive cultivation and commercialization of agriculture in the state. It is probably due to increase in population and shrinking of white collar jobs in the state. Her study shows the changes in cropping pattern, transition from traditional practices in agriculture and the commercialization of the agricultural sector, and the problems faced by the farmers. She further demonstrates that the slow transition is not because of the unwillingness of the farmers to accept new ideas, but due to the lack of infrastructure facilities for the development of the agricultural sector.

R.K. Mandal tries to analyse the role of women in agriculture and takes the inferences from the socio-economic transformation of the Galo community in Arunachal Pradesh. The economic status of women is determined by the role played by them in carrying on economic and non-economic activities in society. The nature and type of economic and non-economic role played by women have undergone continuous transformation in accordance with the changes in socio-economic factors, education levels, technological developments and the changing concepts regarding the extent to which women's contribution is considered desirable and necessary. He finds that the relationship between the percentage of women engaged in agriculture and their age is positive. Despite their hard work, the status of the women in society is lower than that of their male counterparts. He also suggests that the 'Educational System' has to play an important role in this direction, as it is the only medium through which the image of a girl-child as second class citizen can be removed.

Bamboo flowering is one of the rare events and it leads to famine in the hill economy. The essay jointly contributed by R.K.P.G. Singha, Chhuanawṃa, and Bhartendu Singh entitled 'Bamboo Flowering and its Impact on Socio-Economic Life of the Tribal People in Mizoram' attempts to portray the economic impact of Bamboo Flowering in the state. Mizoram is one of the biggest bamboo producing states in the country. Bamboo flowering is a natural phenomenon and it occurs from time to time generally after every 40–50 years. This flower is the best food for rodents (Rats) and helps in multiplying their (Rodent) number. When the flowering is over, rodents find difficult to find food and attack paddy in the field and even in the granaries. This results in mass destruction of food crops and leads to famine in the state. They try to highlight the role of the government in handling the situation and suggest that Bamboo Flowering is not to be taken as a bad omen as perceived by the tribal people; rather the people should accept the reality of such situation in distant future and prepare themselves to face it.

And finally, Singha and Mathew in their essay entitled 'Transition of Agriculture in the Hill Villages of NE India: A Micro Study' focus on the need of commercialization of agriculture in the hill villages. Development of an agrarian village is possible only when commercialization of agriculture is intensified. Due to lack of basic infrastructures like transportation, marketing, credit, and cold storage facilities etc., very often hill village farmers are discouraged from cultivating of cash crops. Over production and under-pricing of hill village agricultural products are very common in the region. As a remedy, they recommend the method of 'Mass Production' and 'Contract Farming System' to protect prices and minimize risk.

Thus, this volume has touched upon almost all the components needed for the development of villages. Though the contributors have given insights and their approaches differ, all of them have highlighted the role of the people, or people's involvement in the development process of villages. According to Santhanam (1984), there are several possible ways of involving people in development projects, based on various case studies. They include (a) Convincing the people about the importance of the programme; (b) Need for planning with the people; (c) Need to consult local organizations before launching a programme; (d) Inviting the villagers for discussion before introducing a programme; and (e) Taking into consideration the felt needs of the people. So, instead of centralization, the concept of people's participation advocates decentralization and that too, not from one level of government to another, but from the bureaucratic level to that of people through a democratic process.

It is hoped that this volume will contribute positively to plan and execute projects and programmes for the development of North-East especially in the hill tribal villages, one of the resource-rich but underdeveloped region of the country.

REFERENCES

Beardsley, R.K. et al. (1959), *Village Japan.* The University of Chicago Press.

Hayami, Y. and Godo, Y. (2006), *Development Economics—From the Poverty to the Wealth of Nations,* Oxford University Press.

Haq, M.N. (1973), *Village Development in Bangladesh: A Study of Monagram Village,* Bangladesh Academy for Rural Development, Comila, Bangladesh.

Madan, V. (2004), *The Village in India,* (ed.). Oxford University Press.

Peet, R. and Hartwick, E. (2005), *Theories of Development,* Rawat Publication.

Rainey, D.V. *et al.* (2003), "Essential Forms of Capital for Sustainable Community Development", *American Journal of Agriculture and Economics,* August.

Singha, Komol. (2003), "Economy of a Tribal Village", unpublished Ph.D. manuscript.

Taylor, J.E. and Adelman, I. (1996), *Village Economies,* Cambridge University Press.

SECTION I

Social Norms, Institutions and Participations

1

VICARIOUSLY LEARNING TO TRANSFORM

An Evolutionary Tale of Economic Development in Indian Trans-Himalaya

K. CHANDRASEKHAR and SARADINDU BHADURI

It may not be wrong to suggest that viewing economic development as a process of transformation owes its intellectual origin to Joseph Schumpeter, who, perhaps, lived and died with a quest to identify the various endogenous forces behind economic change and transformation. He discarded the use of the Walrasian framework to explain economic change and development by pointing out that if economic development involves transformation of "socio-economic norms", any economic theory of development ought to identify endogenous forces behind this process, rather than explaining them away (Schumpeter, 2005). However, the framework laid down by him, purportedly, had two shortcomings: (1) It saw the "private innovating entrepreneurs" as the only agents of such economic change (Sweezy, 1943), and, thereby, (2) *innovations* in the industrial sector as the sole mechanism through which such changes occur. Many developing countries have traditionally had only a marginal presence of "private sector" and very few "industrial *innovations*" to boast of. As a result, the Schumpeterian theory has been considered inadequate to provide any concrete roadmap for economic development of these countries[1]. Hirschman (1958) also had a similar view of economic development, where he emphasized on generation and acceptance of novelty as a prerequisite for economic development. However, novelty, in his case, is broader based and comprehensive, covering aspects of 'new way of life' rather than technological or organisational novelty. And in doing so he emphasized more on cognitive level factors (mind) than other traditional factors like investment. More specifically, he saw the vicious circle of poverty as an outcome of a vicious circle of mind, which is reluctant to accept novelty. A common thread between these two scholars is, however, their acknowledgement that mere economic factors cannot explain the process of economic development in a satisfactory manner. More specifically, both conjectured that the social and cognitive level factors could hold the key to a rigorous theory of economic development. But, while they identified the problems, they stopped short of providing an analytical framework about the exact process through which such factors might operate and bring about desired changes.

After about 5 decades of experimentation with neoclassical theories (see Adelman 2002 for a review), theories of economic development, perhaps, completes a full circle with the Prebisch lecture by Joseph Stiglitz (1998, 2002), where he reasserted the need for conceptualizing development as an uncertain process of socio-economic transformation, which has to be driven by the intellect of the *insiders*. We argue that such a view requires a comprehensive understanding of how (boundedly rational) economic agents take decisions under uncertainty, and change their behaviour.

The research in evolutionary economics can, indeed, prove to be useful in this regard. In fact, the evolutionary theories possess some natural advantages over their neoclassical counterpart in this regard. Some of these are:

(A) Being more open to inter-disciplinary exchange of ideas, evolutionary theory can accommodate the recent development in the fields of social and behavioural psychologies (for instance, Witt, 2001) and can provide a more realistic explanation for generation and dissemination of novelty in artefacts/technology and human behaviour behind every socio-economic transformation.

(B) Its emphasis on historical and cultural bases of human behaviour can throw crucial insights into the inter-country divergence of growth and development, a question that has puzzled many economists for the last several decades.

Our paper analyses the recent transformation of a traditional mountainous society from a, overwhelmingly, barter economy with socially embedded economic exchanges to an economic system characterized by monetized trade and specialized exchanges. We have taken the example of transformation of their cropping pattern, from traditional food crop to modern cash crops. Understandably, while the market for their traditional food crops was largely internal, the new cash crop has a larger market at the national level. While the argument of relative price change may appear to be the most obvious explanation (Demsetz, 1967; Dahlman, 1980), it loses much of its explanatory power when one understands the complex links that existed between their earlier food crop and various social exchange, health care and other occupational needs. Market price, therefore, does not reveal the actual value of such products. There are instances in other such traditional societies where people have refused to respond to relative price changes in such a situation (Rogers, 1995). Stiglitz (2002) puts the burden of failure of such externally imposed policies on their inability to provide adequate incentive to people "to develop their own capacities...using their own intelligence". Hirschman (1958) further argues that an incentive oriented theory of developmental trajectory often fails to explain the 'real life' trajectories of developing societies due to their inadequate attention to issues of uncertainty involved in such complex process of change. This corroborates the findings from studies on institutional reforms that changing institutions does not always set in a process of change in behaviour in desired directions (Rizzello and Turvani, 2002). All these studies seem to point out the necessity of incorporating appropriate models of analysing the introduction and diffusion of novelty (behaviour or technology) within a system. It is, therefore, important to understand the deep rooted dynamics behind their change in behaviour, which included change in their value system (Norgaard, 1994), and preference pattern.

The paper uses social-cognitive vicarious learning theory framework (Bandura, 1986) to explain this change by analysing the dynamic *triadic* interaction between social-cognitive factors (beliefs, values), behaviour and environment (policy and institutions). In the orthodox view following Demsetz (1967), not only the environment was seen as the all powerful force of change, but the impact of environmental factors on personal factors and behaviour was also seen as automatic and undirectional. The social cognitive theory of vicarious learning, in contrast, argues that such interactions are neither one way nor automatic. Rather, the strength of each dimension varies across individuals, activities and circumstances (see also Rizzello and Turvani, 2000).

A proper understanding of cognitive factors influencing agents and associated learning mechanism, which changes their behaviour, would also help design appropriate development policy tools. Recent years are marked by a trend towards homogenization of policy framework, where simple transfer of policies from 'functioning market economy' to a 'developing market economy' is often recommended (Ensminger, 1996). The analysis of this paper would throw important light on both natures of policies as well as the sequence of their implementations.

The paper is organized in the following manner. The next Section II develops the theoretical framework on social-cognitive vicarious learning and behavioural change, which is essential to understand the process of socio-economic transformation and economic development. In section III we briefly describe various facets of the traditional socio-economic system of the Indian Trans-Himalayan region based on our survey. Section IV analyses the recent transformation of the Trans-Himalayan regions towards market based economic activities and monetised trade as a social-cognitive learning process. Section V summarises and concludes the article.

II
Change and Transformation in the Theory of Economic Development: Incentives to Learning

It has indeed been alleged that the conventional analysis of change and transformation in economic theory, as in Demsetz, 1967, is based on a simplistic notion of relative price change and external shocks (Tversky and Kahneman, 1986), giving inadequate attention to the role of social-cognitive factors. Hirschman (1958) also points out that a theory of incentive based behavioural change does not adequately address the issue of dealing with uncertainties that are associated with such changes. There are also more recent studies arguing that human behaviour does not instantaneously react to a change in external conditions (World Bank, 1996; Stahl, 2000) and economic costs are not the only cost to be reckoned with (Norgaard, 1994). Stahl (2000), instead, argues that historical and cultural factors play an important role in shaping subjective perceptions of costs and benefits, thus, being important determinants of change. Witt (2001) and Mokyr (2001), moreover, argue that change in behaviour and socio-economic transformation depends crucially on how preference for novelty emerges and diffuses in a population.

Among the various studies with a critical view of existing development theory, Norgaard (1994) made a pioneering attempt to analyse the process of modernization and economic change as a co-evolutionary process of policy and value system. In biological sciences, coevolution often refers to the dynamics of evolutionary change of two or more closely interacting species, where the fitness of genetic traits within one species depends crucially on the dominant genetic characteristics of the other (Norgaard, 1994:26). Murmann (2003) also points out that two evolving populations *co-evolve* if, and only if, they both have a *causal* impact on each other's ability to replicate, either by altering the selection criteria or only by changing the replicative capacity in a given selection environment (Murmann, 2003:24). Murmann (2003) also emphasizes on the necessity of having a 'causal link' between co-evolving entities (pp. 23).[2] In a nutshell, a coevolutionary process may be conceptualized as a feedback mechanism. However, being its origin in the biological sciences, such an explanation does not adequately account for factors such as human creativity, intentionality, learning and behavioural variety observed among human beings (Witt, 2003a). One, therefore, must pay explicit attention to cultural and cognitive level factors. An understanding of 'mental models', 'attitude to change', and 'learning capacities', are, therefore, important in this regard.

The concept of mental models (Johnson-Laird, 1983; Denzau and North, 1994) helps us understand why and how humans do not react to an exogenous change in a uniform manner. It emphasizes that due to bounded rationality, humans are not capable of processing all sensory perceptions available to him from the environment. Rather, their mental models allow them to receive and process only a limited set of incoming information. The mental models are thus symbolic (subjective) representations of the environment, and are constructed through diverse experience, observation and (cognitively mediated) learning. More than the *actual* environment, therefore, agents' behaviour is influenced by a *perceived* environment, shaped by prior learning and experience. For the sake of this paper we only concentrate on vicarious observational learning, which constitutes a core of the social learning theory a la Bandura (1986). Vicarious learning emphasises that individuals not only learn from their own experiences but also from observing others, more precisely, role models. Mistakes, trial and error and search costs involved in learning may, thus, often be reduced when we take into account learning by observation, as non-rewarding actions or actions leading to failure will not be repeated by the observer. According to Bandura (1986) observational learning can, potentially, help mental models and behaviour to change faster than predicted by the theories where learning is solely based on individual experiences with problem situations (as in Mantzavinos 2001). It should be emphasized that observational learning is not only limited to simple reproduction (imitation) of an observed behaviour, but it also influences judgment and values of an individual.

Observational learning consists of four different phases, namely, attention, retention, reproduction and motivation. When conceptualised in a strictly linear fashion, attention regulates the "exploration and perception of modelled activities". Retention refers to conversion of transitory experiences into symbolic conceptions used as internal models for response as well as standards for response correction. In the next stage re-production process governs the organisation of constituent skills into a new response pattern, and finally, motivation determines whether the observed behaviour will finally, be put to use (*see* Bandura, 1986:51). Motivation is a cognitive process, which guides the action of an individual, influenced by subjective expectations from an action. Subjective expectation can be an unconscious mechanism influenced by vicarious experiences in the past (Bandura, 1989). In reality, however, such a strictly linear description is often problematic. But, dividing the whole observational learning process into such sub groups helps finding the reasons of failures more effectively. A failure to learn, in this framework, may be the outcome of deficiency in any of these sub-processes.

Importantly, one should also distinguish between the phases of acquisition and performance, since people "do not enact everything they learn" (Bandura, 1986:68). The performance of acquired behaviour crucially depends on the likely incentive associated with performance. The reward observed to be accrued to the model as well as rewards of vicariously learned previous behaviour, both can influence the expectations about likely outcomes and the incentives to perform. When feared a punishment, individuals may acquire, and retain a new behaviour or judgement, without ever performing them. In other words, a successful reproduction crucially depends on reward associated with the observed behaviour with its frequency, existing social norms, and the status of the individuals, whose behaviour is observed. An individual with high status is often regarded as role model, and becomes subject of intense attention by others. A new behaviour by such a model signals a change in the social norm, if that individual also occupies a high authoritative position in a community. A new behaviour by them, therefore, attracts faster diffusion without fearing social opposition. The speed of diffusion will be even faster if the model directly propagates a behavioural change. However, not all behaviours can be learned with equal ease; a high cognitive skill is required to *observe* more subtle specialized behaviour (Bandura, 1986:70).

What is the implication of these learning mechanisms for development process and policy making? In this paper we argue that they explain the determinants and the mechanism behind behavioural change more effectively and, in turn, can prove to be important for better designing of developmental policies by highlighting the triadic interaction between behaviour, personal factors (belief, attitude) and the environmental factors. However, such reciprocal interactions are not simultaneous, and often, there is a time gap between cause and effect. Moreover, as mentioned earlier, the strength of these dimensions are far from being uniform, and vary across individuals, activities and circumstances.

It is widely accepted that to be successful (and to spread), a policy induced behaviour must be adopted by a critical minimum mass of people (Witt, 2003b). Mantzavinos *et al.* (2004) argues that such a phenomenon is described as shared behavioural regularity or shared mental models.[3] As emphasised by Denzau and North (1994), sharing of mental models requires intense communication between people (*see* also Mantzavinos, 2001). Interestingly, however, learning theories in this tradition of new institutional economics predominantly focus on individual experiences with problem situations (See Mantzavinos, 2001: 22–33). Each individual develops his/her mental models by confronting a problem situation separately, which is then communicated within a community to build up the shared mental model. As a result, development of a "shared behavioural regularity" or "shared mental models" is believed to be rather slow (*see* Mantzavinos *et al.,* 2004). It can, however, be argued that a critical mass can be more easily convinced, leading to a faster change in "behavioural regularity", a la Witt (1989), in the presence of observational vicarious learning, especially when such behaviours are promoted by individuals with high social status and acceptability. A high degree of social homogeneity further enhances the speed of diffusion.

III
The Trans-Himalayan Societies: A Survey

Data and Sample

This study is based on a census of two villages in the Spiti district of Himachal Pradesh during the period 1997–2002. The district is situated along the northern Sino-Indian borders of India[4]. Its poor natural resource base and harsh climate were the main reasons why this region was not brought under British-India administration for a long (the Statute of 1873)[5]. Even after Independence, Spiti remained under a system of 'local governance' enjoying a special status under the Article 244, Schedules VI and VII to the Constitution until the year 1966, when it was incorporated into the state of Himachal Pradesh. Historically, the "*Nono*" or local landlords have had large influence on administrative decision making. They also enjoy high social acceptability among local people.[6] They continue to occupy a very special position in this regard and play a crucial role in deciding the suitability of a government policy and the means of its implementation. In fact, almost all forms of governmental interventions are implemented taking feedbacks from these local landlords.

Surveys were carried out in two villages (Lidang and Demul) in the Spiti district through participatory rural appraisal (PRA) during 1997–2002. During this period we took an approach of census method of group discussions and interviews with *all* households (a total of 70 households) and government officials. These interviews were held with open-ended, semi-structured questionnaires. The villagers often feel comfortable with informal discussions in social gatherings rather than time bound formal interviews. The process of data collection, in such situations is contingent upon intense social interaction with the community. Obviously what we perhaps do not get is precise data required for smooth statistical analysis. But, such interactions helped gaining their confidence on the objective of probing questions and offers invaluable insight to the researchers about the socio-economic dynamics of these communities. Information was collected on land and livestock holdings, cropping patterns, land-use (meadows/ pastures), relative area under different crops or crop combination, income generation opportunities and socio-cultural attributes.

The Traditional Link between Production, Exchange and Health Care: The Importance of Barley

A prime characteristic of these societies is, like many other traditional societies, an interlinked system of agriculture and live stock management. Being an agro-pastoral society, local people paid equal importance to agriculture and live stock management. As opposed to a purely pastoral society, the value of livestock was not only measured by the production of milk or meat, but by multiple uses ranging from ploughing field to organic fertiliser used for farming.[7] A very short agricultural season (ranging from 3 to 4 months during summer) often restricts them to cultivating only one major crop, barley. The cultivation of barley is a classic example of social embeddedness of economic behaviours in a traditional society (Polanyi, 1944). It is not only meant to satisfy the demand for food or fodder but has also been fundamentally essential for maintaining various forms of social tie-ups and networks, both within and between communities.[8] One such important social tie-up has been with the *Changpa Communities* (Shuttleworth, 1934). *Changpas* are the inhabitants of the *Changthang* region of *Ladakh*, where harsh environmental conditions do not permit cultivation of food crop (Crook and Osmaston, 1994). Our sample villagers exchange barley with these communities for wool. These wools are of high quality and help sustain villagers with their wintertime occupation of weaving.[9] Within these communities, barley is *traded* for various fodders as well as for accessing community owned grazing lands. Indeed, social need based activities and strong principles of reciprocity-based social contracts occupy a central position in their way of living. The reason behind the prevalence of such 'reciprocity-based social contracts' may be found in harsh ecological climatic conditions, which, perhaps, have taught local people to respect the strength of unity and reciprocity.[10] It may also be highlighted that property rights of arable lands are privately owned, while that of grazing lands are *commonly* held by village communities.[11] But, contrary to orthodox economic understanding, common property rights have not led to over exploitation of resources.[12] Moreover, the local people also do not assess the cost of policing common property to be very high, as suspected by Demsetz (1967). In contrast, it seems to confirm the observation made by Barzel (1989) that transaction costs of specifying private property rights can be very high, especially in traditional pre-market societies operating with a high degree of community feelings, since such arrangements (private property rights) contradicts the existing value system favouring community well-being more than exclusive persuasion of private interests.[13]

Importantly, there has been a close linkage between health care and production (cropping pattern). Barley, once again, occupied the central position. Besides providing high protein and energy, it also has substantial folk medicinal value. It seems to provide cure for a range of diseases like bronchitis, cough, debility, diarrhoea, cholera, dyspepsia, and heart disease (Duke and Wain, 1981). Indeed, it is known as the "heart medicine" in Middle-East countries because of its cholesterol reducing capacity. Duke and Wain (1981) also found the effectiveness of barley in treating uro-genital ailments and, more importantly, preventing cancers. Thus, cultivation of barley as the staple food may, arguably, have evolved out of the need to build up a self-sustained health care system in the absence of modern medicine. Indeed, our interviews did not find any instances of major epidemic in the regions.[14]

To sum up, one can see that the cultivation of barley was not only important for food, but also was an integral part of their health care, livestock maintenance, their barter exchange relationship with other tribal communities, and various reciprocal exchanges between themselves. These networks and the need for reciprocity based socially embedded exchanges often constrained the pursuit of individualistic economic gains.

IV

The Socio-Economic Transformation: An Analysis

Exogenous Shocks and Other Explanations

During the last decade, these Trans-Himalayan cold deserts have begun undergoing tremendous socio-economic transformations from barter economy to agricultural commercialization and monetized trade (*see* Mishra, 1997; 2000, Saxena *et al.*, 2005). Our survey findings suggest that the transformation to cash crop, green pea, has been quite rapid in substituting barley in over 30 per cent of cultivated land during our survey period 1997–2002.[15] A most common explanation behind such a rapid transformation has been the change in relative prices and market expansion (Pingali, 2001). Indeed, two major exogenous shocks can be identified as important driving force behind the commercialization of agriculture in this region. These forces are (a) prohibition of production and distribution (agricultural) subsidies under WTO, which compelled the government to encourage the cultivation of commercially viable crops and (b) the emergence of demand for organic foods. The fact that green pea fetches a very high economic reward (*see* Saxena *et al.*, 2005) seems to justify such an explanation.

But, the traditional food crop, barley, had occupied a pivotal role in shaping the communal and social systems of these regions for ages (Asboe, 1933). It is rather difficult to imagine a smooth, albeit drastic, diminution of the importance of barley only due to a singular, external pressure of market expansion and relative price change. It has also been suggested that an explanation solely based on incentive based change in behaviour, as in Demsetz (1967), often ignores more primitive and deeper reasons for such changes, lying within the system (Witt, 1987).

In fact, identifying indigenous forces behind transformations of 'pre-modern' traditional societies have always been a subject of close scrutiny and intense examinations by social scientists (Polanyi, 1944; Hagen, 1962; Salisbury, 1970; Wrigley, 1987; Norgaard, 1994). Salisbury (1970), finds that indigenous innovativeness of these societies play a crucial role in such transformations. Hagen (1962), on the other hand, characterizes traditional societies by near complete absence of innovative ideas; changes are rather brought about by internal conflicts arising out of perceived loss of status. But, these Trans-Himalayan societies are characterized by 'orderly behaviour' (Harcourt, 1870–71; Paske, 1879) with less or no major instances of internal conflicts, and as 'lazy to profit from new ideas' (Harcourt, 1870–71; Asboe, 1937). The pressure of population growth has also been identified as an important factor, driving change in property rights and other institutions (*see,* for instance, Wrigley, 1987). Interestingly, however, population has been rather stable in this region due to the practice of primogenitary inheritance, leading to a stable form of property rights (Mishra, 2000; Mishra *et al.,* 2003).[16] Thus, none of the explanations mentioned above can be said to have played much important role behind the on going transformation. Being a closed system, as mentioned above, these societies developed strong complementarities between various facets of their community life including strong interdependence between agriculture-livestock rearing, exchange, and health care need. A basic characteristic of market economies, namely, the primacy of individual pursuits of economic gains, is not commonly observed in these societies (Polanyi, 1944).[17] A rapid change, in such a situation, purely guided by external forces (incentives or shocks), tends to come in conflict with prevailing informal institutions (North, 1990 and Rogers 1995) due to 'persistent habits', 'mental attitude', and 'point of view', much highlighted by Veblen (1899).[18] It is in this context we believe paying a close attention to indigenous forces is crucial for a deeper understanding of the socio-economic transformation process in this region.

Social Cognitive Learning: The Main Driving Force

It is clear that the barley cultivation was of central importance to the community not only because of it provided food, but also because it helped them maintain the closed agro-pastoral system and interaction with other similar societies. The green peas, on the other hand, are primarily produced for market in big cities and metropolis, devoid of links between consumption, production, livestock rearing and exchange. A successful replacement of barley by green peas, therefore, depended crucially on breaking these links.

The initiation of this change can be traced back to early 1960s, and has been motivated by historical incidents. The Chinese occupation of Tibet, and the subsequent war between India and China on territorial disputes, expedited the need for road construction for better communication between mainland and border areas (Rahul, 1968). A better connectivity was not only to ensure smoother information flow, which was essential for security reasons, but also important to raise the prospect of better integration of local people with mainland India through better governance and developmental work. This was of paramount importance given that these regions were neglected during the British regime. This road construction work provided an opportunity of generating rural employment. Earlier, insufficient income from agriculture had resulted in a social division of labour along the size-class of farm holding. Large landholders often concentrated on agricultural activities, while small land holders supplemented their low agricultural yield by taking up the toiling job of cattle grazing (known as *Doksa*) for large farmers. Let us emphasise, even at the cost of repetition that being an agro-pastoral system (as opposed to a purely pastoral one) the livestock utility was not only limited to production of milk or meat. Rather, livestock were also needed for ploughing fields, transportation, and fertiliser (through manure) for agriculture. In the changed situation, these farmers whose agricultural outputs were low due to a small size of land holdings and had to take up the toiling job of cattle grazers in remote altitudes, found easier employment alternatives and participated in road construction activities in large numbers. Rogers (1995), however, provides strong evidence that external agents often face opposition from local individuals in bringing about socio-economic changes. In this light, one may suspect the acceptability of the government among the local people, particularly in the face of a long absence of any kind of governmental control and interventions in the region. However, local landlords (*Nono*) were popular figures in these regions, and, importantly, these landlords and large farmers were given contracts of such road constructions (see also Rahul, 1968, 1969). It implied less social opposition for small farmers in the event of job-switch from cattle grazing (for large farmers) to road construction. Conceivably, these farmers and local landlords directly motivated the small farmer to participate in these new activities. In line with social cognitive theories, therefore, we have a case where role models directly propagated for change in behaviour reinforcing vicarious learning among local individuals. The construction of roadways changed the local belief system about the efficacy of governmental interventions, not only by raising employment opportunities in particular, but also by raising hopes of good governance by the civil authority in general. The active involvement of individuals with high social prestige in such economically rewarding activities also heralded a change in value judgement, which legitimised the pursuit of individualistic economic profit-centric behaviour among local people, not essentially embedded in social exchange requirement.

Better roadways, gradually, helped strengthen contacts with neighbouring regions and big cities. All this led to more diverse patterns of 'observational learning', to form better economic aspirations towards a higher standard of living through the demonstration effects of urban food habits and life styles. Note that the road construction activities were largely carried out under "food for work" programme. At times, however, such activities had monetary rewards as well. Money, therefore, started to flow into these economies during this period weakening the (barter) link between social needs and economic activities.

This initial success of raising employment opportunities made the governmental initiative more trustworthy to local people, and led to a replication of such forms of policy interventions by initiating a positive feedback loop. The local landlords provided the crucial co-evolutionary link between the government and the local people by conveying the needs and aspirations of local people to policy makers. It must be noted that many such landlords gradually occupied positions of power in various layers of governmental bureaucracy and civil authority. Importantly, they have also been enthusiastic about development related activities. Clearly, these landlords were instrumental in shaping the feedback mechanism between the government and the local people, thereby fostering the adoption of suitable policy measures and alteration of local preference and value systems over time.

From the late seventies the frequency of such developmental projects indeed increased.[19] These policies opened up many new avenues of employment to local people, and reinforced the legitimacy of pursuing economic aspirations over traditional socially embedded activities. The introduction of a public distribution system (PDS) of foodgrains and the system of setting up Primary Health Centres (PHCs) are particularly noteworthy in this regard (the Fifth Plan

Document, Government of India). While the Public Distribution System of food (PDS) was undertaken to provide rice and wheat at subsidized (or zero) prices, primary health centres (PHC) promoted government aided modern curative health care facilities in remote areas.

Both these forces (PDS and PHC) propagated for altering food habits and the reliance on barley. The food habit started shifting towards rice and wheat, largely due to high status associated with the consumption of these commodities (mainly rice) in these societies. It may be noted that while rice (and wheat) are the staple foods in large parts of India, harsh physical conditions and insufficient rainfall prevent cultivations of rice in this region of the Trans-Himalaya. As a result, traditionally, only the rich had access to rice. Rice made items in social occasions were considered prestigious. In a nutshell, rice was a symbol of social prestige (Bourdieu, 1984) mainly due to its scarcity. However, while the so-called status good characteristics may explain the initial switch from barley to rice it does not explain the *sustained* consumption of rice once the access to rice was economised through governmental supply mechanism. Our discussions with local people helped to identify two crucial factors in sustaining the consumption of rice. First, it reduced cooking time since rice was available without husks, which, in the case of barley, had to be removed manually. Secondly, rice primarily replaced barley only at the level of 'ingredients' and not at the level of the final dish. The same final traditional dishes with almost similar tastes (adding similar flavour) could be prepared (e.g. *Thukpa*) with rice as well, but now with less time and less hassles of removing husks. The similarity in tastes, flavour material and cooking methods meant less cognitive and cultural effort to replace barley with rice as a food item. Indeed, anthropological studies seem to point out that tastes, flavour and method of preparations are primary reasons for innateness of food habit (Farb and Armelagos, 1980; Ruprecht, 2005).

However, the health implication of the replacement of barley with rice is questionable. Rice has considerably less amount of protein, energy content, and folk medicinal values compared to barley. As mentioned in Gopalan *et al.* (1985) the protein content in barley is 11.5 per cent compared to a highest of 7.5 per cent (generally around 5%) in rice. The energy content of rice (1.75 cal./gm.) is less than half of that in barley (around 3.36 cal./gm.) One can, in this context, claim that green pea consumption can compensate for the loss of protein since green pea is also known as a rich source of protein. But, interestingly, the protein level of barley-wheat combination can only be compared with that of 'dry green pea' (19.7%). The local people of Spiti, on the other hand, have access only to 'fresh green pea's since the predominant portion of the green peas are exported (sold to big cities) immediately after the harvesting. The amount of protein in 'fresh green peas' is significantly low (7.2%). The energy content of green peas is also considerably less (0.93cal./gm.). All this signals a rather gloomy picture of the disease preventive aspects of the local people. However, an easy access to subsidized curative health care may have mitigated some of these costs. As a result, the preventive aspects of health care attached with the consumption of barley became less important. This reinforced the change in food habits by reducing the risk of health hazards related to loss of disease preventive capacity, at least in the short run. One must also emphasise that high protein-energy diets are crucially important for survival in harsh climatic conditions. A vicariously learned new behaviour, predominantly, on the basis of its immediate reward can therefore lead to undesirable consequences in the longer run.[20]

Since the main demand for barley was internal, changing food habits meant less demand for barley and less incentives for barley cultivation. The introduction of health care facilities reinforced it by weakening the link between barley cultivation and health care need. Such policies also increasingly legitimized the pursuit of individual economic motives, and reduced dependence on social exchange processes. It may also be noted that tourism increased in this region since the early 1990s. The increasing interaction with tourists as well as urban people led to a higher motivation for better standards of living. The local people had, however, continued to produce barley in order to maintain the barter relationships with other tribal communities. But, the reduction of social need for barley with increased flow of money through various governmental projects paved the way for pursuing individualistic economic motives through higher specialization in production.

Due to adverse geographical conditions, this region of Himachal Pradesh is not ecologically suited for fruit cultivation (the major profitable agricultural activities in this state for which it is named the Apple State of India). The enhancement of economic aspirations stemming from greater access to money and more knowledge about material wellbeing had inflicted a sense of relative deprivation among local farmers, and, in turn, intensified the motivation to search for more profitable income generation opportunities. It was, perhaps, easier for government officials and *Nonos* to convince local farmers to adopt green pea cultivation in this situation, where motivations for economic profit were high and barley had lost much of its importance.

Our survey also interestingly reveals a very proactive role of women behind the transformation. One should note that these Trans-Himalayan communities traditionally confer high(er) status and freedom to women and are characterized by a high rate of women participation in social decision-making.[21] Traditionally, there has been instances of a gender based division of labour, where male members of a family engaged in trading (although barter) activities leaving the burden of agricultural including domestic work largely on females (Asboe, 1937). As developmental projects were initiated in large numbers, the overall income and the wage rate increased. A higher wage rate, in some cases, also led to a backward bending supply curve, where male members preferred to spend more leisure time, and indulged in excessive consumption of liquor made from barley. Such activities resulted in an even greater shift of family burden on women and enhanced, associated, family and social conflicts. The prospect of green pea cultivation as a profitable alternative to barley acted in favour of their disliking, and replacement of barley by green peas got a social sanction from the women in these societies. A high social prestige of women in general enabled them to act as role models, which contributed significantly to enhance the speed of the transformation.

V
Summary and Conclusion

To summarise, even though green pea cultivation started in late 1990s, policy measures of last three decades and the consequent learning prepared the ground for a fast and successful agricultural transformation by repeatedly rewarding individualistic economic profit centric activities over socially embedded ones. While these societies demonstrated significant amounts of lethargy and inertia towards novel ideas in the past (Shuttleworth, 1934), the history of the last fifty years is characterized by the gradual acceptance of modernity and change. The initial success of the governmental policy of road construction enhanced the scope of employment in these areas. This success resulted in a positive feedback loop, possibly unintended, where more such policies were demanded and undertaken. The governmental interventions were frequent, consistent and more importantly, supported and mediated by local people with high social acceptability. The involvement of local individuals with high social status, and high social acceptability, in the developmental process led to a fast acceptance of new behavioural regularities through vicarious learning. Their involvement in economic profit generating activities (dis-embedded from social needs) helped legitimize such activities in the community, and encouraged common people to participate in developmental projects in large number without fearing social sanctions and opposition. Such a preference for a new value system also spilled over to the domains of preference for food and health care, which helped diffusion of rice as a food item and modern curative health care practices. These replacements led to severing the links between consumption and production requirement, and, in turn, reduced the cost of introducing novelty in the production system without apprehending its spillover on consumption. An intense communication with tourists and people living in large cities also augmented their aspirations for an improved standard of living. The injection of money into the economy helped local people sustain these changes in their life style. The use of money also obliterated the need for social barter exchanges and sowed the seed for increasingly specialized exchanges and pursuit of individualistic economic goals by local inhabitants. A high degree of communication and cohesion within society and, especially, within the family with a high rate of women's participation in decision making helped to rapidly develop a shared mental model on the efficacy of developmental policies. Finally, their traditional mental models, which was developed through various age old barter-trading activities with other Trans-Himalayan communities, also provides a crucial explanation for a smooth shift towards commercialisation of agriculture, once the pursuit of individualistic economic profit became the overriding objective. For the local community what changed was, possibly, only the basket of commodities and trading partners.

In a nutshell, this paper highlights that not only the elements but also the sequence of policy tools can prove to be important for effective course of economic development in India.

Acknowledgement

We are thankful to Ulrich Witt, Amit Shovon Ray, Christian Schubert, Guido Buenstorf, Andreas Chai, Rohan D'Souza, Uta-Maria Niederle, Bhaswati Das, Amitendu Palit, Simanti Banerjee for insightful comments and discussions.

NOTES

1. See Rimmer (1961) for a summary of these views.
2. In his co-evolutionary theory of the German industry and supporting institutions in the late 19th centuries, this function was served by University professors who were also appointed as industry consultants and policy advisers in the government. They, therefore, conceivably influenced these entities to co-evolve.
3. A behavioural regularity can be observed in a population of individuals if they are confronted with the same decision situation. See, for instance, Witt (1989).
4. The climate of Spiti is arid with most precipitation being in the form of snow. Temperatures range between zero to 30°C in summer (May-October) and –30° to 3°C in winter (November–April). The region is characterized by low precipitation, and short growing season (only in the summer).
5. See Rahul (1968) for detail.
6. It must be emphasised that our case may contrast with many other traditional societies, where land lords are rather well known for their misappropriation of power rather than benevolence.
7. It must be emphasised that they do not use chemical fertilisers at all.
8. A significant proportion of barley is also allotted to the production of beer, used for social entertainments. See also Asboe (1937).
9. There are similar historical evidences of long standing exchange relationship between other tribal communities located in Tibet and Turkestan and the people of this area. See for instance Shuttleworth (1934).
10. Binmore (1998) finds similar instances of reciprocity bound social contracts among the hunter gatherers, who can also survive only through mutual interdependence and reciprocity based altruism. Rodriguez and Pascual (2004) have found similar instances of high prevalence of 'communal organization' and collective resource management among the mountainous Andean communities in Peru. One should also note that contract here does not mean any binding law. As argued by Hagen (1962) reciprocity in such societies can in fact be bound by factors like scruples and faith.
11. This is a typical feature of an open field system as summarised in Dahlman (1980).

12. Some estimates find presence of 87 species and estimates the annual net primary productivity (ANPP) utilisation to be near 52%. Note that an ANPP over 50% is considered sustainable. See McNaughton (1993) for details.
13. Dahlman (1980), however, seems to argue that such forms of common grazing lands existed because cost of fencing and policing under private property rights could not outweigh the gains of grazing in privately owned lands.
14. Historical evidences also do not discuss any major diseases or health hazards affecting these mountainous regions, notwithstanding their continuous fights against harsh climatic condition. Francke (1907) can be regarded as an authentic documentation in this regard.
15. Personal communications suggest a near complete replacement of barley by green peas in these villages in next two years. But, no concrete data could be obtained.
16. According to primogenitary inheritance only the eldest son inherits the whole property, other sons accede to the lamahood. Lamas are the religious priests. Traditionally they also have been the backbone of the cultural developmental process of these regions. See Francke (1907) for a classic exposition of the role of Lamas in these societies.
17. See also Granovetter (1985) for the debate on over and under socialization in the theory of social sciences.
18. In one interesting exposition Witt (1987) argues that reason for choosing more restrictive property rights by Montagnais Indian was gradual increase in population and resultant food scarcity, and not, at least exclusively, the opening of fur trade opportunity as visualised by Demsetz (1967).
19. See Ministry of Environment and Forest (2001), for documentation of various such policy measures.
20. Indeed, when asked to compare the "working capacity" after a barley meal with that after a rice meal, the local people report longer working hours after the barley meal. However, more intense examination is required to substantiate such a claim.
21. As an illustration, one may note that Spitian societies take a very liberal view regarding extra-marital and pre-marital sexual interaction. Also, the decision of the female partners is considered supreme in any paternity related disputes in such cases. This is in sharp contrast with the societal dynamics of adjacent Indian states where women are often marginalized in decision-making processes. See National Family Health Survey, Himachal Pradesh, India (1998–99) for detailed documentation.

REFERENCES

Adelman, I. (2002), "Fallacies in development theory and their implications for policy", in J.E. Stiglitz and G.M. Meier (eds.) *Frontiers of Development Economics,* The World Bank, Washington DC.

Asboe, W. (1933), "Social Functions in Lahul, Kangra District, Punjab", *The Journal of the Royal Anthropological Institute of Great Britain and Ireland*, Vol 63, pp. 189–205.

Asboe, W. (1937), "Agricultural Methods in Lahoul, Western Tibet", *Man*, Vol 37, pp. 74–77.

Bandura, A. (1986), Social Foundation of Thought and Action: A Social Cognitive Theory, Englewood Cliffs (Prentice Hall).

Bandura, A. (1989), "Social cognitive theory", *Annals of Child Development*, Vol 6, pp. 1–60.

Barzel, Y. (1989), "*The Economic Analysis of Property* Rights", Cambridge University Press.

Binmore, K. (1998), "The evolution of fairness norms", *Rationality and Society* Vol 10, pp. 275–301.

Bourdieu, P. (1984), *Distinction: A Social Critique of the Judgment of Taste*, Rutledge, London.

Crook, J.H. and A. Osmaston (1994), (eds) *Himalayan Buddhist Villages: Environment, Resources, Society and religious Life in Zangskar,* Ladakh, Motilal, New Delhi.

Dahlman, C.J. (1980), *The Open Field System and Beyond*, Cambridge University Press, London.

Demsetz, H. (1967), "Toward a theory of property rights", *American Economic* Review, Vol. 57(2), pp. 347–359.

Denzau, A and North D.C. (1994), "Shared mental models, ideologies and institutions", *Kyklos*, Vol. 47, pp. 3–31.

Duke, J.A. and K.K.Wain, (1981), "Medicinal plants of the world". *Computer index,* (from www.hort.purdue.edu/newcrop).

Ensminger, J. (1996), *Making a Market: The Institutional Transformation of an African Society,* Cambridge University Press, Cambridge.

Farb, P. and G. Armelagos (1980), *Consuming Passions*: *The Anthropology of Eating*, Noughton Mifflin, Boston.

Francke, A.H. (1907), *A History of Western Tibet*, S.W. Partridge and Co.

Gopalan, C., B.V.R. Sastri, and S.C. Balasubramanian (1985), *Nutritive Value of Indian Foods,* National Institute of Nutrition, Hyderabad.

Granovetter, M. (1985), "Economic Action and Social Structure: The Problem of Embeddedness", *The American Journal of Sociology*, Vol. 91 (3), pp. 481–510.

Hagen, E.E. (1962), *On the Theory of Social Change: How Economic Growth Begins,* The Dorsey Press, Homewood.

Harcourt, A.F.P. (1870–71), "On the Himalayan Valleys: Kooloo, Lahoul and Spiti", *Proceedings of the Royal Geographical Society of London*, Vol. 15 (5), pp. 336–343.

Hirschman, A.O. (1958), *The Strategy of Economic Development*, Yale University Press, New Haven.

Johnson-Laird, P.N. (1983), *Mental Models*, Cambridge University Press, Cambridge.

Mantzavinos, C. (2001), *Individuals, Institutions, and Markets*, Cambridge University Press, Cambridge.

Mantzavinos, C., D.C. North, and S. Shariq (2004), "Learning, institutions and economic performance", *Perspectives on Politics,* Vol. 2(1), pp. 75–84.

McNaughton, S.J. (1993), "Grasses and grazers: science and management", *Ecol. Appl.* Vol. 3 (1), pp. 17–20.

Ministry of Environment and Forest (2001), *National Action Programme to Combat Desertification*, Government of India, New Delhi.

Mishra, C., H. Prins, and S.E. Van Wieren (2003), "Diversity, Risk Mediation, and Change in a Trans-Himalayan Agropastoral System", *Human Ecology*, Vol. 31 (4).

Mishra, C. (1997), *Livestock Grazing and Wildlife Conservation in the Indian Trans-Himalayas: A Preliminary Survey,* CERC Technical Report # 1,Centre for Ecological Research and Conservation, Mysore.

Mishra, C. (2000), "Socio-economic transition and wildlife conservation in the Indian Trans-Himalaya", *Journal of the Bombay Natural History Society*, Vol. 97 (1), pp. 25–32

Mokyr, J. (2001), "Demand as a factor in the Industrial Revolution: A historical note" in U.Witt (eds.) *Escaping Satiation*, Springer, Berlin.

Murmann, J.P. (2003), *Knowledge and Competitive Advantage*, Cambridge University Press, Cambridge.

Norgaard, R. B. (1994), *Development Betrayed*, Routledge, London.

North, D.C. (1990), *Institutions, Institutional Change and Economic Performance*, Cambridge University Press, Cambridge.

Paske, E. (1879), "Budhism in the British Provinces of Little Tibet", *The Journal of the Royal Anthropological Institute of Great Britain and Ireland*, Vol. 8, pp. 195–210.

Pingali, P.L. (2001), "Environmental Consequences of agricultural commercialization in Asia", *Environment and Development Economics*, Vol. 6, pp. 483–502.

Polanyi, K. (1944), *The Great Transformation*, Beacon Press, Boston.

Rahul, R. (1968), "The Development Programme in the Himalaya", *Asian Survey*, Vol. 8 (8), pp. 666–677.

Rahul, R. (1969), "The System of Administration in the Himalaya", *Asian Survey*, Vol. 9 (9), pp. 694–702.

Rimmer, D. (1961), "Schumpeter and the Underdeveloped Countries", *The Quarterly Journal of Economics*, 75(3), 422–450.

Rizzello, S. and M. Turvani (2000), "Institutions meet mind: The way out of an impasse", *Constitutional Political Economy*, Vol. 1, pp 165–180.

Rizzello, S. and M. Turvani (2002), "Subjective diversity and social learning: a cognitive perspective for understanding institutional behaviour", *Constitutional Political Economy,* Vol. 13(2), pp. 197–210.

Rodríguez, L.C. and U. Pascual (2004), "Land clearance and social capital in mountain agro-ecosystems: the case of Opuntia scrubland in Ayacucho, Peru", *Ecological Economics*, Vol. 49 (2).

Rogers, E.M. (1995), *Diffusion of Innovation*, The Free Press, New York.

Ruprecht, W. (2005), "The historical development of the consumption of sweeteners—a learning approach", *Journal of Evolutionary Economics*, Vol. 15 (3), pp. 247–272.

Salisbury, R.F. (1970), *Vunamani: Economic Transformation in a Traditional Society*, University of California Press, Berkeley.

Saxena, K.G., R.K. Maikhuri, K.S. Rao. (2005), "Changes in agricultural biodiversity: implications for sustainable livelihood in the Himalaya", *Journal of Mountain Science*, Vol. 2(1), pp. 23–31.

Schumpeter, J.A. (2005), "Development", *Journal of Economic Literature*, 43 (March), 108–120

Shuttleworth, H.L. (1934), "People of the Panjab Himalaya", *Man*, Vol. 34, pp. 58-59.

Stahl, S.R. (2000), "Descendence and social genealogies: toward an evolutionary conception of economic history", *Journal of Economic Issues*, Vol. 34, pp. 891–908.

Stiglitz, J.E. (1998), "Towards a new paradigm for development: strategies, policies and process", *Prebisch Lecture, UNCTAD*, Geneva.

Stiglitz, J.E (2002), Participation and development: "perspectives from the comprehensive development paradigm", *Review of Development Economics*, Vol. 6(2), pp. 163–182.

Sweezy, P.M. (1943), "Professor Schumpeter's Theory of Innovations", *The Review of Economic Statistics*, 25 (1), 93–96.

Tversky, A. and D., Kahneman (1986), "Rational choice and the framing of decisions", *Journal of* Business, Vol 59, pp. 251–278.

Veblen, T.B. (1899), *The Theory of the Leisure Class: An economic study in the evolution of institution*, Macmillan, New York.

Witt, U. (1987), "The Demsetz hypothesis on the emergence of property rights reconsidered" in R. Pethig and U. Schlieper (eds.) *Efficiency, Institutions, and Economic* Policy, Springer-Verlag, Berlin.

Witt, U. (1989), "The Evolution of Economic Institution as a Propagation Process", *Public Choice*, Vol. 62, pp. 155–172.

Witt, U. (2001), "Learning to consume—A theory of wants and the growth of demand", *Journal of Evolutionary Economics*, Vol. 11, pp. 23–36.

Witt, U. (2001), "Learning to consume—A theory of wants and the growth of demand", *Journal of Evolutionary Economics*, Vol. 11, pp. 23–36.

Witt, U. (2003a), *The Evolving Economy: Essays on the Evolutionary Approach to Economics*, Part-I, pp. 3–34, Cheltenham, Edward Elger.

Witt, U. (2003b), "Economic Policy Making in Evolutionary Perspective", *Journal of Evolutionary Economics*, Vol. 13, pp. 77–94.

Witt, U. (1987), "The Demsetz hypothesis on the emergence of property rights reconsidered" in R. Pethig and U. Schlieper (eds.) *Efficiency, Institutions, and Economic Policy*, Springer-Verlag, Berlin.

Wrigley, E.A. (1987), *People, Cities and Wealth: The Transformation of Traditional Society*, Blackwell, Oxford.

2

PEOPLE'S PARTICIPATION A KEY FOR EFFECTIVE DEVELOPMENT

Its Relevance in Contemporary Nagaland

CHANDAN DEBNATH

Defining Development

Finding a well accepted definition of development is an arduous task. Scholars across communities differ on its meaning, objective and goal, shaped by their individual and collective perception and experience of the micro and macro aspects of their environment. According to Alexander (1994: 8), developmental is fundamentally a process of change that involves the whole society—its economic, socio-cultural, political and physical structure, as well the value system and way of life. The tools of measuring the level of development ranges from assessing economic factors and other socio cultural and political variables compared against an accepted standard or aspiration. Often the goal of developing planning is to replicate the level of achievements of others who are perceived as superior in the echelon of development. Thus countries and communities can be comparatively studied and the empirical difference between them can be used to illustrate the meaning and level of development. At the macro level the focus of development has always been issues such as: elimination of poverty, social inequality and unemployment and the means perceived to achieve these macro goals was an increase in the GDP. The developmental planning at the macro-level, focused largely on economic growth. It was justified by the overwhelming belief that by increasing the gross national product the base of the economy shall expand and directly or indirectly the benefits of growth shall percolate down to the poorest of the poor and thereby help eradication of poverty, inequality and unemployment in the country (Yadav, 1980:3). The assumption is that quantitative rise in GNP shall automatically percolate to the lower rungs of the population perceived as deprived. From experience we are aware that this has not happened. Nearly 27.5 per cent (2004–05) of the population continues to live in abject poverty, deprived of access to education, health, sanitation, nutrition and other basic amenities of life. Further, one can also ascribe that, their level of deprivation has often been the potent cause of their political and social marginalization offering little or no space to live as dignified entities in the contemporary society. Agriculture continues to employ as high as 39.25 per cent (Census 2001) of the national work force offering little or no respite to teeming millions to break free from the shackles of subsistence farming, a key contributor of poverty. Pattnaik (1986:9–10) states that the general programme of development is concerned with growth in employment and output in different sectors of that economy. As a result there has been development in different sectors—agriculture, industry, mining, and social sciences, spawning islands of prosperity benefiting a select stratum of the society. One of the most contested elections of the 21st century was organized and fought under the theme *India Shinning* and the party in question believed that by selling a dream it could ensure its return to the portals of power. The end result was indeed disastrous for the campaign managers who learnt in the hard way that, winning elections is not similar to promoting sales for consumer durables based on the strength of creative add campaigns. The former required public trust. The party lost power as masses did not believe that their India was truly shinning, so as to mark a difference in their day to day life. For a large section of the society, poverty is real which growth in select segments of the economy could not ameliorate. Thus the election debacle reiterated that few islands of prosperity here and there does not connote development but development is meaningful when it supports concerted efforts that aim to empower the majority in planning and building the developmental process reflecting their aspirations and needs. If one is to analyze the reasons for the developmental *faux pas* in the Indian scenario well, it clearly shows the lack of commitment by all concerned to really empower people in materializing the developmental goals. In a welfare state development was believed to be the sole duty of the government and identification of the means its prerogative. The citizenry are considered to be its beneficiaries and bureaucrats its architects. What is overlooked in the process is the need and importance of participation. Developmental planning is accompanied by a lot of prescriptions rather than adopt an in-depth analysis to asses its strength, weakness, opportunities and threats on which the developmental edifice shall stand to support communities desirous of adding value to their life. Given the freedom to express my opinion on such mode of planning, I would refer to them as bureaucratic arrogance oblivious of the needs of the people and unable to address them by building partnerships. One cannot undermine the importance of evolving partnership *vis-à-vis* developmental policies.

Against this backdrop of the popular perceptions of development, its purpose, utility and experiences so far; the basic question still remains open and unanswered, that is, defining development. Some questions in this regard may be: does development connote change initiated under a top down approach? Is development directed towards matching others' life styles! Can the mode of development be uniform across societies or does development mean westernization enabled by a process of rampant and random imitation? Does development mean urbanization, crass materialism, industrialization or establishing socio-cultural and economic hegemony overtly or tacitly? Is there one best way to initiate development! If the answer to the above questions is a big no, then again we are back at the basic question: what is development? The answer I believe lies in defining society as a collection of creativity that is imbibed, learnt, transferred and sharpened by ones daily experiences gained from the circumstances and unique conditions specific to ones social and economic environment with little or no resemblance with others.

In the literature reviewed thus far, development has a range of meanings but is generally regarded as immanent and desirable and hints at material progress and improved standard of living irrespective of whether initiated under capitalistic or Marxist orientation. This is the premise on which development has to be planned, structured and carried out to have maximum leverage regarding its performance and have utility for those whose lives it purports to change, more on an add on basis rather than replacement. The key to its efficacy in churning out the desired goals lies in evolving and accommodating partnership rather than adopting a straight jacket approach. The UNESCO report of 1995, testifying to this line of thought puts it. "Our Creative Diversity is part of people's culture, and culture, defined as the flourishing of human existence in all its forms truly represents the end aim of development". The report went on to explore and critically evaluate number of ways in which the cultural strategies might contribute to the economic, social and community development. This pertinent realization prompts us to reject an imported concept of development which sees development as a manifestation of a western image which might stand against our own needs, means, social identity, strength, knowledge and skill. In a gist, the western concept of development may not be adequate to address our needs as development has to be as per the need specific to a community. The theme of the paper is identified to reflect the above understanding *vis-à-vis* the Naga society. Its objective is to begin an academic debate on the meaning, and purpose of development as understood and aspired by the Nagas.

Socio-Cultural Environment of the Nagas

The socio-cultural differences between the developed and underdeveloped societies have been explained by Hofstead (1980) in his landmark study *Motivations, leadership and organization: Do American theories apply abroad?* The four dimensions suggested by him to mark the differences between developed and developing countries in an organizational context are: Uncertainty avoidance, Power distance, Individualism-collectivism and Masculinity *versus* Femininity. Using these dimensions Kanungo and Jaeger (1990) have characterized socio-cultural environment of developing countries as high on Uncertainty Avoidance and power distance, relatively low on individualism. On the additional dimension, abstractive *versus* associative thinking suggested by Bhagat and Kedia (1988) developing countries are low on abstractive thinking and high on associative thinking. Each of the five cultural dimensions is assumed to orient our behaviour and approach towards work, having an influence on productivity and the consequent developmental process. Taking note of the above cultural variables the paper tries to understand their implications on development efforts in the Naga society.

Collectivism, a Way of Life for the Nagas

India is categorized as a developing society and Nagaland as a part of India reflects a developing economy having some of the above cultural dimensions at play. From the cultural beliefs and values it can be assumed that Nagas are a collective society where emphasis in the past has been on achieving and promoting collective well-being. Some cultural practices, traditions and beliefs which is felt to support the argument are: (i) community celebrations cum feasting, (ii) group hunting and sharing the game with kith and clan, (iii) existence of clan/village land and forest resources, (iv) clan members assisting one other on agricultural operations as per established custom along with near absence oh hired labor, (v) having places of worship belonging to distinct community/tribe, (vi) low preference for migration outside respective tribal domain or beyond the state, (vii) practice of forming numerous organizations and unions to protect the village, clan, range or tribal interest etc., (viii) villages established and inhabited on clan lines, (ix) the tradition of sovereign village states and the collective responsibility of defending it, (x) practice of community learning enabled through the institution of *Morung*, and (xi) last but not the least, the importance accorded to social recognition by the Nagas. Therefore, from the above citations one can assume that Nagas are a collective society and their collectivism has strengths which can be roped in for effective social and economic transformation of the state.

Power Distance

In the Naga society age and seniority are respected both in the present and in the past. For receiving social recognition and to be accepted as a leader, one had to prove his/her worth and merit to his/her clan/ tribe. In the past the title of chief was bestowed on those who excelled themselves in planning and executing successful head hunting raids, the objective of which was ensuring a better socio-economic status and security for the raiders' village. Further the title was not hereditary to a single family or clan. Rationality guided them in according and accepting power and position. Even for the use of certain status symbols such as special dress and ornaments, one had to pass through elaborate rituals culminating in hosting elaborate feasts for the village and even neighbouring villages for a couple of days. This practice known as feast of merit involved huge expenditures associated with organizing sumptuous meals and accompanying rituals. There was no concept of easy wealth as everything had to be hard earned. Only those with surplus harvest could afford the feast of merit and the beauty of this practice lied in encouraging distribution of wealth (harvest) among the needy through such feasts. The host in return earned social recognition and certain privileges. Thus the analysis of cultural practices *vis-à-vis* power distance brings forth the conclusion that Nagas believed in respecting merit objectively. They also gave credence to seniority because age was equated with experience and experience with wisdom which called for due respect. All issues concerning common interest were democratically addressed. Nagas basically are a classless society and all the cultural beliefs and practices cited above indicate the existence of low power distance in their society.

Uncertainty Avoidance

This basically is a measurement that indicates cultural preference for risk or its avoidance. In the context of Nagas their cultural beliefs and practices point towards low uncertainty avoidance. This belief can be authenticated by the following cultural beliefs and practices: all Naga tribes are essentially head hunting tribes and head hunting expeditions involved colossal personal risk. Being warrior tribes risk was and is part and parcel of their individual and collective life. As individuals Nagas are known as people who do not shy away from challenges thrown at them. The valiant deeds of the Naga regiment during the Kargil war and of late the insurgency operations against the Maoists in Chhattisgarh testify to their risk taking capabilities. There is a particular type of game played by Naga children which consciously and subconsciously has been instrumental in building risk management capacity in them. In the game children divide themselves in two groups, each carrying some toy guns or for that matter anything that resembles a gun or which can symbolize a gun. Hiding themselves they stealthily approach the enemy group and take on them in a mock do or die fight. The rule is—the moment an enemy is sighted and is believed to be within range for a direct hit, one shouts in ecstasy fire... fire... and the opponent so targeted in the mock drill must fall down in order to be presumed dead or immortalized. Thus through such innovative games children learn to master the art of guerilla warfare which in the process can be believed to condition their mind to accept and confront challenges later on as youth and responsible citizenry. From the above analysis one can believe that Nagas are not averse to risk and uncertainty.

Masculinity-Femininity

Nagas as a patriarchal society show the existence of dominant masculinity in their personality. For a Naga loss of face is a major issue and identity is crucial to them. Till today for an average Naga belief in his/her Naga identity is far more precious than the larger Indian identity. The common sentiment among all tribes is first they are Naga's and second Indians, if they wish to be. The desire to compete and excel can be seen in many of their cultural practices. To seek the hand of a beautiful dame an eligible bachelor had to prove himself through his work. This was needed to convince the bride's family of his capability and eligibility as the most natural choice in comparison to his compatriots or similar age groups. An eligible bachelor has to own a house before seeking a bride so that the couple can live independently. Their culture appears to induce in them a sense of independence befitting the image of a complete man. Though in the Naga society women enjoy better status they do not enjoy property rights. Share in the parental property is the sole right of male siblings in the family. In case of agricultural land women enjoy cultivation rights over the property but do not possess the property. Men are expected to be aggressive and the Nagamese phrase '*maikinisena na koribi*' (don't behave like a woman) is indicative of the same. Nagas as warrior tribes are known for their uncompromising nature especially while dealing with foes or with individuals who have wilfully sullied their image or challenged them on something which seriously impacts their life. Conflict arising from any of the above is always carried to its logical end, i.e. fight to the finish and if required go on till victory is achieved. From the above one can believe that Naga personality reflects masculinity features and it guides their approach and attitude towards life in general.

Locus of Control

It refers to the degree of control that people perceive to have on their own lives. When people perceive that they are masters of their own lives, the locus of control is inward or internal and *vice versa.* It reflects a choice between fatalism and self-assurance in shaping ones existence to the best of an individual's capacity. In the context of Naga tribes, though they practiced certain rituals or customs which normally can be termed as superstitious, yet their day-to-day activities directed at adding economic value to their life, reflect their internal locus of control. To substantiate this view, we are aware that the majority of Naga villages is either placed on mountain tops or on ridges. Definitely finding means for daily existence was challenging. Further their economic belief of building and sustaining a self-reliant village amidst the rugged mountains was an arduous community task. The fact that Naga villages in the past were self-sustaining sovereign states proves that they truly achieved what they aspired by dint of hard work, ingenuity and commitment. From salt making to producing other necessities of life along with meeting safety and security needs, they mastered different skills and passed the same to successive generations. All this testifies to their internal locus of control and of their being guided by their convictions. Many other customs such as; beliefs concerning life after death, parting and re-entry of souls etc. can be attributed partly to their ignorance and overwhelming simplicity.

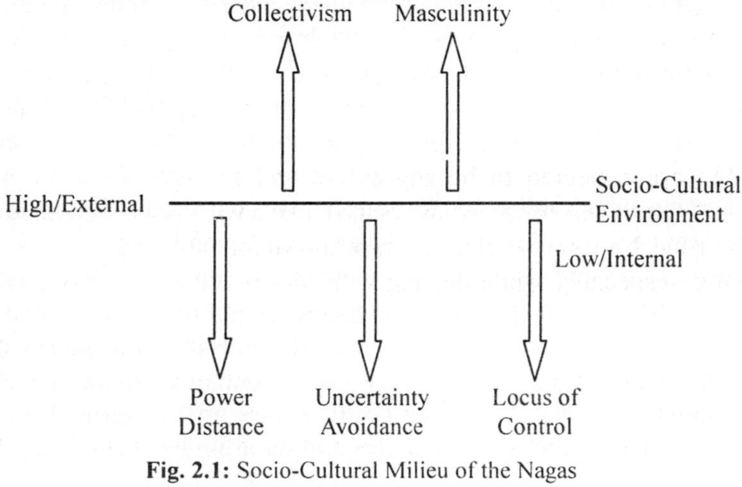

Fig. 2.1: Socio-Cultural Milieu of the Nagas

Cultural Variables—Mental Images—Impact on Work Culture

Based on the above understanding and as depicted in Fig. 2.1, it can be assumed that the culture of the Nagas indicates high on collectivism, dominant masculinity, low power distance, low uncertainty avoidance and internal locus of control. Professor Stevens of INSEAD, a business school in Fountainebleau [see Huib Wursten, 'Mental Images—the influence of culture on (economic) policy'. pp. 14–17] has developed six models representing varied mental images that explain work and motivation based on dominant cultural beliefs and practices as listed above. Mental images are fundamental social structures that we all have in our head and people of the same culture have a similar image and understanding of the way society works and its approaches towards work. The mental image that appears to fit as per the cultural context of Nagas is the Contest Model. The cultural context of this model is low on power distance, lower uncertainty avoidance and communities low on both these aspects are believed to be guided by internal locus of control. The only difference is communities under the contest model are high on individualism whereas Nagas are a collectivist society. The countries whose culture fits the contest model are U.K., U.S.A. and Australia. However, the exception which can be assumed in the context of Naga tribes is: Nagas are high on collectivism as seen in their strong group identity yet they also aspire for individual merit/recognition and have a passion for open competition which indicates cultural transition towards individualism. Based on the above cultural analysis one can believe that Nagas fit the contest model more than any other models.

The implication of this mental image on work values are: (1) People value freedom and autonomy and given the same will compete with each other to be effective and productive in their respective works. (2) Society values hierarchy and seniority and see them as facilitators who are expected to provide guidance, delegate authority and responsibility. (3) Open competition and existence of challenge are source of motivation and rewards must commensurate performance and effort as against the practice of extending general rewards. (4) Solutions to the problems are arrived through open communication between members and an arbitrary decision is not appreciated. The hypothesis that can be framed from the understanding gained thus far is: Naga culture is capable of promoting and sustaining multifaceted and holistic economic growth by drawing on the strengths inherent in their culture. In line with the hypothesis let's examine whether the proposition hold good when evaluated with secondary data available on some select areas of their work culture and economy.

Population Pressure and Impact on Development

Nagaland has been experiencing population explosion to the tune of 5.15 times in 2001 in terms of density of population as compared with the population density of 1961. Increasing population has adverse effect on the demand and supply chain concerning basic amenities of life. Population explosion creates rising demand for resources and other basic amenities. As a natural consequence the quality of supply chain aimed at meeting the demand deteriorate. In the process it spurts malpractices, nepotism, and favouritism both in governance and in distribution networks managed by the government. Rising demand coupled with scarcity of resources breeds conducive ground for corruption and other corrupt practices to capitalize on the opportunity extended by perennial shortfalls. Corruption also spreads in the society for another reason. There is a natural tendency for everyone to tap on all basic and essential services at the cost of others.

Table 2.1: Demographic Aspects of Population of Nagaland

Year	*Total Population*	*Decadal Growth (%)*	*Density of population*	*Sex Ratio*	*Literacy*	*Urban Population (%)*	*Tribal Population (%)*	*Christians (%)*
1961	369,200	14.07	22.34	933	17.91	5.19	—	52.98
1971	516,449	39.88	31.25	871	27.40	9.95	88.61	66.76
1981	774,930	50.05	46.89	867	41.99	15.52	84.00	80.21
1991	1,209,546	56.08	73.19	886	61.65	17.21	87.73	87.47
2001	1,988,636	64.41	120.32	909	67.11	—	89.10	90.00

Source: Census of India, 2001.

In the absence of corresponding increase at the base of economy, a section of the society relatively well placed and advantaged will go to any extent to ensure that their needs are met no matter what the means is or on whose cost it is achieved. Thus the cycle of corruption and poverty moves on unchecked—widening social inequities and impairing developmental activities. Individuals in the society seek to legitimize opportunism in ways and means best suited to them and in the process society experiences de-empowerment instead of empowerment of the truest kind. This analysis though subjective yet appears to be true in the context of present day Nagaland. Shortfalls in essential commodities and other basic amenities in the absence of planned developmental initiatives create class differences, self-centred individualism, lack of belongingness, rampant corruption and much other negativity in a community culture which otherwise was never believed or appreciated by the masses.

Table 2.2: Comparative Data on Population of North-East

States	*Area* (sq.km.)	*Density* (Per sq.km.)	*1991* (lacs)	*2001* (lacs)	*Decadal growth* 81–91	91–01
Arunachal	83743	13.00	8.65	10.98	36.87	26.94
Assam	78438	339.80	224.14	266.56	24.24	18.93
Manipur	22327	102.76	18.37	22.99	29.28	24.71
Meghalaya	22429	103.34	17.75	23.18	32.86	30.59
Mizoram	21807	42.22	6.90	8.99	39.68	28.84
Nagaland	16579	120.03	12.10	19.90	56.13	64.46
Sikkim	7096	76.24	4.06	5.41	28.47	33.25
Tripura	10492	304.89	22.57	31.99	34.29	16.03
North East	262911	148.27	319.54	389.82	27.47	21.99
All India			**8643.03**	**10286.10**	**23.85**	**21.54**

Land and Agriculture Productivity

For the Nagas land is believed God given and hence the community's right over land is inalienable. Hence they are very sensitive to anything that concerns land and property. Agricultural rights from ancient days followed a subsistence pattern i.e., whatever is produced is for consumption and not for sale or for enhancing economic value there from. Other reasons that can be attributed for subsistence mode of cultivation were:

(1) land was surplus in comparison to population and thus need for qualitative improvement in methods of farming was not

felt by the society. There was this general tendency to cultivate on a plot of land till it appeared to be fertile to support the needs of individual families. Thereafter alternative plots were selected in lieu of earlier plots to continue farming.

(2) The food habits were simple involving little variety. Rice was the staple food taken with meat of both domesticated and wild beasts. Use of spices and oil was unknown. The only spice used was ginger and chilly. As needs were simple and nature being bountiful the question of optimum use of land or cultivation through scientific practices was deemed as not necessary.

(3) Guided by their belief which considered land as sacred they were generally averse to the use of in-organic fertilizers to boost land productivity or adopt multiple cropping systems.

(4) Another reason for the continuance of subsistence agriculture even after statehood was iack of transportation and marketing support for Naga farmers for a long period. In the absence of road connectivity transportation of surplus to markets was a daunting task involving high cost.

Further on an average people were not conversant with the cash economy that was replacing their exchange economy and thus they could not effectively en-cash on the market value that their products commanded. This offered them little incentives to shift from subsistence mode to modern farming practices. Table 2.2, highlights the agricultural scenario of Nagaland along with other North-Eastern states.

From Table 2.3, it is evident that things are changing in the agricultural front as Nagaland appears to be enjoying a higher productivity 1420 kg./per hectare after Tripura, 2183 kg./ha., and Megahalaya 1556 kg./ha. as on 1999–2000 with minimum use of fertilizers for the same corresponding period. Farming practices in Nagaland have seen this transformation not purely because of direct plan intervention but more due to the strategy that focused on evolving partnership between the agencies concerned and village level institutions such as village development council. This strategy of building on community partnership induced trust among people culminating in developing and implementing programmes that addressed the needs of the people, suiting local conditions and compatible to their skills and age old practices. By encouraging community participation the government dispelled fears and suspicion normally associated with change and side by side it was successful in motivating farmers to adopt change by visualizing change as a contributor to their overall economic well-being.

Table 2.3: Agriculture scenario of North East

State	*Unit*	*1998–99*	*1999–00*	*2001–01*
Arunachal Pradesh				
Yield Food Grains.	Kg./ha.	205	—	—
Fertilizer consumption	Tonnes	700	—	—
Operational Holdings	Ha/holdings	—	—	—
Assam				
Yield Food Grains	Kg./ha.	1271	1406	1455
Fertilizer consumption	Tonnes	78102	110111	140619
Operational Holdings	Ha/holdings	—	—	—
Manipur				
Yield Food Grains	Kg./ha.	392	376	—
Fertilizer consumption	Tonnes	17109	18672	
Operational Holdings	Ha/holdings	—	—	—
Meghalaya				
Yield Food Grains	Kg./ha.	1404	1556	1604
Fertilizer consumption	Tonnes	3680	4120	—
Operational holdings	Ha/holdings			
Mizoram				
Yield Food Grains	Kg./ha.	136	115	126
Fertilizer consumption	Tonnes	1142	2260	
Operational Holdings	Ha/holdings	—	1.29	—
Nagaland				
Yield Food Grains	Kg./ha.	1340	1420	—
Fertilizer consumption	Tonnes	663	820	—
Operational Holdings	Ha/holdings	7.46	6.82	—
Sikkim				
Yield Food Grains	Kg./ha.	99	103	103
Fertilizer consumption	Tonnes	—	879	1081
Operational Holdings	Ha/holdings	7.10	7.10	7.10
Tripura				
Yield Food Grains	Kg./ha.	1893	2183	2059
Fertilizer consumption	Tonnes	9761	8910	11315
Operational Holdings	Ha/holdings	1.02	0.97	0.97
National average of food grain per/ha.			**1700 kg. per ha.**	

It is true that agriculture scenario in Nagaland is improving due to innovative practices and community partnership but many other aspects concerning agriculture needs to be addressed. Table 2.4 indicates that Nagaland has 64.5 per cent, the highest percentage of work-force involved in agricultural operations in comparison to other North Eastern states. Further women participation in agricultural operation is considered to be important.

Table 2.4: Work Participation and literacy in N.E.

State	*Workers as % of population (2001)*	*Cultivators (%)*	*Cultivators %*		*Literacy %*		
			Male	*Female*	*Persons*	*Males*	*Females*
Arunachal Pradesh	43.90	58.44	50.21	81.10	54.74	64.07	44. 24
Assam	35.88	39.15	51.00	56.90	64.28	71.93	56.03
Manipur	44.77	46.06	55.63	59.56	68.87	77.87	59.70
Meghalaya	41.46	47.80	61.30	72.54	63.31	66.14	60.41
Mizoram	52.75	53.91	53.70	67.57	88.49	90.69	86.13
Nagaland	42.71	64.50	59.40	79.66	67.11	71.77	61.92
Sikkim	48.72	49.91	47.60	71.48	69.68	76.73	61.46
Tripura	36.29	26.88	46.33	62.59	73.66	81.47	65.41
All India	**39.25**	**31.71**	**52.16**	**71.94**	**65.18**	**75.85**	**56.14**

Source: Compiled from Statistical Hand Book 2003 and Census of India 2001.

Nagaland has 79.66 per cent of the total women work force in agricultural operations after Arunachal Pradesh, 81.10 per cent.This indicates agriculture in the state continues to be at subsistence level as mobility towards secondary and tertiary sector stands insignificant in spite of high level of general literacy 67.11 per cent and incase of women 61.92 per cent as per census 2001.

Continuance of gender imbalance in this segment will undermine development. One way the problem can be addressed is mechanization of agriculture and this may not have adverse impact on employment, as basically the composition of hired labour in agriculture is 3.98 per cent of the total workers (849982) and out of which women accounts only for 1.84 per cent of the combined work force. The data by indicating marginal presence of hired labour authenticates that in Nagaland agricultural operations are undertaken collectively by members within the family and with general support from kith, kin and clan. Therefore, a strategy encouraging mechanization in farming practices shall free hands who alternatively can concentrate on weaving and other traditional crafts in which Naga men and women are highly dexterous at.

Table 2.5: Per Capita Income (at current prices)

(in Rs.)

State	*1996–1997*	*1997–1998*	*1998–1999*	*1999–2000*	*2000–2001*	*2001–2002*	*2002–2003*
Arunachal Pradesh	10816	11642	12955	13669	14683	14771	15616
Assam	7394	7966	8826	10080	10718	11132	12074
Manipur	7961	9039	10504	12721	12823	13213	12230
Meghalaya	8785	9668	11090	12083	13114	14510	15983
Mizoram	12210	12393	13479	14909	18491	19696	—
Nagaland	11805	13052	12408	12594	17629	18911	—
Sikkim	9901	11324	12645	13356	16658	18822	20456
Tripura	7440	8647	9613	10213	10913	17459	—
All India	**11564**	**12706**	**14395**	**15625**	**16555**	**17823**	**19041**

Source: NEDFI data Bank, October 2005.

Per-Capita Income and Poverty Ratio

The data on per-capita income indicates that as on 2001–02, Nagaland with a per capita income of Rs. 18911.00 stands second among the states in the region. Mizoram with a per capita income of Rs. 19696.00 tops the region. This is definitely a commendable achievement. In this context it is pertinent to note that the percentage of workforce in Nagaland is 42.71 per cent of the total population whereas in Mizoram it is 52.75 per cent of the total population (Table 2.3). Nagaland in spite of being an agrarian state and with a comparatively lesser working population is standing very close to Mizoram in per-capita income which incidentally, also enjoys higher literacy rate at 88.49 per cent as compared with Nagaland, 79.66 per cent (Census 2001). Directly or indirectly the figures reveal higher work motivation and commitment towards productivity. This is a strength for the society and when effectively channelized can bring economic wonders in the state. Naga culture being low on uncertainty avoidance indicates higher risk taking capabilities which is an entrepreneurial quality. Society by collectively sustaining and promoting this entrepreneurial talent among its work force can usher rapid economic refurbishment to the state.

On the poverty dimension as per data indicated in Table 2.5, Nagaland and Assam have the highest poverty ratio among North-Eastern States as on 2004–05. One reason that can be attributed for high incidence of poverty in Nagaland is the massive decadal growth of population, i.e. 64.41% (Table 2.1) between 1991 and 2001. Going by this rate the annual average growth of population works out at 6.44 per cent and it is bound to affect poverty alleviation programmes.

Table 2.6: Poverty Ratio in North-East

State	*1973–74*	*1993–94*	*1999–2000*	*2004–05**
Arunachal Pradesh	51.93	39.35	33.47	17.60
Assam	51.21	40.46	36.09	19.00
Manipur	49.96	33.78	25.84	17.30
Meghalaya	50.20	37.92	33.87	18.50
Mizoram	50.32	25.66	19.47	12.60
Nagaland	50.81	37.92	32.67	19.00
Tripura	51.00	39.10	34.44	18.90
All India	**54.88**	**35.97**	**26.10**	**27.50**

Source: *Manpower Journal,* May 2006 p. 256 and **Kurukshetra,* May 2007, p. 45.

Management of population is a major issue that needs to be addressed in the context of development initiatives in Nagaland. One distinct advantage of Naga society is the existence of strong and vibrant traditional institutions and involving these institutions in population control and management mechanism shall be beneficial. Besides, the society being relative non-conservative, it offers the opportunity to debate on the problems and threats of population explosion and thereby through open debates can generate consensus on means to control population. It is felt that by addressing the issue on a community basis involving traditional and mass based institutions can add strength to any strategy directed towards this end. The involvement of traditional and mass based institutions can be facilitated through social agreements. One interesting observation made by Sampath Kumar (2007), is worth our attention as it testifies to the need to evolve partnership between the administration and social institutions in order to gain success in poverty alleviation programme. In his capacity as Deputy Commissioner of West Garo Hills, entrusted with implementing the National Rural Employment Guarantee

Programme, he noticed that often the administration takes the support of grassroots institutions in dealing with law and order issue and the effort bears fruit. But when it comes to the issue of involving them in developmental process there is tendency to keep them out of the process. Citing his experience he states that by involving traditional and other village level institutions in Garo hills the NREGS was a great success and it could achieved the desire goals as planned. This point is worth considering in the context of poverty alleviation programmes in Nagaland and also in dealing with issues concerning population explosion in the state.

Another aspect which poverty alleviation programmes needs to tackle is over dependence of the state in the primary sector, i.e. 64.50 per cent (Table 2.3) of the working population contributing 31 per cent of the NSDP as in 2001. For the same corresponding period the share of industrial workers numbering 2.21 per cent of work force contributed 15.17 per cent of NSDP and 29.83 per cent of total workers in the tertiary sector contributed 53.80 per cent of the NSDP. Thus the data indicates that the strength of Nagaland lies in industrial and tertiary sectors as productivity per worker is high here. Hence poverty alleviation programme would be most successful if more and more workforce is trained and transferred to industrial and tertiary segments.

Table 2.7: Sectoral Composition of Net State Domestic Product at Current Prices

(Rs. in lakh)

State	*1999–00*	*2000–01*	*2001–02*	*2002–03*
Arunachal Pradesh				
Primary Sector	58618	64265	62405	67332
	(40.20)	(40.34)	(38.11)	(38.53)
Secondary sector	26576	25899	24022	25833
Tertiary Sector	60514	69148	76352	81582
NSDP	145708	159312	162779	174747
Assam				
Primary Sector	1283069	1241289	1319182	1434424
	(48.85)	(43.97)	(44.25)	(44)
Secondary sector	326222	397384	334997	353369
Tertiary Sector	1017969	1187541	1313837	1470492
NSDP	2627260	2826214	2968015	3258284

(Contd.)

(Contd.)

State	1999–00	2000–01	2001–02	2002–03
Manipur				
Primary Sector	87803	95699	101046	—
	(30.72)	(32.49)	(31.52)	
Secondary sector	57280	58378	66579	—
Tertiary Sector	140692	140425	152853	—
NSDP	285775	294502	320478	—
Meghalaya				
Primary Sector	95304	100900	112105	—
	(32.83)	(31.24)	(30.57)	—
Secondary sector	33565	36788	42173	—
Tertiary Sector	161495	185308	212377	—
NSDP	290364	322996	366655	—
Mizoram				
Primary Sector	30628	47283	47142	49240
	(23.77)	(28.92)	(26.52)	(24.27)
Secondary sector	17340	12396	19591	28188
Tertiary Sector	80850	103782	110997	125321
NSDP	128818	163461	177730	202749
Nagaland				
Primary Sector	71421	106296	—	—
	(27)	(31)		
Secondary sector	60067	52015	—	—
	(22.63)	(15.17)		
Tertiary Sector	133931	184409	—	—
	(50.46)	(53.80)		
NSDP	265419	342720	—	—
Tripura				
Primary Sector	131661	143007	—	—
	(34.53)	(34.18)		
Secondary sector	51441	58640	—	—
Tertiary Sector	198200	216703	—	—
NSDP	**381272**	**418350**	—	—

However as per statistical data reported in statistical handbook 2003, the number of trainees declared successful in craftsman and industrial training during the year 2000, 2001 and 2002 is 173, 122 and 165 respectively. This indicates that policy planners are not seriously assessing the efficacy of industrial training both in augmenting employment and also in reducing poverty. It would be advantageous for all concerned if due is attention is given to the above issues.

Education

Quality of human resources is a key factor that facilitates developmental process in any society. Data in Table 2.8 reveal that Nagaland stands second with 6.58 teachers per school in the primary and upper primary level. However when the data for secondary and senior secondary school is considered the state with a ratio of 20.15 stands third with Tripura leading all the North-Eastern states with a ratio of 29.12. The data reveals that all the states in the region appear to be neglecting the importance of primary education and in the long run it is bound to undermine the quality of human assets.

Table 2.8: Comparative analysis of school education (2004–05)

State	*No. of Primary and upper primary schools*	*Teachers*	*Teacher/school ratio*	*Secondary and Sr. Secondary Schools*	*Teacher*	*Teacher/school ratio*
Arunachal Pradesh	1697	6139	3.61	204	3951	19.36
Assam	33749	91386	2.71	4502	67883	15.10
Manipur	3346	17402	5.20	652	12899	19.78
Meghalaya	9890	20289	2.05	596	7355	12.34
Mizoram	2100	10867	5.17	385	3637	9.44
Nagaland	1779	11714	6.58	255	5140	20.15
Sikkim	626	4407	7.04	138	3638	26.36
Tripura	2489	14739	5.92	643	18727	29.12

Source: Compiled from NEDFI data bank quarterly, July 2004.

The reason is pretty simple. Primary schools are the centres which initiate learning process in the tender minds. Children spend roughly 40 per cent of their productive time in school. Therefore, when schools are understaffed it is obvious that children shall be deprived of required attention from the teachers. Absence of adequate attention makes learning for a child incomplete. Adding to his/her woes are the numerous tests and assignments where a child has to prove its merit both to the parents and the school. Seldom do we realize that learning is effective for a child only when imparted giving due attention to the child. The child needs attention to boost his confidence and also to satisfy his emotional needs. A child lacking in requisite attention runs the risk of loosing natural interest for learning and learning for him/her becomes mechanical hindering its creative and innovative abilities. The end result is either under-performance or mediocre performance. In the context of Nagaland one is aware that schools have been communitized and thus school committees at grassroots level have to ensure that schools are optimally staffed. As an earnest step towards that direction the government may even consider involving the school committees at sub-divisional levels to assess, plan, co-ordinate and control issues concerning management of schools at all levels. Collective cultures have a great strength of building public opinion and a public opinion in collective society is never overlooked as trivial or irrelevant. For any guidance concerning fine tuning of education in the state they can draw strength from past experiences when the society could promote excellent centres of integrated learning through institutions like the Morung.

Handloom and Handicrafts

The segment of the population that works in the cultural industries and production process use traditional knowledge inspired by nature. Work is guided by the inner motivation to produce goods of ethereal beauty. North East India is home to diverse ethnic groups who are rich in crafts, having immense potentialities to shape the socio-economic milieu of the region. As indicated in Table 2.9, Manipur tops having 9.29 per cent of the total artisan of the region and Nagaland stands fourth with 1.95 per cent of the total number of artisans of the region. In terms of production value Nagaland tops the region generating 35.98 per cent of the value. The data reiterates the fact that Naga handlooms, a cultural product of the people command higher market share as compared to others. This is a position of strength and development initiatives have to build on this strength to the advantage of the weavers. Analyzing further one can establish that this unique strength in a way is supported by their culture, which promotes open competition, appreciates innovation and creativity in all facets of life. As one is aware in the past Naga society encouraged creativity and excellence in an individual was accorded social recognition. The strength of their handlooms and handicrafts can be assumed to stem from this fact.

Table 2.9: Profile of Handloom and Handicraft Sector

State	*Number of Units*	*No. of Artisans*	*Production (lakhs)*	*Artisans employed (lakhs)*		
				Male	*Female*	*Total*
Arunachal Pradesh	30360 (2.39)	100482	7820.94	0.39	0.69	1.00
Assam	4044 (0.31)	15735	855.56	0.87	0.70	1.57
Manipur	98051 (7.74)	379988	1476.00	1.85	1.95	3.80
Meghalaya	11512 (0.90)	53564	2580.67	0.24	0.29	0.53
Mizoram	2213 (0.17)	5260	5.93	0.02	0.03	0.05
Nagaland	17603 (1.39)	79878	9463.99	0.40	0.40	0.80
Sikkim	2198 (0.17)	9768	5.59	0.26	0.72	0.98
Tripura	77375 (6.11)	244495	60.80	1.32	1.13	2.45
North-East	231844 (19.18)	889170	20941.08	—	—	—
All India	**1266009 (100)**	**4103293**	**26312.13**	**—**	**—**	**—**

Table 2.10 shows that artisans of Nagaland have the highest average income, i.e. Rs. 9350.00 when compared to other states in the region. The position of the state reflects the strength of intrinsic motivation among weavers which prompt them to produce things of beauty besides offering full value for the money exchanged. Another pertinent fact that the data reveals is the enterprising skill and zeal among the artisans which directly or indirectly enabled them to command 35.98 per cent (Table 2.9) of the total market share in the North East. Therefore, one can reasonably believe that the culture promotes enterprising spirit and the state by recognizing this strength can build programmes and policies that facilitate weavers and artisans to capitalize on the market opportunities wherever they exists.

Table 2.10: Share of Handloom and Handicraft in the income of the artisans

State	*Monthly average total income*	*Monthly average income from handloom and handicrafts*	*Income from other sources*	*% share of income from handloom*
Arunachal Pradesh	10750.00	5250.00	5500.00	48.84
Assam	8088.89	6437.04	1651.85	79.58
Manipur	8468.42	7768.42	700.00	91.73
Meghalaya	7860.00	5320.00	2540.00	67.68
Mizoram	6866.67	6700.00	166.67	97.57
Nagaland	12125.00	9350.00	2775.00	77.11
Sikkim	1725.00	962.50	762.50	55.80
Tripura	5458.33	3875.00	1583.33	70.99
North-East	8479.79	6664.36	1815.43	78.59

Source: NEDFI quarterly data bank October 2005.

Table 2.11: Working Status of full time weavers in North Eastern States

State	*Weavers*	*Production of clothes per loom*
Arunachal Pradesh	545	1.26
Assam	384262	0.63
Manipur	107148	1.86
Meghalaya	480	1.58
Mizoram	1074	0.22
Nagaland	26899	1.21
Sikkim	—	—
Tripura	17216	2.30

Source: NEDFI quarterly data bank October 2005, p. 23.

Table 2.11 shows that Nagaland stands fourth in production with 1.21 metres per loom and is preceded by Tripura, Manipur and Meghalaya. Before forming any opinions regarding loom productivity one has to recognize that weaving in Nagaland is mostly undertaken by women, as cultural beliefs prohibit men from weaving. Secondly, weaving in Nagaland is not a full time occupation, women pursue it in addition to other normal chores in the family. Further, Table 2.4 indicates that 79.66 per cent of women take active part in agricultural operations and thus it becomes clear that most of the weavers are also farmers and weaving for them is a part time engagement. Further while assessing the productivity of weaving one has to take note of the level of mechanization that has gone into it. In the absence of data concerning mechanization, one can fairly assume that Naga weavers and artisans are a productive lot despite several constrains.

State Support Towards Development

The government machinery in India by default undertakes the responsibility of procuring funds, planning and implementing development activities in the country. Citizens in the existing process of development remain at the end of the developmental pipeline more as its mere beneficiaries/recipients. For development to be encompassing it is essential that there exists some debate in order to achieve some consensus on the following issues:

1. Targets that the developmental plan desires to seek such as: reducing poverty, increase in employment and income, increase in the quality of education, health and sanitation, and additions to the general infrastructure etc.
2. Availability and strength of resources to support the programmes and the means through which it can be achieved. Basically the question wishes to address issues such as: level of government and private participation, need for roping in traditional and modern institutions, level of expertise and the source of such expertise etc.
3. In what ways does it add to the quality of life or how does it make peoples' life better?
4. Roles and responsibilities that parties concerned have to undertake and execute.

Basically the questions attempts to ascertain public opinion regarding community approach to development and in what ways community participation can make development effective and meaningful. In the context of Nagaland, we know that Nagas are collective societies having strong mass based public organizations, a strength for them in all respects. The concept of community participation in development is not new to them. For them it is part of their belief both in the past and in the present. The vibrant institution of morung, owning community land and community cultivation practices etc. is a pointer in that direction. Village development programmes existed in the state since the early part of the 1970s and its noble objectives were incorporated and institutionalized in the Panchayati Raj Act. Thus, it appears that culturally and socially community development programmes can be very effective in contemporary Nagaland in all respects. In short development initiatives supported by evolving community partnership can be instrumental in ushering in freedom as termed by the noble laureate Amartya Sen.

Referring to Table 2.12, it is seen that Nagaland as on 2002–03 spent 52 per cent of its total receipts in development, whereas states like Arunachal Pradesh, Meghalaya, Assam and Tripura have higher allocations for developmental purpose. Further, the percentage of spending of central grants received for the purpose is mere 76 per cent of the total grant as on 2002–03. The data indicate two things: (1) the state suffers from resource constrains and lack of resources make development less meaningful. The state is not doing much to improve the resource base to facilitate concerted development programmes. (2) Even out of the grants received it appears that there is a significant diversion to other areas rather than for the purpose for which the fund is earmarked. Continuance of this trend will put the state behind other states in the North-East. Further curtailing on developmental expenditure in the long run will simply affect the poor thereby widening inequities among the people. One distinct advantage that community participation shall usher in is that society will develop a sense of belonging thereby helping in reducing the mistrust that people generally carry about developmental programmes when pursued in a top down approach.

Table 2.12: Public Finance: Government spending on Developmental Activities

(Rs. in crores)

State	*1999–00*	*2000–01*	*2001–02*	*2002–03*
Arunachal Pradesh				
Aggregate Receipt	1052	1117	1506	1444
Aggregate Expenditure	1098	1026	1523	1369
Development Expenditure	794(72)	824(80)	1129(74)	921(67)
Assam				
Aggregate Receipt	6585	7509	8927	9684
Aggregate Expenditure	7086	7631	10380	10494
Development Expenditure	3980(56)	4627(61)	6570(63)	6350 (60)
Manipur				
Aggregate Receipt	1622	1244	2035	1922
Aggregate Expenditure	1780	1381	2186	2010
Development Expenditure	1160(65)	762(55)	1206(55)	1014(50)
Meghalaya				
Aggregate Receipt	1206	1458	1721	1844
Aggregate Expenditure	1195	1424	1746	1839
Development Expenditure	811(68)	891(63)	1173(67)	1235(67)
Mizoram				
Aggregate Receipt	1261	1131	1343	1221
Aggregate Expenditure	1161	1288	1403	1224
Development Expenditure	840(72)	873(68)	970(69)	791(64)
Nagaland				
Aggregate Receipt	1539	1686	1924	1992
Aggregate Expenditure	1495	1836	2019	1962
Development Expenditure	843(56)	1070(58)	1134(56)	1038(52)
Sikkim				
Aggregate Receipt	1073	958	1152	2016
Aggregate Expenditure	1620	947	1129	1996
Development Expenditure	458(28)	504(53)	688(61)	717(35)
Tripura				
Aggregate Receipt	1899	2085	2427	2694
Aggregate Expenditure	1773	2135	2668	2733
Development Expenditure	1164(66)	1409(66)	1742(65)	1693(62)

Table 2.13: Grants from the Centre and Utilization for Development

(Rs. in crores)

State	*1999–00*	*2000–01*	*2001–02*	*2002–03*	*Development expenditure*	
Arunachal Pradesh	598	760	1063	988	921	(93)
Assam	1722	2018	2714	3230	6350	(197)
Manipur	599	790	1108	944	1014	(107)
Meghalaya	415	762	928	987	1235	(125)
Mizoram	576	686	919	1358	791	(58)
Nagaland	543	1237	1271	1360	1038	(76)
Sikkim	321	436	625	634	717	(113)
Tripura	731	1181	1373	1500	1693	(113)

Source: NEDFI, Data Bank Quarterly October 2005.

Conclusion

The need for development is never static but is always progressive. It expands with the increasing need of the people. In fact there is no limit to the developmental process in any society. The question that automatically follows from the above understanding is: how do we make development meaningful for us in spite of varied odds and constrains. In our analysis one thing has been shown as conducive that the government alone cannot be expected to make development matter. The reason is that development does not resemble a one-way traffic to flow utilities from one end to the other. Development is a participative exercise which involves common strength, combined resources and collective wisdom to make it effective. Anything which calls for common strength, resources and wisdom has its source in the culture of the people. Culture in the broad anthropological sense connotes 'design for living' and development in this context can be understood as community policies and practices in planning and implementing that design for living. Therefore one can say that development is a community approach, where people's participation holds the key for its effectiveness. Alemtoshi (2002:2) quoting the Sukla Commission report cites that, for infrastructure alone Nagaland needs a whopping amount of Rs. 11000 crores. The question is, wherefrom will such enormous amount come. Government alone cannot provide the funds but at the same time the need for infrastructural growth cannot be overlooked. The answer lies in evolving a mechanism that supports people's participation at all levels. The roots of community development as a means for collective well-being can be traced to the early hunting expeditions of pre-historic man. However its importance as an alternative approach to development can be linked to the first Mechanics' Institute set up in 1823 by Lord Brougham, an aristocrat turned philanthropist (Mayo, 2000:85–90). Community development in the current context cannot be understood simply as some basic programmes in literacy, health, vocational training etc. It does not mean only digging of wells, roads, occasional social works; it is more properly the development of stable, self-reliant communities with an assured sense of social, political and economic responsibility among people. In the truest sense communitisation means democratization aimed at generating a sense of equity. Nagas as a collectivist society can make community development process very meaningful and the reasons are same as cited earlier. Their culture supports and accommodates participation and hence community development based on people's participation can place the state higher in the developmental plane of the region. What is required for its success is commitment and dedication to the cause, open communication, transparency and respects for partnership—its core strength. Analyzing different segments of the state's economy vide the data we could identify some strengths and weakness along with cultural compatibility. The commitment that has just been referred to is nothing but continual evaluation of the cultural and developmental beliefs so as to make culture effective for development and in the same breath make development responsive to culture and economic goals of the people. The advantages of community participation in development especially in the context of ethnic societies like the Nagas can be manifold: (1) Community participation can evolve a community perspective in building broader understanding on diverse issues that confront the society. Side by side it shall pull the society out of narrow loyalties which often is believed to be the potent cause of lopsided development. (2) It can be instrumental in developing a consensus on long term and short term economic and social goals. (3) Community participation can harness the patterns of influence of kin and clan is development and modernization. In doing so it shall rebuild the integrated structure and solidarity that traditional order contained. Community participation by synthesizing the old and the new, tradition and modernity can stimulate economic growth by cutting down on dependency. Dependency can never be a facilitator of meaningful development. (4) Lastly participation shall minimize the stress and strain any society undergoes in the transitional phase as it brings change as per requirement of the people and not on whims and fancies of those in authority or power.

REFERENCES

Alemtoshi Jamir (2002), Keynote Address, delivered at National Seminar, Dimensions of Development in Nagaland, Kohima.

Baidyaṇath Saraswati (1998).*The Use of Cultural Heritage as A Tool For Development*, New Delhi: Indira Gandhi National Centre for the Arts.

Bag, G.N. (2001) *Rural Transformation in Tribal Areas,* New Delhi: Akansha Publication House.

Dube, S.C. (1990), 'Social and Cultural Factors in Development' in *Tradition and Development.* New Delhi: Vikas Publication House. pp. 1–16

Hofsted, G. (1980) *Cultures Consequences: International Differences in Work Related Values.* C.A: Sage Publications.

Huib Wursten (____) *Mental Images: The Influence of Culture on Economic Policy.*

Hutton, J.H. (1969) *The Angami Nagas*, Oxford University Press.

Kanungo, R.N. and Jager, A.M. (1990), The Need for Indigenous Management in Developing Countries. In A.M. Jager and Kanungo, R.N. (eds.), *Management in Developing Countries*. London: Routledge.

Marjorie Mayo (2000), *Cultures Communities, Identities: Cultural Strategies for Participation and Empowerment,* New York: Palgrave, pp. 85–90.

Pattnaik, K.M. (1986) *Rural Industrialization*, Cuttack: Kitab Mahal, pp. 9-10

Sanjay T. Menon (1994), Designing Work in Developing Countries In Rabindra N. Kanungo and Manuel Mendonca (eds.)*Work Motivation Models for Developing Countries*, New Delhi: Sage Publication. pp. 95–96.

Sen, Amartya, (2004), *Argumentative India,* London: Penguin.

Simray, U.A. (2006), *Tribal Land Alienation in North East India*, Guwahati: North East Social Research Centre.

Statistical Hand Book (2003), Government of Nagaland, Kohima.

Vedayi Nyekha (1994). *The Naga Work Culture,* Kohima: Naga Cultural Society.

Yadav. R.P. (1980), *People's Participation: Focus on Mobilisation,* Local Level Planning and Rural Development, Bangkok.

3

COMPLEXITIES OF COMMON AND RURAL LIVELIHOOD

An Empirical Study of Rural Households in Nine Villages of Arunachal Pradesh

A. IBOTOMBI SINGH and A. MITRA

Introduction

In contemporary literature of economics the term 'Common Property Resources' (CPRs) includes three dimensions which are essential to any definition of CPRs:

- Community, i.e., village or subset of people in a village (tribe or caste based),
- Ownership, i.e., legal or there is a perception of ownership through habitual usage (which is free),
- Accessibility to indivisible bodies of land, water, air and public spaces where a group people exercises rights of use and carry responsibility of management.

Resources which are collectively used by a group of people are defined as CPRs. (Pasha, 1992:249). Alternatively they can be defined as "those (non exclusive) resources in which a group of people have co-equal use rights. Membership in the group of co-owners is typically conferred by membership in some group, generally a group whose central purpose is not the use or administration of the resources (*per se*) such as a village , a tribe etc." (Jodha, 1990:65A). Another definition of CPRs is "a property on which well defined collective claims by an exclusive group are established, the use of the resource is subtractive, having the characteristic of a public good such as indivisibility, shall be termed as common property resource" (Kadekodi, 2004:19). From these definitions two important characteristics of CPRs. stand out: (i) consumption of the resources is rivalry and (ii) the principle of exclusion cannot be applied. By rival consumption, we mean that the exploitation of the resource by a group of people or a village or a tribe or an individual reduces the stock of the resource. It not only affects the consumption of others but also deteriorates the environment. The second criteria refers to the fact that a resource user cannot be debarred from using the resource as each resource user is a co-owner, having equal rights of usage. However, CPRs. can be divided into two groups: (a) Community Property Land Resources (CPLRs) and (b) Community Property Forest Resources (CPFRs). The CPLRs refer to lands identified with a specific type of property rights whereas the CPFRs are the forest area where the state has exclusive rights on the stock resources. The CPLRs include community pastures, cultivable wastelands, fallow other than current fallow, grazing lands etc. Similarly, the CPFRs include reserved forest area, protected forest area, un-classed forest area etc. Hence, an attempt is made in this article to measure the degree of degradation of CPRs in Arunachal Pradesh by taking into account the variables like un-classed forest area, cultivable waste lands and fallow other than current fallow which can be accounted as a CPRs. It is often not easy to measure the role of specific factors that are associated with the decline of these resources since it is a byproduct of multiple forces and also investigate to the extent to which rural households use and depend on CPRs for their daily livelihood.

The paper is organized into four sections. Section-I deals with changes in land utilization and district-wise distribution of population, density and percentage of urban population in Arunachal Pradesh. Section-II discusses changes in characteristics of CPRs. in Arunachal Pradesh during the last three decades. Section-III investigates the diverse intricacies of the dependence of rural households on community forests and develops an econometric model to analyse the degree of variation in forest dependency as well as dependency on different forest products of poor and non-poor rural households with the socio-economic status of user households. The final section (Section-IV) summarizes the findings and conclusion.

SECTION-I

Changes in Land Utilization in Arunachal Pradesh

The total geographical area of the State is 83,743 sq. kms., out of which 70 per cent constitute broad and narrow valleys, 10 per cent foothills and flat areas and 20 per cent snow clad peak areas. Because of being a mountainous and hilly region state, the state is not conducive for permanent/settled and terrace cultivation. There are also two other reasons for it. First, the population density is low (13 people per sq. km. as per 2001 Census). And secondly, jhum/shifting cultivation seems to be the main viable alternative to the villagers (i.e., highlanders) as they have no other income earning opportunities than agriculture. Thus, the agricultural operations are confined to around 5 per cent of the total geographical area of which a large portion is under shifting cultivation. About 62 per cent of the total forest area of the state is under un-classed forest where the local people exercise their traditional rights. There are three types of land ownership system existing presently in Arunachal Pradesh: (a) Private ownership, (b) Community ownership and (c) Clan ownership. Community ownership system mostly prevails in the state. It will be difficult for anybody in the rural areas to say about the extent and value of the land since they do not have surveyed village maps and land records. In the absence of land records, a community or a clan of a tribe owns a demarcated area of land, which is known among the village community or clan. The traditional village councils headed by *Gaon Burah* (Das, 1995; Mishra,1983) are the traditional institutions for decision making, natural resource management, conflict-resolution and collective action in the villages of Arunachal Pradesh. This institution has the authority and thus directs all activities in the village including the allocation of land and forests to every households of the village. Sachin Roy writes in his book, *Aspects of Padam Minyong Culture*, that all matters of common interest are placed before it for decision and nothing can be done without its approval and sanction (Roy, 1960). The villagers enjoy the rights over community lands, which are distributed by this institution to them, and they conduct agricultural activities on it. When the land becomes less fertile, they shift from the present area under cultivation to another place. This process of shifting land for agricultural activities is known as jhum/shifting cultivation. It seems to be the main reason for the degradation of CPRs and the environment as a whole. But the people living in the urban area have individual rights to the lands under the Arunachal Land Revenue Act, 1991, and have freedom to utilize it according to their own conveniences.

The custodianship of CPRs presently in Arunachal Pradesh rests with the village community; represented by village councils/ Panchayats and *Gaon Burah*s. In the traditional tribal society, village councils or Panchayats and *Gaon Burahs* did not impose any taxes and levies on CPRs users. The maintenance and upkeep of CPRs suffered as they depended more and more on funds for assistance from the government. The main reason for the ineffectiveness of these institutions seems to be the conflicts between the traditional and the modern system of judiciary. There is also the lack of environmental awareness among the masses, especially the villagers.

Therefore, an attempt has been made to analyze the changes in land utilization in Arunachal Pradesh during the period 1980–81 to 2000–01.

Table 3.1 compares the changes in land utilization in terms of net sown area and gross area under agricultural operation in Arunachal Pradesh from 1980–81 to 2000–01. The net sown area had declined in all districts of the state except East Kameng and Changlang districts where the percentage variation of net cropped area stood at 6.56 and 17.94 respectively. However, the gross area under agricultural operation has a negative variation in all districts except Tawang. For example, the state has a negative variation in both the indicators –8.94 and –44.45 per cent over the years. The negative variation in net cropped area and gross area under operation seems to be because of diversification of economic pursuits or non-availability of surveyed land records.

Further, increased population is widely considered to be an important contributor to shrinkage and depletion of CPRs. In Arunachal Pradesh, the role of population in the decline of CPRs seems to be dominant. The decadal population variation is 37 per cent (which increases from 6.32 lakhs in 1981 to 8.65 lakhs in 1991). Table 3.2 gives a brief account of district-wise distribution of population, density and percentage of urban population. The decadal population growth in Lohit district is very alarming as it is recorded as 57.85 per cent. The percentage decadal growth rate of population during 1991–2001 shows that the population of the state increased by 26.20 per cent as against an increase of 21.34 per cent at all India level. The density of population as per 2001 Census is 13 persons per sq. kms. as against 10 persons in 1991 Census, which is an increase of 30 per cent in a decade. However, the density is found to be the lowest among the states. In 2001 Census, as many as 79.59 per cent of the people reside in rural areas and the remaining 20.41 per cent of the people reside in urban areas. The degree of urbanization has substantially improved in 2001 as compared to 1991. The trend is towards more and more urbanization. The percentage of urban population to total population was 11 per cent in 1991, which has increased to 20.41 per cent in 2001.

Table 3.1: Changes in Land Utilization in Arunachal Pradesh (1980–81 to 2000–01)

(in hectare)

District	*Net Area Sown*		*Percentage Variation over*	*Gross Cropped Area*		*Percentage Variation over*
	1980–81	*2000–01*	*1980–81*	*1980–81*	*2000–01*	*1980–81*
Tawang	7911	4495	–43.18	4471	5506	23.15
West Kameng	12944	4616	- 64.34	14242	4770	- 66.51
East Kameng	9994	10653	+ 6.56	30173	11217	- 62.82
Papum Pare	N.A.	13053	N.A.	N.A.	13760	N.A.
Lower Subansiri*	40686	35585	–12.54	46542	39427	- 15.29
Upper Subansiri	8407	8409	0.02	12325	8457	- 31.38
West Siang	20136	19354	- 3.88	59860	19619	- 67.22
East Siang	36464	26555	- 27.17	102771	29670	–71.13
Upper Siang	N.A.	3277	N.A.	N.A.	3359	N.A.
Dibang Valley**	19852	14591	- 26.50	20244	13478	- 33.42
Lohit***	23932	19163	–19.93	25948	19525	- 24.75
Changlang	22992	27117	+17.94	28280	27472	–2.86
Tirap	16545	13342	- 19.36	40530	15240	- 62.40
Arunachal Pradesh	**219863**	**200210**	**- 8.94**	**385386**	**214066**	**- 44.45**

Note: The symbol (*) includes Kurung Kumey , (**) includes Lower Dibang Valley and (***) includes Anjaw Districts.

Source: Statistical Abstract of Arunachal Pradesh, 1987 and 2007. Directorate of Economics and Statistics, Government of Arunachal Pradesh, Itanagar.

Table 3.2: District-wise Distribution of Population, Density and Percentage of Urban Population

(1991–2001)

District	*Population*		*Density (per sq. km.)*		*Percentage of urban population*	
	1991	*2001*	*1991*	*2001*	*1991*	*2001*
Tawang	28287	38924	13	16	—	12.84
West Kameng	56421	74599	8	10	10	8.96
East Kameng	50395	57179	12	14	—	26.22
Papum Pare	72811	122003	25	35	43	50.83
Lower Subansiri*	83167	98244	8	10	11	12.59
Upper Subansiri	50086	55346	7	8	—	28.13
West Siang	89936	103918	7	13	15	19.95
East Siang	99653	87397	15	22	15	25.13
Upper Siang[a]	—	33363	—	5	—	—
Dibang Valley**	43068	57760	3	4	16	17.56
Lohit***	109706	143527	10	13	21	18.54
Changlang	95530	125422	20	27	—	9.85
Tirap	85508	100326	36	42	8	15.25
Arunachal Pradesh	**864568**	**1097968**	**10**	**13**	**11**	**20.41**

Note: (1) The symbol (*) includes Kurung Kumey , (**) includes Lower Dibang Valley and (***) includes Anjaw Districts.

(2) The symbol ([a]) indicates population being included in East Siang.

Source: Statistical Abstract of Arunachal Pradesh, 1987 and 1995, Directorate of Economics and Statistics, Government of Arunachal Pradesh, Itanagar.

SECTION-II

Changes in Characteristics of CPRs in AP: A District-wise Comparative Study

An attempt has been made to calculate the total approximate CPRs. (land and forest) of the state. Table 3.2 gives a district-wise comparative study of the changes in CPRs characteristics in Arunachal Pradesh. It has been found that the un-classed forest land of Arunachal Pradesh under study stood at 28462.54 hectare in 2006–07 where West Siang district recorded the highest un-classed forest area of 9806.82 hectare and Lower Subansiri district followed it with 4388.46 hectare. In case of cultivable waste lands, Tirap district recorded the highest of 12,514 hectare and Upper Subansiri followed with 2,912 hectare. As far as fallow other than current fallows is concerned, Tirap district recorded the highest with 23,368 hectare followed by Upper Subansiri with 6,079 hectare. Regarding the total approximate CPRs, Tirap district marked the highest CPRs. stock of resources and West Siang and Upper Subansiri ranked second and third recording 13.39 and 10.03 per cent of the State CRPs. It can be reflected from the above analysis that the percentage of total district-wise break-up of CPRs is the highest in Tirap district (15.19 per cent of CPRs to total area of the district), Changlang district (2.46) and West Siang district (2.12).

SECTION-III

Diverse Intricacies of the Dependence of Rural Households on Community Forests: An Econometric Model

In order to explain the diverse intricacies of the dependency of rural communities on community forests, an econometric model was developed to understand the relationship between forest dependency and socio-economic determinants. (Yanggen and Reardon, 2001 also adopted the same procedures). The extent of forest dependency is measured on the basis of the CPR based collections like timber, firewood, bamboo, leaf litter, herbs and medicinal plants, vegetables, eatable roots and wild animals hunted for consumption, as part of total consumption expenditure by rural households as it was done in the 54th round of NSS data (1999). It was hypothesized that household level benefits from common property forest resources (CPFRs) would be associated with the household and community attributes. Hence, variation in forest dependency among rural households can be explained by the socio-economic status of user household. This relationship can be represented as:

$$\sum_{i}^{N} Y_{ij} = f(COSEX_i, HSIZE_i, LANDHO_i, GEN_i, EDU_i, LIVECOST_i, VIDMKT_i, CONNECTY_i)$$

Where, Y = Household consumption value derived from commons, (a proxy for household income from community forest in '000 rupees).

COSEX = Total consumption expenditure of household (a proxy for income status of household in '000 rupees).

HSIZE = Size of household, i.e., number of family members in a household.

LANDHO = Size of land holdings in hectare

GEN = Gender, i.e., male = 1, female = 0

EDU = Average education of family members (number of school years).

LIVECOST = Value of livestock owned by household in '000 rupees.

VIDMKT = Average distance between house and market (a dummy variable for a house 17 km. and above =1 and below 17 km.= 0)

CONNECTY = Road connectivity between village and a constructed road (metal or non-metal) in kilometre.

'j' = Forest products (timber, firewood, bamboo, leaf litter, herbs and medicinal plants, vegetables, roots and wild animals etc.) and, 'i' = (1,2,3,.........N) observations.

Taking log in both sides, the standard equation is given as:

$$\text{In} \sum_{i=1}^{N} Y_{ij} = \beta_0 + \beta_1\text{InCOSEX}_i + \beta_2\text{InHSIZE}_i + \beta_3\text{InLANDHO}_i + \beta_4\text{InGEN}_i$$
$$+ \beta_5\text{InEDU}_i + \beta_6\text{InLIVECOST}_i + \beta_7\text{InVIDMKT}_i + \beta_8\text{InCONNECTY}_i + \varepsilon_i \text{.............(1)}$$

The corresponding equation is defined as double-log model and it is based on a similar model by Di Falco and Perrings (2003) used to understand the effect of co-operative production on inter-specific crop genetic diversity.

It would have been better if the household level income from community forests is taken as a dependent variable. However, the estimation of income in Arunachal economy is, on the one hand, very difficult since the production at the village level is meant mainly for home consumption and on the other hand, the level of monetization is very low. Even after intensive survey, the income data suffers from a lot of errors. This is because the respondents normally hesitate in reporting his/her income. The level of literacy is very low in the study areas. It is not possible to get reliable income data at the household level. Hence, we have no other alternative but to take a proxy variable of household level consumption value from the community forest as well as total consumption expenditure of the household. For consumption purpose again various edibles, fuel, house building materials etc. gathered from the CPRs. are not generally marketed and their valuation is a problem. We have taken their imputed value in estimation of consumption. The data on quantities of different items gathered from forests is dependable but the problem is the non-existence of their village level prices. Some of these forest products are, no doubt, locally bartered but the exchange rate in barter does not reveal the absolute prices which are necessary to arrive at the value. Under these circumstances, we have to take into account the prices of these products prevailing in the nearest local market.

The results of regression for determinants of household consumption value (Y) derived from commons on the above explanatory variables in the estimated equation are represented as:

$$\widehat{\ln Y_{ij}} = \underset{(5.992)}{11.646^{*}} + \underset{(6.624)}{0.190^{*}}\ln COSEX_i + \underset{(0.969)}{0.165}\ln HSIZE_i + \underset{(2.173)}{0.490^{**}}\ln LANDHO_i$$

$$+ \underset{(1.120)}{1.927}\ln GEN_i - \underset{(-4.295)}{0.825^{*}}\ln EDU_i + \underset{(0.992)}{0.043}\ln LIVECOST_i$$

$$+ \underset{(9.447)}{16.413^{*}}\ln VIDMKT_i - \underset{(-4.139)}{0.458^{*}}\ln CONNECTY_i \ldots\ldots\ldots (2)$$

$R^2 = 0.54$ $\bar{R}^2 = 0.53$ $F = 44.356$ $N = 312$

Note: 1. The figures in parentheses are t-values.
2. The asterisk symbol (* and **) denote significant at 0.01 and 0.05 level.

It is evident from the analysis that in addition to constant term, most of the estimators of explanatory variables are significant with the expected sign such as 'COSEX', 'EDU', 'VIDMKT' and 'CONNECTY' at 0.01 level and 'LANDHO' at 0.05 level (2–tailed). The R-square and adjusted R-square ($\bar{R}^2$) for the estimation are as high as 54 per cent and 53 per cent respectively. The F-statistics for overall goodness of the model is 44.36 which is highly significant at $\mu = 0.000$. The parameters of the log transformation variables like β_1, β_2, β_3, β_4, β_5, β_6, β_7 and β_8 in the double log model are different elasticities of the explanatory variables which are measured in different units. The reason for transforming the equation in double-log model is to pull outlying data from a positively or negatively skewed distribution closer to the bulk of the data in a quest to have the variables to be normally distributed.

From the point of interpretation, it is very often difficult to say which explanatory variable is most important in determining the consumption value from community forest (Y) since the values of estimators like b_1, b_2, b_3, b_4, b_5, b_6, b_7 and b_8 depend on the choice of units to measure the explanatory variables.

Therefore, the standard interpretation of estimators in the model is that one per cent change in 'COSEX' results in the respective estimator say (β_1) change in the expected value of Y while all the predictors are held constant. Thus, the elasticity of 'COSEX' reveals the rate of forest dependency as necessity since the estimator, $\beta_1 < 1$. In this model we find all β's as necessity except 'VIDMKT' and 'CONNECTY'. The necessity of forest dependency arises because of (i) climatic condition and altitude from the sea level and (ii) non-availability of alternative fuel. For example, when there was no change in the average value of COSEX (rupees 46,650 per annum), the average value of consumption value from community forest was found to be rupees 25,998 per annum. Hence, the forest dependency in the study area was found to be 55.71 per cent. In other words, if average value of 'COSEX' increased by one per cent, the average value of Y would increase by 0.19 per cent at 0.01 levels (2–tailed) and *vice versa.* Thus, the study shows that the dependency of community forest has direct bearing on the total household consumption expenditure and it is highly significant at 0.01 levels.

In case of the explanatory variables like 'LANDHO', it has a positive relation which is statistically significant at 0.05 levels. The variable 'EDU' is negatively related and significant at 0.01 levels. This is due to the fact that higher level of schooling may have better exit options (Ostrom, 2000) due to high opportunity cost and hence, forest extraction activities may be less attractive for those households. Besides, availability of government sector jobs may well divert people from dependency on forests. A similar finding of Gunatilake (1998) observed that education of the family members was negatively related to forest income in the tropical biosphere reserves in Sri Lanka.

Livestock is sometimes regarded as an asset of the rural community. The average value of livestock per household in the study area is rupees 10,132 and it is positively related but insignificant to the consumption value from commons. This may be due to the fact that the value of livestock is likely to be skewed among the rural households in the study area. In other words, livestock reared in the plains and foothills may be higher than the livestock reared in the hill terrain.

The dummy variable 'VIDMKT' (distance between house and market) was positively related to consumption from community forests and it was statistically significant at 0.01 levels. This indicates that the availability of market nearer the village may divert rural communities from forest dependent activities and other gainful activities due to alternative earning opportunities. At the same time, the rural communities living far away from market may have to depend more on community forests in order to sustain their livelihoods. Gunatilake (1998) also showed similar results in the Sinharaya forest of Sri Lanka.

With regard to road connectivity, it was observed that it is negatively but significantly related with the consumption of community forests. That means the villages having more connectivity have to depend less on community forests and *vice versa.* Probably with more accessibility, alternative livelihood options become available for the villagers and as a result dependence on community forest is reduced.

In common literature, gender was often used to test the effect of gender difference on the level of consumption in CPRs management (Grossman, 1996). Some experimental studies on the gender and cooperative behaviour indicate that women contribute more than men in managing commons due to greater interdependent utility and altruism. However, in the present study one of the aims was to see whether access to and consumption from CPRs was significantly different between male-headed and female-headed households. It was found that the consumption from CPRs was positively related but not significantly affected by gender issue. This may be due to the fact that there were very few female-headed households in the study area.

In order to understand the relationship between the extent of rural community's dependency on consumption of different forest products and socio-economic variables, three more regression models, i.e.

regression on consumption of firewood ($\sum_{i=1}^{312} Y_{i1}$), consumption of timber ($\sum_{i=1}^{312} Y_{i2}$) and consumption of bamboo and other minor forest products ($\sum_{i=1}^{312} Y_{i3}$) were estimated. These are represented as:

$$\ln\sum_{i=1}^{312} Y_{i1} = \beta_0 + \beta_1 \ln COSEX_i + \beta_2 \ln HSIZE_i + \beta_3 \ln LANDHO_i + \beta_4 \ln GEN_i + \beta_5 \ln EDU_i + \beta_6 \ln LIVECOST_i + \beta_6 \ln VIDMKT_i + \beta_7 \ln CONNECTY_i + \varepsilon_i \text{.........} (3)$$

$$\ln\sum_{i=1}^{312} Y_{i2} = \beta_0 + \beta_1 \ln COSEX_i + \beta_2 \ln HSIZE_i + \beta_3 \ln LANDHO_i + \beta_4 \ln GEN_i + \beta_5 \ln EDU_i + \beta_6 \ln LIVECOST_i + \beta_6 \ln VIDMKT_i + \beta_7 \ln CONNECTY_i + \varepsilon_i \text{.........} (4)$$

$$\ln\sum_{i=1}^{312} Y_{i3} = \beta_0 + \beta_1 \ln COSEX_i + \beta_2 \ln HSIZE_i + \beta_3 \ln LANDHO_i + \beta_4 \ln GEN_i + \beta_5 \ln EDU_i + \beta_6 \ln LIVECOST_i + \beta_6 \ln VIDMKT_i + \beta_7 \ln CONNECTY_i + \varepsilon_i \text{.........} (5)$$

To quantify the magnitude of the effect of forest products on the above explanatory variables, the results are represented in estimated equation form as:

$$\ln\hat{Y}_{i1} = \underset{(11.203)}{14.634^*} + \underset{(4.579)}{0.088^* \ln COSEX_i} + \underset{(0.852)}{0.098 \ln HSIZE_i} + \underset{(0.096)}{0.015 \ln LANDHO_i}$$
$$+ \underset{(0.318)}{0.367 \ln GEN_i} - \underset{(-4.566)}{0.590^* \ln EDU_i} - \underset{(0.217)}{0.006 LIVECOST_i}$$
$$+ \underset{(12.357)}{14.427^* \ln VIDMKT_i} - \underset{(-5.196)}{0.387^* \ln CONNECTY_i} \text{.................................} (6)$$

$R^2 = 0.55$ $\overline{R}^2 = 0.53$ $F = 45.372$ $N = 312$

$$\ln\hat{Y}_{i2} = \underset{(-2.100)}{-2.868^{**}} + \underset{(4.375)}{0.088^* \ln COSEX_i} + \underset{(0.123)}{0.015 \ln HSIZE_i} + \underset{(3.029)}{0.480^* \ln LANDHO_i}$$
$$+ \underset{(1.031)}{1.246 \ln GEN_i} - \underset{(-1.929)}{0.260^{**} \ln EDU_i} + \underset{(1.190)}{0.036 \ln LIVECOST_i}$$

$$+0.628\ln VIDMKT_i - 0.046\ln CONNECTY_i \quad \ldots\ldots(7)$$
$$(0.514) \qquad (-0.586)$$
$$R^2 = 0.24 \qquad \overline{R}^2 = 0.22 \qquad F = 12.161 \qquad N = 312$$

$$\ln \hat{Y}_{i3} = -0.119^{**} + 0.014^{*}\ln COSEX_i + 0.053\ln HSIZE_i - 0.004^{*}\ln LANDHO_i$$
$$(-0.307) \qquad (2.371) \qquad (1.557) \qquad (-0.096)$$
$$+0.313\ln GEN_i + 0.025\ln EDU_i + 0.001\ln LIVECOST_i$$
$$(0.915) \qquad (0.646) \qquad (0.052)$$
$$+1.358^{*}\ln VIDMKT_i - 0.026\ln CONNECTY_i \quad \ldots\ldots(8)$$
$$(3.921) \qquad (-1.180)$$
$$R^2 = 0.15 \qquad \overline{R}^2 = 0.13 \qquad F = 6.582 \qquad N = 312$$

Note: 1. The figures in parentheses are t-values.
2. The asterisk symbols (* and **) denote significant at 0.01 and 0.05 level.

The estimated equations show that most of the explanatory variables have the expected signs which are statistically significant at different levels. Out of these three regressions, firewood consumption from community forest appears to be the best model since $R^2 = 0.55$ and $\overline{R}^2 = 0.53$. Therefore, firewood contributes significantly to total household consumption expenditure from forests irrespective of poor and non-poor households. In other words, when average value of 'COSEX' increased by say 10 per cent, i.e., around rupees 51, 320, the average value of firewood consumption increased by 0.19 per cent at 0.01 level, i.e., rupees 20, 360 and vice versa. Though, the average consumption of timber and minor forest products also show a significant dependency at 0.01 and 0.05 levels to consumption value from community forest but R^2 and $\overline{R}^2$ are comparatively lower than the firewood consumption and the effect on timber and minor forest products was negligible.

Finally, an attempt was made to see the forest dependency between poor ($\sum_{i=1}^{196} Y_{ijP}$) and non-poor ($\sum_{i=1}^{116} Y_{ijN}$) households. It is represented in equation form as:

$$\ln \hat{Y}_{ijP} = 11.789^{*} + 0.252^{*}\ln COSEX_i + 0.185\ln HSIZE_i - 0.211\ln LANDHO_i$$
(6.136) (5.270) (1.253) (–0.861)

$$+1.215\ln GEN_i - 0.503^{*}\ln EDU_i - 5.113E-02\ln LIVECOST_i + 10.639^{*}\ln VIDMKT_i$$
(0.974) (- 3.476) (- 0.790) (5.983)

$$-0.259^{**}\ln CONNECTY_i \quad \ldots\ldots (9)$$
(- 2.508)

$R^2 = 0.57$ $\overline{R}^2 = 0.54$ $F = 29.537$ $N = 196$

$$\ln \hat{Y}_{ijN} = 17.443^{*} + 0.115^{**}\ln COSEX_i + 0.253\ln HSIZE_i + 0.502\ln LANDHO_i$$
(2.868) (2.361) (0.712) (1.316)

$$+5.982\ln GEN_i - 1.404^{*}\ln EDU_i - 0.082\ln LIVECOST_i + 23.406^{*}\ln VIDMKT_i$$
(1.043) (–2.860) (–1.059) (6.696)

$$-0.700^{*}\ln CONNECTY_i \quad \ldots\ldots (10)$$
(–2.984)

$R^2 = 0.49$ $\overline{R}^2 = 0.45$ $F = 12.574$ $N=116$

Note: 1. The figures in parentheses are t-values.
2. The asterisk symbols (* and **) denote significant at 0.01 and 0.05 level.

The study shows that the poor households are found to be benefiting more from community forest than non-poor households. The estimator of 'COSEX' of the poor households was found to be 0.25 and it was significant at 0.01 levels and for the non-poor households it was 0.12 which was significant at 0.05 levels. The poor stakeholders had the estimators of 0.21 (firewood), 0.03 (timber) and 0.02 (minor forest products), and for the non-poor households the estimators were 0.05 (firewood), 0.05 (timber) and 0.02 (minor forest products) respectively. In other words, the poor household's dependency on firewood is for higher consumption than the non-poor households. In timber consumption, non-poor households had higher dependency than the poor households. And, in minor forest products, both poor and non-poor households had a similar share. Further, if we look at different minor forest products, it was found that the poor households consumed more of bamboo, leafy vegetables, eatable roots and leaves but the non-poor households had higher consumption of the marketable products like honey, medicinal herbs, seeds and wild animals. Therefore, socio-economic heterogeneity in the rural community determines the different levels of consumption from the community forests. At the same time, heterogeneity in the extraction of forest products between poor and non-poor households was also observed in the study area since these resources were very significant sources of rural livelihood to the Arunachalee people who reside in the ecologically fragile and economically poor State.

SECTION-IV

Findings and Conclusion

The study reveals that CPRs play a very important role in the economy of the surveyed villages although the consumption value from community forest is higher for the non-poor households in absolute terms and in relative terms, the poor households' dependency on community forest is very important and crucial for their survival. Hence, there is urgent need to form sustainable management of CPRs, particularly the forests in order to avoid 'the tragedy of commons'.

Secondly, there is an urgent need to strengthen the age-old traditional system of village council headed by *Gaon Burah* or *Village Chief* in addition to the village Panchayat with specific aims of management of these resources.

Finally, the success of restoration and sustainable use of CPRs depends on the overall socio-economic development of the rural masses.

Hence, it calls for higher agricultural productivity through modernization of agriculture along with the expansion of horticulture so as to reduce the degree of forest dependency to some extent. It should be noted that any policy intervention to ensure livelihood security of rural communities in Arunachal Pradesh has to be based on a properly framed institutional strategy particularly in relation to the CPRs management.

Table 3.3: Changes in CPRs characteristics in A.P.: A district-wise comparative study 2007

(In hectare)

District	*Un-classed forest 2006–07*	*Culti-vable waste lands 2006–07*	*Other than current fallows 2006–07*	*Total Approx. CPRs 2006–07*	*% of CPRs to District 2006–07*	*% of CPRs to State Area 2006–07*
Tawang	—	68	107	175.00	0.08	0.15
West Kameng	3060.93	248	718	4026.93	0.54	3.34
East Kameng	537.74	892	5600	7029.74	1.70	5.82
Papum Pare	—	465	785	1250.00	—	1.05
Lower Subansiri*	4388.46	738	2218	7344.46	0.66°	6.08
Upper Subansiri	3112.00	2912	6079	12103.00	1.72	10.03
West Siang	9806.82	1670	4694	16170.82	2.12	13.39
East Siang	3806.73	2535	6027	12368.73	1.14°°	10.24
Upper Siang	—	668	1405	2073.00	—	1.72
Dibang Valley**	3050.54	319	1130	4499.54	0.35	3.72
Lohit***	572.48	2249	3551	6372.48	0.56	5.28
Changlang	63.42	2543	8852	11458.42	2.46	9.48
Tirap	—	12514	23368	35882.00	15.19	29.70
Arunachal Pradesh	**28462.54**	**27821**	**64534**	**120817.5**	**1.44**	**100.00**

Source: Statistical Abstract of Arunachal Pradesh, 2007, Directorate of Economics and Statistics, Government of Arunachal Pradesh, Itanagar.

Note: (1) The symbol (**o**) indicates the average % of CPRs of Papum Pare, Lower Subansiri and Kurung Kumey districts and (**oo**) refers the average % of CPRs of East Siang and Upper Siang districts.

(2) The symbol (*) includes Kurung Kumey , (**) includes Lower Dibang Valley and (***) includes Anjaw Districts.

REFERENCES

Ahuja, V. (1998), 'Land Degradation, Agriculture Productivity and Common Property from Cote d'Ivoire' *Environment and Development Economics*, Vol. 3, pp. 7–13.

Berkes, F. (1989), 'Introduction', in Berkes, F., ed., *Common Property Resources: Ecology and Community based Sustainable Development*, Belhaven Press, London.

Das, Gurudas (1995), *Arunachal Tribes in Transition*, Vikas Publishing House, New Delhi.

Di Falco S. and C. Perrings (2003): 'Crop Generic Diversity, Productivity and Stability of Agro-Ecosystems: A Theoretical and Empirical Investigation', *Scottish Journal of Political Economy*, Vol. 5, No. 2, May.

Gunatilake, H.M. (1998): 'The Role of Rural Development in Protecting Tropical Rainforests: Evidence From Sri Lanka', *Journal of Environmental Management*, Vol. 53, pp. 273–279.

Jodha, N.S. (1990), 'Rural Common Property Resources: Contribution and Crisis', *Economic and Political Weekly*, Vol. XXV, No.26, pp. A65–A78, New Delhi.

Kadekodi, G.K. (2004), *Common Property Resource Management*, Oxford University Press, New Delhi.

McKean, M., and E. Ostrom (1995), 'Common Property Regimes in the Forest: Just a relic from the Past', *Unasylva*, Vol. 46, pp. 3–15.

Mishra, S.N. (1983), 'Arunachal's Tribal Economic Formations and Their Dissolution', *Economic and Political Weekly*, Vol. 18, No.43.

Mitra, A. (1999), 'Planning for Forestry and Environment Development in Arunachal Pradesh', in Amalesh Banerjee and Biman Kar (ed.) *Economic Planning and Development of North-Eastern States*, Kanishka Publishers, New Delhi.

Mitra, A. (2003), 'Forestry Planning in Arunachal Pradesh—Need for an Alternative Approach', *Assam Economic Journal*, Vol. XV, pp. 74–81.

Pasha, S.A. (1992), 'CPRs. and Rural Poor: A Micro Level Analysis', *Economic and Political Weekly*, Vol. XXVIII, No. 46, pp. 2499–2503.

Roy, S. (1960), *Aspects of Padam Minyong Culture*, NEFA, Shillong.

Yanggen, D. and T. Reardon (2001): 'Kudzu-improved fallows in the Peruvian Amazon', in A. Yangelsen and D. Kaimowilze (ed.), *Agricultural Technologies and Tropical Deforestation*, CABI Publishing in Association with Centre for International Forestry Research, Bogor, pp. 213–229.

Government Publications

Govt. of A.P. (1987), *Statistical Abstract of Arunachal Pradesh*, Directorate of Economics and Statistics, Itanagar.

Govt. of A.P. (1995), *Statistical Abstract of Arunachal Pradesh*, Directorate of Economics and Statistics, Itanagar.

Govt. of A.P. (2001), *Statistical Abstract of Arunachal Pradesh*, Directorate of Economics and Statistics, Itanagar.

Govt. of A.P. (2002), *Statistical Abstract of Arunachal Pradesh*, Directorate of Economics and Statistics, Itanagar.

Govt. of A.P. (2007), *Statistical Abstract of Arunachal Pradesh*, Directorate of Economics and Statistics, Itanagar

NSSO (1999): *Data Documentation for NSS 54th Round*, Department of Statistics, Government of India, New Delhi.

4

THE ROLE OF SOCIAL CAPITAL IN THE DEVELOPMENT OF VILLAGE ECONOMY

A Study of Tribal Village in Manipur

KOMOL SINGHA

Introduction

Development is the primary goal of thinking beings. With the emergence of global capitalism, many village communities have been shut off from the mainstream development. The rural-urban inequality gap has been widening due to rapid industrialization and urban centric or unidirectional development (Schmidt, 2006) policies. The dynamics of the centres do not tend to penetrate deeply to the social structure of the periphery. In contrast, the centre propagates and spread in the periphery its technology, forms of consumption, life-styles, institutions, ideas and ideologies. Peripheral capitalism increasingly draws its inspiration from the centres and tends to develop in its image and likeness. This imitative development takes place belatedly in a social structure which differs in major respects from the developed structure of the centre. The penetration of technology takes place through capital accumulation, in terms both of physical means and of the training of human beings (Prebisch, 1997). For many rural communities, the consequences of global capitalism have resulted in declining real wages, high under-employment, and increasing rates of income inequality (Rainey *et al.*, 2003). Despite the unprecedented growth that has occurred in the service and trade sectors, the rural trade sector has steadily lost market share in recent years (Henderson,

2002). In recent years, trends towards global capitalism have made these issues more prominent.

The United Nations Development Programme (UNDP), determines the Human Development Index (HDI) on three main parameters, viz. Per Capita Income (sufficient resource to live a decent life); Education (adult literacy and mean years of schooling); and Life expectancy at birth (result of health care, safe drinking water, nutrition, etc.). This index takes into account the efficiency of social, political and cultural variables. It also calculates, a Human Freedom Index (HFI), that measures political participation, the rule of law, freedom of expression, and non-discrimination because, as one commentator puts it, 'Life expectancy and literacy could be quite high in a well- managed prison. Basic physical needs are well met in a zoo.' (Streeten, 1995)

Development in today's world and all the modern advances in science, technology, democracy, values, ethics, and social organization fuse into the single humanitarian project of producing a far better world (Peet *et al.,* 1999:1–5). Perhaps the most important thematic deficiency of traditional development economics is its concentration on national product, aggregate income and total supply of particular goods rather than on 'entitlements' of people and the 'capabilities' these entitlements generate (Sen, 1997). Development is not complete with some physical inputs; it includes social system or the norms of the society. Debnath (2007) argues that, development does not resemble a one-way traffic where utilities flow from one end to the other. Development is a participative exercise which involves common strength, combined resources, and collective wisdom to make it effective. Anything which calls for common strength, resources and wisdom has its source in the culture of the people; it is nothing but a social capital. To cope with the modern development, the village community has to adopt an alternative measure that takes into account social variables more attuned to development than just economic growth.

Conventional views of development ignore the ability of indigenous communities to articulate and negotiate their local identity in the midst of global pressures. It is generally assumed they face cultural extinction when confronted with modernizing forces, which are frequently given the label of 'Progress' (Long, 1996). The alternative views not only encompass both the indigenous people and their environment; they also challenge the linear, top-down approaches of mainstream development efforts, such as conventional conceptions of 'sustainable development', that all too frequently ignore the cultural and social capital of these so-called traditional societies (Sillitoe, 2002). This paper analyses the role of social norms and social institutions of a tribal village in formulating their (village) economy to cope up with economic complexities brought about by global capitalism. Since the norms of traditional villages are also independent, they are to be incorporated hand in hand with conventional factors in designing development model. We also need to recognize that so-called traditional norms and practices are not isolated, static or obsolete artifacts that only have a place in museums, and that so-called global force of change are not homogenously hegemonic (Schmidt, 2006).

In the recent past, social scientists including Robert David Putnam have started examining the role of social system in the process of sustaining economic development. As they seek to expand our understanding of local social structure and how it affects the welfare of people and places, these researchers have begun to shift attention from conventional models of development to alternative, community-based models that put the interests of workers and community sustainability over markets (*op. cit.*). For example, Porter (1990) proposes that clusters play a significant role in economic growth. Prebisch (1997) also advocated that in peripheral development, technology accompanied by continuous changes in their social structure play a fundamental role.

The Idea of Social Capital

Social capital (Putnam, 1993) is defined as the norms, networks, and social trust that make society/community function more smoothly. Social capital theory explains development from a structural rather than an economic perspective. Its emphasis is on the 'embeddedness' within which economic relations take place, based on the notion that both individual and group decisions are embedded in a particular social context that includes community traditions, norms, networks, and the like (Granovetter, 1985). The diversity of village institutions is instrumental in how government policies and economy, and environmental changes affect village economic activities and incomes

(Taylor and Adelman, 1996: 14–15). In the first phase, the village community is primarily a political society; in the second, a body of co-owners of the soil, while in the third phase it becomes the emblem of traditional economy and polity (Dumont, 1966). So, the norm of a community or a society or social norm (Basu, 2008), that enhances the economic activities in a society is considered as social capital.

'Social capital is the aggregate of the actual or potential resources which are linked to possession of a durable network of more or less institutionalized relationships of mutual acquaintance and recognition' (Bourdieu 1983: 249). 'Social capital is defined by its function. It is not a single entity, but a variety of different entities, having two characteristics in common: they all consist of some aspect of a social structure, and they facilitate certain actions of individuals who are within the structure' (Coleman, 1988: 302). Whereas physical capital refers to physical objects and human capital refers to the properties of individuals, social capital refers to connections among individuals—social networks and the norms of reciprocity and trustworthiness that arise from them. In that sense social capital is closely related to what some have called "Civic Virtue." The difference is that "social capital" calls attention to the fact that civic virtue is most powerful when embedded in a sense network of reciprocal social relations. A society of many virtuous but isolated individuals is not necessarily rich in social capital (*op. cit.*, 2000:19). 'Social capital refers to the institutions, relationships, and norms that shape the quality and quantity of a society's social interactions. Social capital is not just the sum of the institutions which underpin a society—it is the glue that holds them together' (The World Bank, 1999). For John Field (2003: 1–2), the central thesis of social capital theory is that 'relationships matter'. The central idea is that 'Social networks are a valuable asset'. Interaction enables people to build communities, to commit themselves to each other, and to knit the social fabric. A sense of belonging and the concrete experience of social networks (and the relationships of trust and tolerance that can be involved) can, it is argued, bring great benefits to people.

Types of Social Capital

Michael Woolcock (2001), a social scientist with the World Bank has helpfully argued that many of the key contributions prior to

Bowling Alone[1] failed to make a proper distinction between different types of social capital. He distinguished between: (1) Bonding Social Capital which denotes ties between people in similar situations, such as immediate family, close friends and neighbours. (2) Bridging Social Capital, which encompasses more distant ties of like persons, such as loose friendships and workmates. (3) Linking Social Capital, which reaches out to unlike people in dissimilar situations, such as those who are entirely outside of the community, thus enabling members to leverage a far wider range of resources than are available in the community.

Which Type of Social Capital?

It has been noted that social capital may not always be invested towards positive ends. An example of the complexities of the effects of social capital is violent or criminal gang activity that is encouraged through the strengthening of intra-group relationships. This points to the importance of distinguishing between bridging social capital as opposed to the more easily accomplished bonding of social capital. In the case of deleterious consequences of social capital, it is a disproportionate amount of bonding *vis-à-vis* bridging. Without "bridging" social capital, "bonding" groups can become isolated and disenfranchised from the rest of society and, most importantly, from groups with which bridging must occur in order to denote an "increase" in social capital. Bonding social capital is a necessary antecedent for the development of the more powerful form of bridging social capital. Bonding and bridging social capital can work together productively in balance, or they may work against each other. As social capital bonds and stronger homogeneous groups form, the likelihood of bridging social capital is attenuated.

Putnam and his team looked at whether social capital is bonding (or exclusive) and/or bridging (or inclusive). Putnam suggested that the former may be more inward-looking and has a tendency to reinforce exclusive identities and homogeneous groups. The latter may be more outward-looking and encompasses people across different social divides (Putnam, 2000: 22).

> Bonding capital is good for under-girding specific reciprocity and mobilizing solidarity... Bridging networks, by contrast, are

> better for linkage to external assets and for information diffusion.... Moreover, bridging social capital can generate broader identities and reciprocity, whereas bonding social capital bolsters our narrower selves..... Bonding social capital constitutes, a kind of sociological superglue, whereas bridging social capital provides a sociological WD-40. (*ibid*: 22–23)

'Community' literally means a group of people standing together for common interest or social cause. A traditional view on 'community' in sociology, from Karl Marx to Ferdinand Tonnies, and Max Weber has been that of a small group of people (or families) bounded by blood and locational ties, in which different economic principles operate from those of the capitalist market economy. In this view, while the prime motivation in the capitalist economy is private profit-seeking by individuals, the principle of community is mutual help for guaranteeing subsistence to all its members. Theoretically, communities range from family to the national community and further to the 'global (or international) community' (*op. cit.*: pp.310–28). However, the community discussed in this paper covers only the village level, characterized by personal relationship as close as a family.

The purpose of this paper is to examine, how Social Capital works in uplifting a hill tribal village in the fast-changing global economy. For examining at the micro level, a hill tribal village in Manipur, called Maram Khullen is selected on the basis of its primitiveness. Using primary village survey and personal interviews, this paper discusses the economic structure, norms, and laws of a hill village. It is also possible that the social system in a village fits in the present global capitalism. If a village social system is not in a position to cope with global capitalism, what are the reasons for it? A well-structured questionnaire and administered and the field survey was conducted in the month of October 2006.

Maram Khullen

Maram Khullen is the original village of the *Marams*, the lone primitive tribe in the State of Manipur. The name of this village 'Maram Khullen' is of Manipuri (Meitei-lon) origin which means biggest and original village of Maram tribe (Maram—name of a hill tribe in Manipur, Khullen—biggest and original village). Maram Khullen covers approximately an area of about 5 sq. km. The village is situated on the top of the Maram Khullen Hill mainly as a defensive strategy since inter-tribe clashes were the orders of the day in the earlier periods. It is one of the biggest villages in the State and the biggest among the villages of Maram with 432 households and a population of about 2400 at the time of survey in 2006. It is 94 km. away towards north from the capital city, Imphal and 25 km. from the district headquarter, Senapati. It lies approximately 5 km. inside the hills in the West from the National Highway 39 (NH 39 or Imphal–Dimapur road). In the south and just below the foothill of Maram Khullen, a tarred road runs from the Maram Centre which is on the NH 39 to Willong, another Maram village. New Magaimei, a Maram village and Mao Pungdong, a Mao village lies in the west and north respectively.

All the members of the Maram tribe inhabiting different villages/ towns today were migrants or their descendents from this mother village, Maram Khullen. Almost all the historical monuments, relics, traditions, cultures, and customs of the Maram tribe are still alive in Maram Khullen. They speak the Maram dialect and the village is at an altitude of about 3000 m (approximately) above the mean sea level. Maram Khullen receives an average annual rainfall of 1467.5 m.m. The relative humidity varies from 36 per cent to 100 per cent and temperature from 0.5°C to 36°C. The nearest market place of this village is Maram centre, which is on the NH 39 in the east and 5 kms. from the village.

Maram Khullen's Social Structure

The Maram society is a patrilineal society. The principle of primogeniture is strictly followed. The eldest surviving son succeeds to a clan headmanship. The Sagong[2] is the *de facto* and *de jure* head of the village; he is the executive, legislative and judicial authority. The present day welfare schemes and governmental projects are handled through the office of the *Khullakpa*[3] (Athickal, 1992: 61–63). In Maram Khullen, each Sagei (Makha, Khullakpa and Mathak) is headed by a Chairman in a hierarchical order and Sagong is the over all chief (King of the village) of the three Sageis in the village. Each Sagei has one organization to look after their own Sagei and they are headed by a Chairman (*see* Table 4.1). Any matter related to Sageis which is to be discussed at the village council level is brought out by their respective Chairman. By and large, Maram society is a simple and primitive society. It is characterized by certain customs and traditions, and moreover what binds the Maram society or the village together is its kinship relations.

Table 4.1: Moieties-Clans-Sub-clans of the Village

Section/Colony	*Moiety*	*Clan*
Makha Sagei	Ng'kiikui/ Kagamna	1. Kishumai 2. Majangmai 3. Puinamai
Khullakpa Sagei	Dikakuina/ Lamkhana	1. Dinamei 2. Rangnamei 3. Karangnamei
Mathak Sagei	Rangbiing Raiyinamai/ Magai-Bognamai	1. Magai-Bognamai 2. Bishunggnamai

Note: These clans have many sub-clans and these sub-clans take after the name of the one from whom it is descended.
Source: Compiled from Athickal (1992: 54) and James.

Village Authorities Hill Areas Act, 1956: The Village Authorities Hill Areas Act was passed in 1956 by the Indian Parliament. Section 58 of the Act repeals the Manipur State Hill People's Regulation of 1947, in which the power was vested in the Maharaja (King) of Manipur. Sections 3–8 of the Act deal with the constitution and function of village authority and sections 19–56 deals with the administration of justice by village authorities. In Maram Khullen, though the Act 1956 vested power on state machineries (DC, SDO etc.), it does not have any tangible effect as far as the administration of the village is concerned. Almost all the welfare schemes and government funded projects in the village are handled through the Office of the Sagong/Khullakpa. Still the Sagong or the village chairman has got the executive, legislative, and judicial authority.

Village Structure

Even today, the Maram Khullen is an independent unit. It was recognized as a single community for all religious purposes, festivals, and social functions. Even though ninety per cent of the tribal have converted to Christianity; this village still preserves the traditional religion, Paganism. It is mandatory for the Sagong to follow the traditional Maram religion; if he does not, he cannot be a Sagong in Maram Khullen. There are three religious groups in Maram Khullen now, they are Paganism (though small in number), Christianity (Baptist), and Christianity (Roman Catholic).

It is only in recent years, that the people began to form new communities of villages, based on conversion to a new religion (Christianity), access to modern amenities of life and nearness to government offices, market places, cultivable lands etc. The village owns the village gate and still follows the dormitory system. The village has sufficient forest wealth and land.

Land Ownership System

Land use system of this village is more or less same as in other tribal villages in the state. Nevertheless, there are some unique features in regard to land use system of this village. Land ownership system of this village can be classified into four categories. They are as follows:—(1) Common village land. (2) Clan land. (3) Morung land. (4) Individual land. The whole Maram Khullen is classified into three Sagei (colony)—Mathak Sagei (Upper Colony), Makha Sagei (Lower colony) and Khullakpa Sagei (Chief's colony). Each Sagei is divided into two sections each, i.e. A and B. Each section is again further divided into different Clan ranging from 4 to 6. Some of their name are: Karang namei, Hoibi namei, Besii namei, Rairai namei, Bishung namei, Kannki namei, Pung namei, Ngiimei, Katai namei, Psiikatauba namei etc. (*see* Table 4.1).

First, the common village land includes those areas which are too far for cultivation—forest land, cattle grazing land, places for worship, play ground, public entertainment place and land reserved for public purposes etc. The village authority takes care of these lands and these are used for the welfare of the village. This common land/ property is neither inheritable nor transferable nor can it be sold to other village or tribe. There is one provision for addition to village land—if there is any dispute about land of an individual with another tribe or village which he cannot settle by himself, it is normally handed over to the village authority. The village authority fights for it and becomes village property.

Secondly, the clan lands belong to a particular clan and are passed on from one generation to the next. It has got a very specific significance as the clan always extends a helping hand to the needy and provides a portion of it if one of its members is in need of it to survive. The clan also gives land to immigrants on the condition that the immigrant agrees to become one of them. The clan also generously helps divorced women or widows if they decide to live with them and remain faithful. This system is not in practice in Maram Khullen now.

Thirdly, Morung land includes woodlands from where firewood is gathered for their common use. During alternative years, the land is utilized for certain vegetables either for commercial or domestic use. It is not transferable to any of the members or to an outsider. Occasionally, fire wood is cut for commercial purposes for Morung fund. At times this land is cultivated by the members of the Morung for common purposes. In certain Morung land plantation of trees is also done as afforestation.

Finally, Individual land includes forestland, Jhum land, wet rice field, grazing ground and large grassland for hunting purposes. These lands are well demarcated by stones, hill range, rivulets etc. This is normally inherited permanent property. All these lands are held individually are inheritable and transferable but this is not recognized by customary laws. No restriction is made nor is any tax imposed on the community by the land owner for keeping animals on a particular land meant for grazing purposes. The forest and grass lands which are too far to cultivate or are yet to be cultivated are reserved for future cultivation. These can also be utilized for hunting or trapping animals. The breast and leg of any animal killed in those forests by traps are given to the land owner as tax. Nevertheless, no tax is levied on animals killed with a spear or gun in the case of individual hunting. No individual can sell land to other communities, tribe or, village whether it is individual land or community land. Wet rice cultivation is being practiced on this type of land (Individual Land). They do not practice double cropping particularly in the rice cultivation. It is due to the two reasons. First, lack of irrigation, physical infrastructure does not favour double cropping. Secondly, and equally important,

Marams have a belief that double cropping is a bad omen or bring bad luck to the people. This is the reason why they never practice double cropping since time immemorial. They do not use fertilizer in the cultivation because they do not need for double cropping.

As far as land succession is concerned, Marams being a patriarchal society, it is inherited by the sons after the death of their father. If the father does not have son, the inheritance right goes to his nearest male kinship. The eldest son gets the lion's share although all the sons inherit the father's landed property almost equally. The house and the best wet rice field will go to the eldest son and the rest are distributed among the other sons. Daughters are debarred from inheriting paternal land/landed property. Nevertheless, on the day of their wedding they are given a necklace depending upon the capacity of the parents. If mother has lands (given in her marriage by her parents), that will be distributed among the daughters. The only provision for a daughter to inherit the property of the parents is that acquired during her married life.

Individualization of Land

The transition of community land to individuals dates back to time immemorial. The inhabitants of Maram Khullen are fortunate indeed to be blessed with forest land, agricultural land and pastural land as well. There are many instances where large tracts of land in a village or over several villages have become private possessions through land accumulation by indigenous ruling elite or plunder by colonizers (Hayami and Godo, 2006:324–25; Hayami and Kikuchi, 1981; Hayami *et al.,* 1990). The examination of the village history reveals that when the population was small and there had been surplus land for various usages, there was no controversy over land or individual land. As population grew, and land use by the people became intense, there grew a situation where the need for personal landownership arises. The tragedy of commons appeared in the absence of a particular proprietor. This led to the selling of certain common land to private individuals. Another important factor responsible for transfer of common land to individuals was, when a community wanted to invest cash for common purposes or for meeting exigencies and sold land to individuals. This trend still continues in the village.

The Dormitory System

Marams have the institution of Dormitory popularly known as Morung in Nagaland. The Marams call their boys' dormitory as 'Rehangki' and the girls' as 'Riiliiki'. The 'Rehangki' and 'Riiliiki' are made separately. It is a tradition for Maram Khullen that the clan chief has to build a Morung and it is a pride for them to own it. In the Morung, there is a fire place in the middle squired by four logs of wood used as seats. There are two long beds on both sides of the fire place made of single plank/wood each. It can accommodate a minimum of 13 to 16 persons and is open for ever for male members. Fire wood is provided by the Morung owner. But now-a-days it is used very occasionally during the feast in the village. Produces like firewood collected from the Morung land are mainly used for Morung purposes.

Argument of the Study

Maram Khullen is considered a single independent economic unit. It is the village law or social norm which binds the people of this village from time immemorial. Traditional norms and beliefs deeply rooted in people's minds, are more difficult to change than formal laws so that they are likely to become more fetters on modern economic development (North, 1994). Trust is the social capital, which can reduce social transaction cost. Community institutions and organizations are inflexible and fail to adjust to changing economic needs. Traditional norms and conventions in communities have been formed slowly over many, many years (Hayami and Godo, 2006: 346). In Maram Khullen, the role of the village council or student organization is very great, and community is strongly locked-in with the trust and the beliefs of the village system. Trust accumulated through personal interactions in the community increases efficiency and reduces costs associated with the division of labor. In this regard, trust is a kind of 'social capital' similar to social overhead capital such as roads and harbours (Arrow, 1974; Dasgupta, 1988; Putnam, 1993; Seabright, 1993). The law of the village is so strong and powerful that there is no case which the village council could not settle within the village jurisdiction. No individual can violate village laws and customary laws of the village/society. The village council headed by the Sagong has got full judiciary power in the village and no state interference is needed. There is no question of court procedure in the village, and consequently the transaction cost (expenditure and procedure for government law) is less.

Practically, social and traditional norms of this village have no influence on economic formation. Despite strong laws of the community and village level institutions (refer Table 4.2), the village could not make any head way towards economic ends probably due to negative bonding social capital. There is also another factor about which we do not like to speak much—it is our social backwardness. Growth does not depend on economic policies alone. It requires a certain social climate (*Yojana,* May 2004: pp. 10). For example, any of the village organizations mentioned above could not save the dying passion fruit farms in the village funded by International Fund for Agricultural Development (IFAD). This organisation spent huge amounts of money for Passion fruit cultivation (approximately 5 acres of land) in the village land/community land through different clusters of people in the village. Unfortunately, after digesting the funded money, these clusters have disappeared from the project.

Table: 4.2: Organizations in the Village and their activities

Name	*Type*	*Activity*	*Cover Area*	*Approx. Members*
Maram Khullen Village Council	Non-Profit Organi-zation	Socio-economic-politico activity	Entire Village	Minimum 4 members from each Sagei + Sagong
Maram Khullen Youth Club	Non-Profit Organi-zation	Develop-mental Activities	Entire Village	All Young People in the village
Maram Khullen Students' Union	Non-Profit Organi-zation	Educational and Deve-lopmental	All students in the village	All students in the village

Source: Survey.

The government of Manipur, some time in the 1980s undertook a project of water supply taking from a gorge source called '*Lakshe Maidui*' about 4½ km. from the village. A reservoir was built, pipe line laid and a water motor pump was installed at the source. Just a day before the operation of the project could start, the motor pump was stolen, and it was believed to be secretly sold out by the engineer-cum-contractor of the project. Despite heavy investments and the labour incurred in the said project, motor pump was not replaced, which led to the complete failure of the project. A year following this incident, the Assam Rifles camped at Maram Bazar collected the pipes for their use with some payment of cash, and with the same materials, they are getting sufficient water.

A decade later, in 1992 with the initiative of the then constituency candidate (Ex-MLA), the late Mr. Luikang, the government engineered a rain water harvesting project and installed ordinary hand pumps in the village as an alternative to the failed project of 1980s. As a result, 7 hand pumps were installed and 4 tanks were built. But only 2 hand pumps could draw water effectively. Unfortunately, this hand pump's water could neither be used for cooking nor for washing as the water had strong arsenic contamination, strong toxic levels irritating odour and was creamy and muddy. To the dismay of the people, the tank did not do any better as it withered with holed-patches, as it was thinly walled, fulfilling no purpose as a reservoir.

Similarly, a Public Health Centre, the Government Primary School and the Sub-Veterinary centre became cow sheds of the village (*see* Table 4.3) due to the negligence of the people. No organization or individual has so far raised voice for reviving these community projects in the village. The Village Council and other strong organizations like the Students' Union do not give much importance to these types of long term sustainable social wealth. Traditional village institutions have negligible influence on the economic development front in the village. It is also seen (Table 4.3) that the SBI branch, the Post Office, and the College are running smoothly and efficiently in and around the village because it is run by external agencies. The village institutions are more concerned with the social, religious, and political activities. Religious, political and social activities are considered more important than economic activities in the village. This is why church related activities are successful in the village. The school runs by Catholic Church functions successfully, whereas the government school in the village cannot function at all. Any external funding projects in the village, especially government, is generally considered as free goods and the people do not take any interest in it or responsibility for it.

Table 4.3: Physical Infrastructure in the Village

Institution	*Available/Not available*	*Condition at present*
ICDS/Anganwadi Centre	Available	Functioning Well
Primary School (Govt.)	Available	Dormancy/Not functioning
Electricity in the village	Available	Functioning Well
Community Centre	Available	Infant Stage
Road	Available(Not Black top)	Functioning
Public Health Centre	Available	Dormancy/Not functioning
Veterinary	Available	Dormancy/Not functioning
Telephone	Available only Mobile (BSNL)	Functioning
Private School	Available	Functioning Well
Water Supply	Not Available	—
Livestock Aid Centre	Available	Dormancy/Not functioning
Transportation	Available	Functioning
Market Centre	Not Available	—
Post Office	Available in the Bazar	Functioning Well
Bank	Available in the Bazar	Functioning Well
College	Available in the next Village	Functioning Well
Internet	Available in the next Village	Functioning Well
Theatre Hall	Not Available	—
Club	Available	Infant Stage
Play Ground	Available	Functioning Well
Sale Centre	Not Available	—

Source: Survey.

Recently, the Airtel (Mobile Phone) company came to install a tower as part of expanding their network in the rural areas and since this village is on the top of the mountain, it is very much convenient to cover larger areas. Unfortunately, the company could not cope up with the huge ransom amount. Now the question is: where has the village authority gone? It is not a big deal to nab any culprit in a tribal village. Either it is because of lack of interest or because it does not give direct benefit to the people who investigate it. The strong social capital of this village cannot be used efficiently towards the direction of economic sustainability. If a proper policy direction is applied, the collectivism and common property system of this community could have been used as a strong force of economic agent to uplift the community or the village. It is not that social capital is weak, but it is used in a different direction.

Bridging Social Capital

Given the continuing difficulties in quantifying social capital and its imperfectly established effects, social capital should be a means rather than an end of development. Social capital is not, and cannot be, the panacea that Putnam optimistically proposed in his 1994 book 'Making Democracy Work'. Nevertheless, fostering social capital in less developed countries, when achieved in tandem with other components of a development strategy, offers the opportunity to speed the successful achievement of development objectives. As Putnam aptly stated, social capital may be the 'key to making development work'—its greatest strength lies in its ability to help individuals open doors that would otherwise be closed to them (Holm, 2004).

As Michael Woolcock (2001) suggested, without Bridging Social Capital, development of a traditional community would be isolated and disenfranchised from the rest of society. For example, Rainey *et al.,* (2003), 'a sense of community', Harris (1996: 26) 'Organising Tradition', and Pulver (1995: 59), 'Economic Development Literacy' are to be embedded in the traditional village development model. Sustainable development of a village requires active participation from the village concerned and development policies are to be made as the framework of the village norm. The intent of economic development literacy policies is to enable local communities to understand critical changes in global economic forces, analyse their specific economic problems and opportunities, and build comprehensive strategies to address them. Holm's (2004) recommendations on how to improve the social capital divide fall under two main categories; improving the institutional environment, and working on building horizontal networks with in each society—especially among the poor. These two recommendations can be thought of as advocating micro and macro level of solutions, respectively. At the micro level, one of the main roles of development organizations is to spread social capital by training government officials, educators, and grassroots organisers in the successful utilisation of social capital. Another approach that foreign donors can adopt is to fund projects that work to enhance a community's stock of social capital. Additionally, at the macro level, donors can encourage or pressure recipient governments to implement policies that are conducive to group formation and raise the level of trust within society.

Conclusion and Suggestion

Education is the institution which unlocks the rigid laws of the village. Rural educational system can no longer focus on providing the bare basics to meet state educational requirements. If they are to take an active part in creating sustainable village development, they must be proactive in ensuring that students not only understand basic math and science but also are able to think creatively and work within diverse groups to solve problems. In this regard, 'Economic Development Literacy' (Pulver, 1995) is quite imperative. The intent of economic development literacy policies is to enable local communities to understand critical changes in global economic forces, analyse their specific economic problems and opportunities, and build comprehensive strategies to address them (Rainey *et al.,* 2003).

Developing societies/countries require a rapid growth of good/ quality higher education for their very survival in the highly competitive globalize world. Only those nations having high ratio of enrolment in higher education, say about 20 per cent (Tilak, 2005) could become economically advanced and *vice versa.* Most 3rd World Nations have been led to believe or have wanted to believe that it is the rapid quantitative expansion of educational opportunities that holds the basic key to national development; the more education, the more rapid the development. All countries have committed themselves, therefore, to the goal of universal education in the shortest possible time (Todaro, 1993). Quality education (not quantity) is the only real asset and inevitable capital for sustainable development in the society. No matter the type of unemployment, quality education takes care of it. It helps in changing mindset and attitude of the people. This is what we need in the village at present. An individual who successfully completes the necessary schooling for entry into the modern sector labour market has a high probability of getting that well-paid urban job than someone who does not (*Ibid.*).

The category belongs to government employee which constitutes 19 per cent (81 families) of the total households in the village spends 22 per cent of its total expenditure on education, which is much higher than the national average (12.76). The village's cultivation class constitutes 65 per cent of the total household in the village spend 17.10 per cent of its total expenditure on it (Singha, 2008). This village has changed tremendously in the educational front. It is the contribution of Christian Missionary Institutions which work as catalyst in the village. It is not an exaggeration to say that, 99 per cent of the educated youth of this village are from Missionary institutions. It is interesting to note that the quality of life of this village is far better than some villages in Assam like, Rongpur I of Silchar, Rupaibali in Lakhipur Sub-division in Cachar district, and Kayang in Along of West Siang District in Arunachal Pradesh (Singha, 2006). So, quality education takes care of social backwardness and rigid village norms.

Acknowledgements

I am very much indebted to my colleague, James Karaiba for supplying his valuable information in preparing this paper.

NOTES

1. Bowling Alone (1995), is the most famous (and controversial) work of Robert David Putmam, he argues that the United States has undergone an unprecedented collapse in civic, social, associational, and political life (social Capital) since the, with serious negative consequences.
2. Sagong is the traditional chief (King) of Maram village. Mr. Kangnamba is the present Sagong of Maram Khullen and his mother Mrs. Hinga is the queen of the village. She looks after the continuation of the traditional customs. Though she is like 'regent', she cannot involve herself in village activities actively since she is a woman and old. Sagong (her son) takes charge of her responsibilities.
3. Khullakpa is the elected chief of the village, but in case of Maram Khullen, Sagong itself is the Kullakpa. He is the hereditary Monarch in the village. By the Act of 1956, the Khullakpa became the ex-officio Chairman of the village authority.

REFERENCES

Athickal, J. (1992), *Maram Nagas: A Socio-Cultural Study,* Mittal Publication, New Delhi.

Basu, Kaushik (2008), ICSSR Special Lecture at Manipur University on 8th January.

Bourdieu, P. (1983) 'Forms of capital' in J.C. Richards (ed.) *Handbook of Theory and Research for the Sociology of Education,* New York: Greenwood Press.

Coleman, J.C. (1988) 'Social capital in the creation of human capital' *American Journal of Sociology*–94: S95–S120.

Debnath, C. (2007), 'Peoples' Participation a Key for Effective Development: It's Relevance in Contemporary Nagaland' presented in the National Seminar at Kohima on 14–15 September.

Field, J. (2003), *Social Capital,* London: Routledge.

Hayami, Y. and Godo, Y. (2006), *Development Economics—From the Poverty to the Wealth of Nations,* Oxford University Press.

Henderson, J.R. (2002), 'Will the Rural Economy Rebound with the rest of the Nation' *Economic Review*—Federal Reserve Bank of Kabsas City 87.

Holm, Andrew. (2004), 'A (Social) Capital Idea,' *Harvard International Review,* (Winter), pp. 24–27.

Peet, R. and Hartwick, E. (1999), *Theories of Development,* Rawat Publications.

Porter, M.E. (2000), 'Location, Competition, and Economic Development: Local Clusters in a Global Economy', *Economic Development Quarterly,* February, pp. 15–34.

Prebisch, Raul (1997), "The Latin American Periphery in the Global System of Capitalism" in Kanth, Rajani (Ed.), *Paradigms in Economic Development,* Rawat Publications.

Putnam, R.D. (1993), *Making Democracy Work. Civic traditions in modern Italy.* Princeton N.J.: Princeton University Press.

Putnam, R.D. (1995), 'Bowling Alone: America's Declining Social Capital'. *Journal of Democracy* 6:1, Jan, 65–78.

Putnam, R.D. (2000), *Bowling Alone: The collapse and revival of American community.* New York: Simon and Schuster.

Rainey, D.V. *et al.* (2003), "Essential Forms of Capital for Sustainable Community Development" *American Journal of Agriculture and Economics,* August.

Schmidt, E. (2006), 'Sustainable Community for Sustainable Development: A Case Study of the Mujeres Reunidas Co-operative in Hidalgo, Mexico' *Journal of Developing Societies,* Sage Publications, Vol. 22, Issue 4, Dec. pp. 379–400.

Sen, Amartya (1997), "Development: Which Way Now" in Kanth, Rajani (Ed.), *Paradigms in Economic Development,* Rawat Publications.

Streeten, P. (1995), in Ul, Haq. M. (Ed.) *Reflections on Human Development,* Oxford University Press.

Tilak, J.B.G. (2005), "Higher education in Trishanku—Hanging between state and market" *EPW,* September 10, 2005. Mumbai. pp.4029–4036.

Todaro, M.P. (1993), *Economic Development in the 3rd World,* Orient Longman Ltd., Hyderabad. pp. 330.

Woolcock, M. (2001), 'The Place of social capital in Understanding social and Economic Outcomes', *Isuma: Canadian Journal of Policy Research* 2:1, pp. 1–17.

SECTION II

Education and Human Resource Development

5

EDUCATION AND DEVELOPMENT OF NORTH-EAST'S TRIBAL REGION

A Seed-Corn Relationship

T.K. BASANTIA and R.K.P.G. SINGHA

North-East India—A Profile

North-East India (NEI) comprising eight states, viz., Assam, Arunachal Pradesh, Meghalaya, Mizoram, Manipur, Nagaland, Sikkim and Tripura, is situated in the outskirts of the country. Though the entire north-eastern region constitutes 7.98 per cent of Indian geographical area (an area of 262,179 sq. km.), its population is only 3.91 per cent of the country's population (40.2 million of population) as per the 2001 Census. Despite being rich in natural resources with fertile land, rich forests and mineral deposits, the region is still very poor. At the national level, the forest constitutes about 19.39 per cent of the geographical area of the country; whereas 64 per cent of the total geographical area of the north-east is covered by the forest (Ao and Kharmawphlang, 2002). The entire NE region except Sikkim is connected to the rest of the country through a narrow 20 km. wide Chicken's neck corridor near Siliguri (West Bengal). Sikkim is also connected with the Indian mainland via West Bengal but it remains at a distance from other NE states. Out of six international boundaries touch the whole of India (i.e. China, Pakistan, Bangladesh, Nepal, Bhutan and Myanmar) five of them touch North-East India (namely, China, Nepal, Bhutan, Myanmar and Bangladesh). The bio-diversity of NEI is considered as one of the 19 identified biodiversity "*hot spots*" of the world. A large number of national parks, wild life sanctuaries and bio-diversity reserves are found in this region, and prominent among them are the Kaziranga National Park and the Manas Wild Life Sanctuary. Endangered species like the wild boar, wild cat, rhino, mithun, Sangai etc. are really assets to North-east India.

Around three-fourth of NEI is filled with hills and mountains where mainly the tribal people of various races, especially the different mongoloid stock are found. The Indo-Aryan population is concentrated mainly in the Brahmaputra and Barak valleys of Assam, and the plain areas of Tripura. In an average, the density of population is very low in the hill areas as compared to the plains or valleys. The entire NEI is called a "*melting pot*" because of the people from varied religious sects, linguistic groups and cultures live there. While the plains and valleys are dominated by Hindu religious groups and Muslims, the hill areas are dominated by Christian religious groups followed by Buddhists/Hindus. The North-East is composed of numerous linguistic and dialectical groups like Assamese, Nagamese, Tripuri, Mizo, Manipuri, Khasi, Garo etc. and among them Assamese is widely spoken. The biggest state of NEI is Assam which is the largest tea producer of the world, and it (Assam) is also one of the biggest supplier of petroleum products and agricultural products like rice, jute etc.

Problems in the Process of Development of North-East India

During the time of the British Raj, most of the present States of NEI were mainly under the political and economic jurisdiction of Assam with its headquarters at Shillong. Through the passage of time, the hill tribes of North-East India strived for their separate identity, and they became separate from Assam. For example, the present state of Mizoram was the Lushai Hill District of Assam for a long period of time and became a Union Territory in 1972 and attained statehood in February 1987 and became the twenty-fourth state of the country. In the same way, most of the other hill tribes of North-East also became separate from Assam from the political and administrative point of view. In reality, it is true that most of the states of NEI especially the hill states are very young in terms of life style and development. After India got her independence, the Government of India took strong steps to bring sustainable development in NEI. In order to bring quick and sustainable development in NEI, the Government of India established the North Eastern Council (NEC) under an Act of Parliament (North Eastern Council Act, 1971). During the inception of NEC, the state of Sikkim did not come under the purview of the NEC, but now Sikkim is also included in the NEC. From 2003, the NEC gets its budgetary allocations/funds from the Ministry of Development of North Eastern Region, but before 2003 the NEC was getting all its budgetary allocations/funds from the Ministry of Home Affairs since there was no Ministry of Development of North Eastern Region. Besides the NEC, through different plans, programmes and activities, the Government of India does a lot for sustainable development of the region. The Government of India directly as well as indirectly encourages the State Governments of North-East region to launch immediate and long term strategies for solving the existing problems of their respective states and to achieve the tasks of development. Also, the non-governmental organizations are taking a lot of initiatives for bringing a desirable change in the North-eastern region.

After *sixty* years of Independence of India, NEI is not able to achieve the basic and essential tasks of development despite a lot of intervention by central and state governments. Where one problem is solved, another problem comes up. The common problems found in the process of development in NEI are given below:

Problems from Political Standpoints: Regional imbalances, geo-political problems, insurgency, strikes and *bandhs,* inter-state and intra-state conflicts, migration Problems etc.

Problems from Social and Cultural Standpoints: Cultural differences, linguistic fights, racial fights, ethnic fights, religious fights, insider and outsider feeling, alienation, frustration, shyness, inferiority and superiority complex, traditional beliefs and prejudices etc.

Problems from Educational Standpoints: Educationally unreached, under reached and half reached, failure to achieve quality education, science and mathematics education is very poor in the entire hill regions, illiteracy and ignorance is very common in rural hill areas etc.

Problems from Economic Standpoints: Unplanned economic growth, massive unemployment and under employment, lack of well developed industries in the entire region, very slow industrialization, problems of infrastructure for industrialization, rampant poverty in rural areas, lack of productive ethos, irregular and uncontrolled markets, capturing everything by the neo-rich people, wastage and stagnation of business resources due to lack of proper facilities.

Problems from Health and Life Style Standpoints: Water crisis in the hilly areas, drug addiction and alcoholism, lack of information and communication, lack of proper transport facilities for goods and services, lack of proper medical facilities etc.

Problems from Geographical Standpoints: Problem of flood in the valley, problems of land slide in the hill areas, geographical inaccessibility, topographical disadvantages, soil erosion etc.

Problems from Environmental Standpoints: Climatic change and destruction due to jhum/shifting cultivation and deforestation, destruction of bio-diversity and threat to wild life, desertification of jungles by the common people, green house effect in the entire region etc.

Education and Development of North-East Region: A Relationship

J.S. Mill, the famous English Philosopher once told, "*Education does not perform everything but there is hardly anything which education does not perform*". Education is the key to all the processes of development. The importance of education towards the development of the whole country in general and development of NEI in particular is realized by all in recent years. The Nobel Laureate Amartya Sen stresses a lot on the importance of education in general and elementary education in particular for achieving the development of a country. Education is a means through which the long term and stable development of a society is possible. In this context, a Chinese saying can be quoted:

If you are planning for one year, plant grains
If you are planning for ten years, plant trees
If you are planning for hundred years, plant man

Man power planning or planning of human resource is the most valuable planning which takes a country towards development, and education acts as the prime means for man power planning.

The North-East India is lagging behind a lot in terms of socio-economic development, modernization etc. not because of its geographical, socio-economic, and communication problems but because of its poor educational parameters. The greatest stumbling block to the development and growth of north-east India is its poor standard of education. Education is the basis of all types of development of a society, viz. political, economic, cultural and social. A well planned and well developed educational system can help the people to solve all their problems in one way or the other. Their relation is just like a relation between a seed and a corn. If a seed is properly cared for and provided its basic requirements for growing, then it can provide the desired corn; otherwise it is not. In a similar fashion, for achieving a dynamic, liberal, desirable and sustainable development in the North East, the educational system of the North East needs to be planned meticulously and executed with great sensitivity.

Educational Strategies for Development of the North-East Region

North-East India urgently needs a well developed and well planned educational system for its multisided development. The entire region is lagging behind a lot relating to many areas and many aspects of education. A lot of issues relating to the qualitative and quantitative education are found in the hill states of the North-East, as well as in the valley. For example, the status of science, commerce and technical education is very low in almost all the hill states of the North East whereas the quality of school education is very poor in almost all the states of the North-East. Almost all the schools of North-East region irrespective of hill or valley areas suffer a lot from many qualitative issues, like high drop-out rate, lack of adequate number of trained and specialized teachers, lack of sufficient infrastructure facilities etc. In 1998–99 the drop-out rates in classes I to VIII in the state of Assam was *70.08* per cent, in Meghalaya *77.91* per cent, in Tripura *70.26* per cent and in Mizoram it was *67.20* per cent whereas the drop-out rate in classes I to VIII in the state of Kerala was 4.49 per cent, in Goa was 7.88 per cent, in Punjab *27.91* per cent and the national average was *56.82* per cent (National Human Development Report, 2001). As per NIEPA (2004), only *4.55* per cent male teachers and *8.33* per cent female teachers in Mizoram, 10.03 per cent male teachers and *12.44* per cent female teachers in Assam, *15.33* per cent male teachers and *19.49* per cent female teachers in Meghalaya and *16.35* per cent male teachers and *20.05* per cent female teachers in Nagaland teaching in upper primary with secondary/higher secondary schools are trained with professional qualifications whereas in Chhattisgarh *78.33* per cent male teachers and *71.83* per cent female teachers and in Haryana 75.09 per cent male teachers and *67.81* per cent female teachers teaching in upper primary with Secondary/Higher Secondary Schools are trained with professional qualification. And the national average in this regard is *58.89* per cent in case of male teachers and *47.95* per cent in case of female teachers. This clearly shows how the educational system of North-East India suffers. The following strategies may be used as the basic parameter for improving the qualitative and quantitative aspects of the educational system of North East India and consequently for bringing about a desirable and sustainable socio-economic and cultural change in the North-East region.

Quality School Education for all Children

The status and quality of School education are very poor in the North-eastern region. The drop-out rate (as discussed above) in the schools of North-eastern region is very high as compared to national average. *Further, the schools in the North-East suffer a lot in terms of training of teachers, availability of infrastructural facilities, availability of required number of teachers etc. The problem of shortage of teachers in primary schools is mainly a rural phenomenon. The country has about 89.00 per cent of its schools in rural areas carrying the burden of multi-grade teaching* (Sixth All India Educational Survey, 1993). The North-eastern states share a greater burden; *94.3* per cent of the schools in the region are rural schools. And this burden is most acutely felt by single teacher schools. The survey identified that *21.68* per cent of primary schools are single teacher schools and *42.67* per cent primary schools are two-teacher schools. For the development of the region, there is need for providing quality school education to all the children which is also our *constitutional obligation*. Therefore, the schools in the North-East need to be re-structured and re-facilitated with adequate number of trained and committed teachers, with better infrastructure and academic and non-academic facilities.

Facilities of Quality Higher Education in the Region

Cotton College, Guwahati, established in 1901 is the first college in the NE India and Gauhati University, Guwahati, established in 1948 is the first University in the region. North-Eastern Hill University (NEHU), Shillong, Meghalaya was established in 1973 as a Central University and all other Universities of the North-eastern region were established after the establishment of NEHU. Most of the Universities except a few are in infancy stage and they rarely have good departments. Especially the science, commerce and technical education in the North-Eastern Universities is very poor. One would really be surprised if s/he compared the status of physical sciences, mathematical sciences, chemical sciences, engineering sciences and many other basic sciences in the North-eastern region with that of the rest of the country. Higher educational institutions in the NE face several problems of infrastructure, adequate and competent teaching faculties, shortage of students in different departments, use of slow pace of technology in the teaching learning process etc. Also, the institutions face a lot of problems relating to administration, students admission, maintenance of academic calendar, linkage between under graduate and post-graduate studies, evaluation, *bandh* culture, students' indiscipline etc. For the wholesome development of the North-eastern region, there is need of trained man power. Higher education has to play a vital role in this direction. Therefore, the higher education system of the North-East needs to be changed and modified in the light of the above problems. In this regard, the Universities themselves, the state governments as well as the central government should take a lot of initiatives to impart quality higher education in this region.

More Open/Distance and Non-formal Education Centres for off School Students

In the previous page(s), it has already been discussed that in the North-eastern region the drop-out rate at school is too high. Besides that, there are many school-age children who are educationally unreached, half-reached and under-reached due to many psycho-social, economic and geographical reasons. A strong base of open/distance and non-formal education is necessary in order to educate such off-school children. Besides the off-school children, the workers and adult illiterates of this region also require proper distance/open and non-formal education for developing their quality and competency in their work place, so that they can contribute more to the development of this region.

Improve Facilities for Science and Technical Education in the Region

One of the foremost reasons for underdevelopment of the North-eastern region is the low level of its science and technical education. Degree and Diploma courses in science and technical education in the educational institutions of the NE started too late, *i.e.* mostly in or after the seventies. Also it is a fact that the technical institutes and technical courses are not evenly distributed in the region and are mostly concentrated in the plains. *Even after more than six decades of independence, the region continues to witness a situation of inadequate sectoral and in-house R&D base for industrial development* (Abrol and Pulamate, 2005). A strong base of research and development in science and technology is needed in this region for the industrial, technological and agricultural development of the region.

Health and Medical Education

The North-eastern region is one of the most un-served region so far as medical education and medical facilities are concerned. The following table gives us the sad data about the spread of medical education in the North-eastern region.

Table 5.1: Population and Medical Colleges

States	Assam	A.P.	M.P.	Meghalaya	Mizoram	N.L.	T.P.	Sikkim
*No. of Medical Colleges	3	Nil	1	**Nil**	Nil	Nil	Nil	Nil
**Population as per 2001 Census	266.38 lakhs	10.91 lakhs	23.88 lakhs	23.08 lakhs	8.91 lakhs	19.88 lakhs	31.91 lakhs	5.40 lakhs

Source: *Basic Statistics of NEC 2002. ***www.censusindia.net*

Besides medical education, the medical facilities are also very poor in the region. Shortage of adequate number of hospitals along with necessary staff and facilities, non-availability of sophisticated instruments in the hospitals, non-availability of medical and first aid facilities in the rural and hill areas, communication barriers in the way of getting medical facilities etc. are some of the important problems relating to medical facilities in this region. Whole hearted steps are to be taken by the Governments as well as the common people in providing better medical education and medical facilities in the region for better development of the region.

Agro-based and Craft Centred Education

North-East India is very rich in forest products like different types of bamboos, woods, medicinal plants, canes, forest fruits and numerous types of other forest products. Besides the forest products, the region is also very rich in coal mines and many other natural minerals resources. The hill areas of North-East are famous for producing ginger, squash pineapple etc. The entire Brahmaputra valley and Barak valley are famous for rice, tea and jute production. Assam is the largest tea producing state of India, and only because of Assam, India secures first position in tea production in the world. If the people in this area would get a strong base of agricultural education and craft/handicraft training, then they can use the existing agricultural lands/resources in the proper manner and can develop the small scale/cottage industries or craft centres with the help of available local products from different sources and consequently they can help the economy grow. Agricultural education and craft/handicraft education should constitute an important part of the school as well as University education and special training centres/institutes must also be opened for the same.

Vocational, Industrial and Commerce Education

Growth of industries, trade and commercial activities is very less in the North-eastern region not because of its geographical problems but because of lack of proper training and motivation of its people. In spite of having rich natural/forest and mining resources, agricultural products and petroleum products, North-East India is still an industrially and commercially undeveloped area. In no part of North-East is a mega/big industry found. Vocational and commerce education along with a strong base of political and community will is necessary in this region in order to make the entire region an industrial and commercial centre.

Forest and Environmental Education

There was a time when the entire north-eastern region except some plain areas was filled with dense forests. These forests were the happy abode of wide ranging animal species and it had very significant role in maintaining the ecological balance. Due to the increasing pressure of population on forests and the demand for forest products from inside and outside North-East India, the forests in North-East India is decreasing very fast. Jhumming method of cultivation; clearing the forest for dwelling/constructing houses, food and fuel, illegal trading and sale of timbers etc. are some of the main causes of forest destruction. In a study undertaken by the Forest Survey of India, it was estimated that during 1987–97 an area about *0.38* million hectare has been affected by shifting cultivation in Mizoram. *Though shifting cultivation has many ill effects, it is still widely practiced due to the compatibility of the system with the physical environment, steep and undulated topography, socio-economic and cultural factors, physiographic remoteness and isolation, lack of awareness and unfavourable environment* (Singh and Singh, 2000). It is observed that since last few years the temperature of Mizoram is rising faster in comparison with other parts of the country and perhaps the destruction of its forests and natural environment is the main reason for it. The destruction of forests in North-eastern region is affecting the life of the people and besides climate of the region/country it affects also its natural beauty, rich bio-diversity and eco-tourism. Environmental and forestry education is urgently needed in this region in order to make the people aware of the positive implications of protection, preservation and promotion of forest resources. Scientific study of the forests, ecology and environmental studies should be given special status in the educational institutions of this region. Extension departments should be opened to popularize the fruitful effects of the departments of forestry and environmental education among the common masses.

Education and Tourism

The natural beauty of North-East India is really surprising. The wide range of mountains, high and beautiful hills and terrains, rich forests and jungles, wonderful rivers and riversides, green river valleys, diverse and wide ranging bio-diversity, vast and unending tea gardens in the valley areas, God gifted climate especially in most of the hill areas etc. make the north-eastern region one of the best tourist spots of the world. A large number of national parks, biospheres and wild life sanctuaries are found in North-East India. In spite of having such natural and man made beauty, it has not been till today a popular tourist destination because of many socio-political and geographical reasons. The main barriers in the process of tourism development in the region is the religious and racial fights, insurgency, cultural rigidity, communication problems, lack security to the tourists and failure in presenting North-East India at the national as well as global level as a popular tourist destination. Education can to do a lot for removing the existing barriers of tourism of this region and spreading tourism in this region. North-East's Universities/Higher education institutions should open Departments of tourism education for facilitating tourism in this region. The state governments of the North-eastern region should encourage tourism education because tourism can provide a lot of economic benefits to the region.

Women Empowerment and Education

Even after *60* years of Independence, the women of North-East India have not attained the basic socio-economic and educational facilities. The following data gives clear indication about the state of female literacy in comparison to male literacy in North-East India.

Table 5.2: Literacy rate in NE

State	*A.P.*	*Assam*	*Mani-pur*	*Megha-laya*	*Mizo-ram*	*Naga-land*	*Sikkim*	*Tripura*
Percentage of Female Literacy	44.24	56.03	59.70	60.41	86.13	61.92	61.46	65.41
Percentage of Male Literacy	71.93	77.93	77.87	66.14	90.69	71.77	76.73	81.47

Source: Based on Preliminary Census 2001 Estimates.

Till today, we find hardly any woman from the north-east of the country who holds important political/administrative position at the national level. Also at the state level women have less access to power in comparison to their men counterparts. Similarly, in many other fields of life, like the economy, culture, style of living, social status etc. women in the North-East remain far behind the men. In the rural areas of the North-East, women hardly enjoy a decent life because of ignorance and poor educational status. In traditional Thadu-kuki, Mizo, Naga societies and many other tribal societies' women occupy a very low position and this has a lot on impact for their present day social status. For the total development of this region, the women of the region who constitute about *50* per cent of its population need to be empowered. Special care for women in the educational system of North-East India should gain momentum. All the factors which hinder the education of women of this region should be eradicated. Special care should be taken for training and placement of girls for their development and ultimately for the socio-economic prosperity of the region.

Encouraging ITC Education in the Region

The world is moving very fast due to the impact of Information Communication Technology (ICT) in every field of life and society. The role different information and communication technologies and techniques, like the internet, e-mail, digital networking, audio and video conferencing, computer based software programmes etc. play a vital role, and the developing societies are getting a lot of benefits from it. Wide use of information and communication technologies is necessary for the faster progress and prosperity of underdeveloped regions and countries. *Communication and information technologies have been recognized to have enormous potential especially for developing countries and in furthering their sustainable development* (Mansell and When, 1998). For shaping a new and broad based of economy and producing rapid changes in the north eastern society, information and communication technologies have to play a major role. Significant transformation in trade and industry, business, agriculture and food production, health and medicine, engineering, transport is possible through the wide use of improved communication technologies like telephone, radio, television, computer generated activities like teleconferencing internet, satellites, etc. Therefore, at the school level, each and every student should be given basic training in computer/ICT, and ICT should constitute both core as well elective part of their school curriculum. At the University/Higher education level, ICT education should get special status. Special degrees, diplomas and certificates should be awarded to the students in these fields. Knowledge of ICT should be the desirable/mandatory qualification for the entrants/in-service persons in any field. Software based jobs/works are to be given higher priority in the region.

Conclusion

Education has to play a vital role for the total development of the north-eastern region. In this regard quality education should reach every student of the region. The educational institutions especially the higher educational institutions/universities should play the strategic role in changing the destiny of the region through its curricula and teaching learning programmes. Along with a general and liberal education, a strong base of technological and business education is needed for its economic and socio-geographic emancipation. To accomplish the task of development of this region, a triangular relationship ought to be established among governments, the general public and the educational system.

REFERENCES

Abrol, D. Pulamate, L. (2005), 'An assessment of the S & T imbalances in North-Eastern Region of India' in S.K. Soiu, and C. Mahanta (eds.) *Science and Technology for Regional Development: Case for North-East India* Tejpur University. IIT Guwahati and C-MMACS, Bangalore.

Ao, I. and Kharmawphlong, B.S. (2002), 'Conserving Rich Natural Resources of the North-East: The Constraints and Opportunities' Paper presented in the 11th Annual Conference-cum-Seminar of NEIES, Department of Education, NEHU, Shillong, 27 and 28 February.

Basantia, T.K. (2006), 'Quality Management of Elementary Education in the state of Mizoram: Some strategies' paper presented in 15th NEIES Conference-cum-Seminar on Management of Education in North-East: Problems and Prospects, Department of Education, Mizoram University, Aizawl, 26th and 27th October.

Behera, L. and Basantia, T.K. (2006), 'Evaluation of elementary Pre-service Teacher Education Syllabus in Orissa,' *Indian Educational Review.*

Mansell, R. and When, U. (1998), *Knowledge Societies: Information Technologies for Sustainable Development.* New York: Oxford University Press.

NEIPA (2004), 'Elementary Education in India—Where we stand? Analytical Report 2004', New Delhi: NIEPA.

Panda, B.N. and Basantia T.K. Two-Year B.Ed: Aiming at making professionally Competent Teachers, Unpublished Manuscript.

Singh, A.K. (1994), *Approaches to Tribal Development,* Sarup and Sons New Delhi.

Singh, M.K. and Singh, N.P. (2000), 'Agro-forestry, A sustainable land use system for shifting cultivation in N.E. India', Proceeding International Workshop on Agro-forestry and Forest Production, Aizawl, November 28–30, pp. 32–34.

Singha, R.K.P.G. and Singh, Bhartendu. (2006), 'Need for Reform in Commerce Education' in Goswami, P.J. (ed.), Department of Commerce, Assam University, Silchar and Silchar Chapter of ICAI of India, New Delhi. pp. 28–38.

Yogi, A.K. (1991), *Development of North-East Region-Problems and Prospects,* Spectrum Publication.

6

EDUCATED YOUTH IN NAGALAND

Aspirations vis-à-vis Employment Opportunities

KEDILEZO KIKHI

I

Nagaland, the 16th state of the Indian Union is one of the hill tribal states of North-East India. It is a state having a weak industrial sector and an underdeveloped agriculture, bulk of the educated population being dependent on the service-sector. We can see that the educational institutions in Nagaland are continuously producing educated youth but employment opportunities are limited in relation to supply of labour. There is no balance between the supply of workers and the demand for their services. Thus, open unemployment occurs because able and willing educated persons are in search of work, but there is no work for them.

The problem is menacing because: (i) these intelligent people, can become dangerously vocal and influential not to accept any unenviable position lying down and can give constant threat to the security and stability of the state; (ii) it is a waste for educated people to remain idle for they constitute the best of our human resources, valuable human capital (Puttaswamaiah, 1977).

Dholakia (1977) sees unemployment as a state of being without gainful work and generally considers it as an involuntary failure to get income yielding work. Thakur (1985) states that when an individual even after his best possible efforts, does not get work on the existing wage rate or even at low wage rate to earn his means of subsistence, he is termed as 'unemployed' as well as "poor'. Sinclair

(1987) has stressed the need to define unemployment negatively by stipulating what it is not, i.e. unemployment is clearly not employment and so the unemployed are a subset of those who are employed. Bajpai (1992) refers to unemployment as the condition of joblessness in one's life.

Unemployment refers to a situation where persons who are able to work and also willing to work at the prevailing rate of wages, does not find work. This is an involuntary idleness leading to wastage of labour. It is not confined to any category of persons. It may be among the unskilled, high skilled and technically qualified persons. Able-bodied persons who voluntarily remain unemployed are excluded from the concept of unemployment. It has three elements: (i) An individual should be capable of working; (ii) An individual should be willing to work; and (iii) An individual must make an effort to find work.

Youth has been defined as the early part of life especially the period between childhood and adult age; and the youth population constitutes a significant segment in any given society. In order to launch any meaningful policy and programme for the youth, it is essential to determine the age bracket that constitutes youth. But it is difficult to accurately assign lower and upper age limits for the youth, because this varies from time to time, and also from society to society. The time span required for biological maturation differs from person to person. Kuppuswammy (1984), early youth would refer to the 13 to 19 years age group. To some others, it refers to the 12 to early 30s (Chauhan, 1990). The UNO has categorized youth to be between the age group of 15–24 years. In India, for census operations, and in accordance with the practice of the Government of India, the age group of 15–34 is recognized as youth; which is further classified into three groups: (i) 15–19 years as sub-junior, (ii) 20–24 years as junior, and (iii) 25–34 years as senior youth (Saraswathi, 1988).

Ahamad considers the educated to be all those who have completed at least eleven years of schooling and are matriculate and above (1973). The comprehensive working definition of an 'educated unemployed youth' for the present study is identified as anyone between the age group of 15–34 years from matriculate, who is capable of working, willing to work and making an effort to find work but is unable to get any remunerative job.

In Nagaland there has been an alarming rise of educated unemployed youth. The total number of unemployed, which was 22,069 in 1991 on the live register, had risen to 37,090 in 2000, which is a percentage increase of 68.06 and had further risen to 49,960 in 2006 with is a percentage increase of 126.38 (taking 1991 as base). The state had 10,534 registered educated unemployed in 1991, whereas the figure rose to 22,119 in 2000 and further rose to 31,277 in 2006.

II

When young men find they have to wait for years to get employment and then to content themselves with petty jobs, they feel greatly upset. The youth seek a stable life but cannot secure it; they are hungry for opportunities, recognition and status. They feel that instead of sympathy and consideration, they get general denunciation and condemnation. They have to frequently bear derogatory remarks agaist the whole lot of youth (Bajpai, 1992). The youth of today, who are the nation builders of tomorrow complain of mounting frustration, and are largely a discontented lot. Their vast energies and labour force, intelligence and knowledge are being wasted and remain untapped.

Any solution to the problem would require information on the aspirations of the unemployed and the availability of job opportunities. The aspirations of job seekers are reflected in their preferences and desires for particular jobs.

Indian youths tend to nurture materialistic aspirations like their Western counterparts. Hardly anyone wants to be a Gandhi or a Nehru, Buddha or Mahavira, Rama or Krishna; rather most of them want just a secure and prosperous life. It is true that in the contemporary materialistic society money and material resources form the core of human aspirations. Money gives power over men and materials (Bajpai, 1992). The study reveals that this is the case with the educated unemployed youths of the Nagaland state. The study finds out that the most desirable jobs are in the organized sector of the economy, i.e. government jobs, for the simple reason that they promise stability and security of tenure with assured levels of wages and salaries along with guaranteed retirement benefits. Moreover, the society also attaches glamour, prestige, status and relative importance to government jobs. At the same time, the educated youths on completing their studies are under pressure from parents and relatives who not only have high expectations but also want their educated wards to secure government jobs. Interestingly, it is a reflection of Cooley's theory of 'looking-glass-self', according to which in the course of socialization, the individual develops 'self' and 'social consciousness' simultaneously and looks for his image in the society. And since Naga society pays high regard for government jobs, every youth prefers government jobs to any other opportunities.

The study shows that 67.01 per cent preferred government jobs to self-employed jobs (26.18 per cent) or private jobs (6.81 per cent). It indicates that most of the educated youths do not like hard work, but they prefer sedentary jobs. Their first choice is relatively for white collar jobs. However, in case of no other alternative, the educated youths are ready for manual jobs. It has been shown that 83.25 per cent are ready for manual jobs in case of no other alternative. We can thus conclude that, though the youths prefer government jobs, their final goal is getting any job in order to earn a livelihood.

III

Like students throughout the world, Indian students seek education for a number of reasons. The motivations might well be simultaneously mundane, noble and realistic (Dhar, 1976). For some, a respective degree ensures respect and status in the community, particularly when opportunities are less or in short supply. For others, the main purpose is to achieve a competitive edge in the job market. While some pursue their studies as being desired by parents and relatives; yet some others do, for not getting any jobs. Some others are motivated by genuine love for learning.

As shown in Table 6.1, the educated unemployed youths are asked to indicate and rank the reasons that prompted them to seek college/ university/technical education. An analysis of their responses indicates that 68.59 per cent ranked 'acquire more education' as the most important reason for seeking education; 15.71 per cent ranked 'prospect of a higher paying job'; 12.04 per cent ranked 'respect and status in the community'; 2.62 per cent ranked 'could not get a job'; and 0.52 per cent ranked desire by parents and relatives as the most important reason that has motivated them for education respectively.

The desire to acquire more knowledge emerged as the primary reason for the youth to seek further education after matriculation. In other words, the majority of the educated youth are motivated by genuine love for learning. As also shown in the table, 39.79 per cent marked 'respect and status in the community' as the second most important reason for seeking higher education. It indicates that the community and the respect in community influence the choice of many students. The students go for higher education because it can enable them to have respect and better status in the community.

Table 6.1: Reasons for seeking College/University/Technical Education

Sl. No.	*Reasons*	*Students ranking it (in % ages)*	
		Most Important	*Second most Important*
(i)	Respect and status in the community	12.04	**39.79**
(ii)	Prospect of a higher paying job	15.71	24.08
(iii)	Desired by parents/relatives	0.52	12.57
(iv)	Acquire more knowledge	**68.59**	16.75
(v)	Could not get a job	2.62	6.81

Note: One respondent remarked "concern for society" as the most important reason.

One would assume that the youth's motivations would vary with differences in the socio-economic status of the family and the positional and occupational status of the father. Those with little status in the community are likely to seek higher education for gaining communal respect, while those whose families enjoy higher status will use higher education for further enhancing their economic position. However, the data show that the desire 'to acquire more knowledge' emerged as the main reason for all occupational groups and all income groups. Prospects of highly paid jobs that a degree opens up for its holder and gaining community respect through attainment of higher education are the other reasons.

The study shows a general satisfaction among the sample respondents about their current choice of subjects. In response to the question, 'Are you satisfied with your education and faculty?,' about 53.93 per cent indicated *yes,* while 46.07 answered *no.* In their study, Dhar, Ilchman and Ilchman find that engineering and medicine emerged as the most preferred faculties, which are noted for better and more remunerative employment opportunities (Dhar, 1976). The present study, in contrast shows that the respondents of the different subject groups prefer their own fields. These two responses contradict, because on the one hand 46.07 per cent answered that they are not satisfied with their education and subjects, while on the other 63.08 per cent prefers their own subject if they are given a chance to study again.

IV

The occupational choices of the educated youth are influenced by a variety of factors: (i) The economic returns associated with a job, (ii) The social prestige that it carries, (iii) The type of education and exercise, and (iv) Security and future prospects considered suitable to it. Of the four factors, about 41.88 per cent feel the type of education and training as the most influential, about 35.08 per cent marked the economic returns associated with a job as the second choice, while the social prestige that it carries is marked as the next preference. As the study shows it is obvious that the most influential factor for occupational choices is the type of education and training one has. For the job seeker should know what kind of job one is qualified and accordingly looks for it. For instance, an Arts graduate cannot apply for a medical profession, likewise an MBBS or MD cannot teach in an Arts college. In other words, a realistic appraisal of suitability seems to lead the educated youth to choose and expect occupations more in line with their training, whether they prefer them or not. It has to be noted that all the four factors are complimentary and no single factor alone solely influences the youth for choosing their occupation.

One may assume that, what the educated youths prefer may not necessarily be the vocation they choose. However, their preferences do have substantial influence on occupational choice, especially when educational choices have been made based on future occupational goals. It is obligatory to make a distinction between the occupations the educated youths prefer and the occupations that they expect to get. Dhar, in his study of the college and university students showed little discrepancy between preferences and expectations (Dhar, 1976). On the other hand, Foster found a great discrepancy between the occupational preferences and the occupational expectations of Ghana school students (Foster, 1963). The present study of educated youth in Nagaland showed a great discrepancy between the occupational preferences and the occupational expectations.

There is no correspondence at all between the proportions indicating preference for occupation and those indicating the occupations that they expect to get. The difference between the two ranges from a low of –33.51 per cent and a high of +12.04 per cent. For instance, 48.69 per cent of the educated youth preferred to be administrative officials but only 15.18 per cent expected to get it resulting in a wide discrepancy of –33.51 per cent. On the other hand, only 6.28 per cent preferred salesman/business job, but 18.32 per cent of them are expecting to get it showing a discrepancy gap of +12.04 per cent (Table 6.2).

Table 6.2: Occupational Preferences and Expectations

Sl. No.	*Occupations*	*Proportion of students*		*Differences between*
		Preferring i	*Expecting ii*	*Preference (i) & Expectation (ii)*
1.	Administrative Official	48.69	15.18	**- 33.51**
2.	University Teacher	5.76	12.04	+ 6.28
3.	Secondary School Teacher	0.00	8.38	+ 8.38
4.	Higher Research	5.76	3.14	- 2.62
5.	Legal (Law) Practitioner	1.57	4.19	+ 2.62
6.	Engineer	5.76	4.71	- 1.05
7.	Physician/Surgeon	9.95	6.81	- 3.14
8.	Salesman/Business	6.28	18.32	**+ 12.04**
9.	Contractors and Suppliers	2.09	0.52	- 1.57
10.	Clerk	0.00	6.28	+ 6.28
11.	Farmer	1.57	1.57	0.00
12.	Politician/Political Agent	0.52	4.19	+ 3.67
13.	Journalist	2.09	1.57	- 0.52
14.	Military/Police	6.81	7.85	+ 1.04
15.	Others	3.14	5.24	+ 2.10

The study reveals that high administrative positions emerged to be very attractive. Perhaps the preference for this occupation is strongly influenced by the perception of the change in the economic and social position. The occupation of high administrative official has become scarce and the competition to the position even stiffer. Consequently, this job acquires better economic position, higher status, higher prestige and glamour than before. On the other hand, some occupations like secondary school teacher, clerkship, etc. which have been perceived to have declined in economic and social position, are not generally preferred even by those whose qualifications would make them more suitable for them.

The youths wanting to acquire more knowledge, at the same time preferring for administrative jobs to academic jobs in occupation is itself contradictory because, the salary of administrative officials and university/college teachers is more or less at par.

The present study also tries to understand the willingness or unwillingness of the educated youth to work in the rural or urban areas. They are asked to indicate their preferences when it comes to higher pay or lower pay, work that is more interesting or less interesting, more job security or less job security, nearer home or distant location. They are asked to indicate their preferences for two jobs, which are similar to each other in all but two respects.

The data in Table 6.3 show that the jobs which offer scope for interesting work and security, are preferred even when they offer less monetary rewards. The location of the job is not the primary consideration, especially when higher salary and more interesting work are the factors. In such a case the disincentives are associated with the job rather than where it is located. According to the study, given interesting work and job security, to work in rural areas is not particularly disliked by the youths. The preference for distant urban locations is slightly greater than rural areas nearer home. In other words, when the choice of urban and rural areas is offered, majority of the educated youths prefer urban areas though it would have been far from home. The primary option to urban areas can be attributed to the expectations that are created among students in urban-based universities. This attitude may be because of the livelihood that works in the rural areas are less stimulating professionally, immobile and dull.

Table 6.3: Preferences for Jobs/Locations

Sl. No.	*Job Characteristics*	*Proportions*
1.	Higher pay with less interesting work/Lower pay with more interesting work	33.51/66.49
2.	Higher pay with less job security/Lower pay with more job security	34.03/65.97
3.	More interesting work in distant location/Less interesting work nearer home	69.63/30.37
4.	Nearer home with lower pay/Distant location with more pay	26.18/73.82
5.	Urban location with lower pay/Rural area with higher pay	53.93/46.07
6.	Nearer home in rural area/Distant but in an urban area	47.64/52.36

V

The educated unemployed youths are studied as to how they perceive acquiring a satisfactory job. In response to the question, "Will you get a satisfactory job?" About 71.73 per cent of the youths are not sure of getting a satisfactory job. Form the point of view of manpower planning, how the youths perceive acquiring a job is nearly as important as the job that they might choose. As shown in Table 6.4, the educated youths are asked to rank in order of importance, the factors that are important in getting a satisfactory job. The study reveals that education (51.83 per cent) and hard work (34.03 per cent) are regarded as the most and second most important criteria for satisfactory jobs.

The factors have been categorized into (i) 'achievement oriented' and (ii) 'tradition oriented' (Dhar, 1976). The first three factors as shown in the table—education, hard work, and ability—can easily fall into the achievement oriented category, but placing of some of the other criteria presents problems. Using this rough scale we find that about 88.48 per cent of the youths regard achievement criteria to be the important factor for getting satisfactory jobs; 6.28 per cent regard personal contacts, influential friends, and recommendations of important persons to be the crucial factor; while 4.72 per cent felt that bribery and luck are helpful to get a satisfactory job. The study indicates that more than 4/5th of the educated youths perceive achievement criteria as the primary factor for acquiring a job. While, it is usual for personal contacts and recommendations to play a crucial part in job seeking, it is also obvious that some respondents rely on bribery because it is prevalent in the state.

Table 6.4: Factors Important for getting Satisfactory Jobs

Sl. No.	*Factors*	*Proportions ranking it as*	
		i *the most important*	*ii* *the second most important*
1.	Education	51.83	12.04
2.	Hard work	27.23	34.03
3.	Ability	9.42	27.23
4.	Personal contacts	0.00	2.10
5.	Influential friends and contacts	0.52	1.05
6.	Recommendations from important persons (politicians, government officials)	5.76	10.47
7.	Luck	3.67	6.28
8.	Bribery	1.05	6.28
9.	Others	0.52	0.52

VI

Manpower planning aims essentially at striking a balance between the supply of workers and the demand for their services. In the case of educated manpower, the aim is to regulate the outflow from, and consequently in the flow into the educational institutions in relation to the requirements of trained manpower for the economy (Dhar, 1976). It is imperative to know the state government policy for manpower planning; whether it is a successful plan or not; whether it is balanced between supply and demand or outflow and inflow. It is imperative to study: (a) the literacy growth rate and the job structure in the state, (b) the existing state of the information that the youth have about the employment market, (c) the extent to which the educated are concerned with their occupational future, (d) the perceptions of the employment situation like the varying incidence of unemployment, the increase or decrease in availability of jobs, etc.

The picture in the state is the increasing trend of educated unemployment, the continuous increase of students in schools and colleges and the high literacy rate which are all indicators of high supply of workers. They remain as educated unemployed, for they are not fitted into the employment scenario. The number has grown very fast compared to the expansion of job opportunities in the state. The future of the educated youths is expected to be bleak in view of the shrinking employment opportunities, particularly in the organized sector.

The literacy rate has steadily increased since the last six decades. It has increased gradually from 10.52 per cent in 1951 to 67.11 per cent in 2001. The percentage of literate men and women to the total respective population has steadily increased from 15.18 in 1951 to 71.77 in 2001 in the case of men and 5.75 in 1951 to 61.92 in 2001 in the case of women. The population growth, the literacy growth, the job structure and the growth of employment correspond to the growth of unemployment in the state. The government policy on curbing the problem of unemployment among the educated youth is related and can be closely examined based on these factors. The data demands of the policy makers and planners to create jobs suitable for the educated population based on its proportion.

The entire population can be classified into three main occupational categories as is done by the Census department: (i) Main workers, (ii) Marginal workers, (iii) Non-workers.

Main workers are those who have worked for the major part of the year preceding the date of enumeration, i.e. those who are engaged in any economically productive activity for 183 days or six months or more during the year. Main workers are further classified into four broad industrial categories:

(a) **Cultivators:** A person is considered as a cultivator if he or she is engaged either as employer, single worker or family worker in cultivation of land owned or held from the government or held from private persons or institutions for payment in money, kind or share of crop. Cultivation includes supervision or direction of cultivation.

(b) **Agricultural Labourers:** A person who works in another person's land for wages in cash, kind or share of crop is regarded as an agricultural labourer. Such a person has no risk in cultivation but merely works in another person's land for wages. An agricultural labourer has no right of lease or contract on land on which he works.

(c) **Household Industry:** Household Industry is defined as an industry by the head of the household himself/herself or by the members of the household at home or within the village in rural areas, and only within the precincts of the house where the household is situated in urban areas. A household industry is one that is engaged in production, processing, servicing, repairing or making and selling of goods.

(d) **Other Workers:** All those who work in any field of economic activity other than cultivation, agricultural labour, or household industries are *'other workers'*. The types of workers that come under this category include factory workers, plantation workers, those in trade, commerce, business, transport, mining, construction, political or social work, all government servants, municipal employees, teachers, priests, entertainment artists, etc.

Marginal workers are those who work any time at all in the year preceding the enumeration but did not work for a major part of the year, i.e. those who work for less than 183 days or six months.

If an individual has not worked at all during the last six months, he or she is treated as a non-worker. *Non-workers* include: (a) those attending to household duties at home, (b) students, (c) dependents, (d) retired persons or pensioners, (e) beggars, (f) inmates of institutions and (g) other non-workers which includes educated unemployed youth.

In view of the job opportunities and job expectations of the educated youth, it is relevant to examine the existing job structure in the state. The economic activity of the entire population has been classified as shown in Table 6.5. In 1981, the total number of main workers is 3,68,321 which constitutes 47.53 per cent of the total population, 5,433 marginal workers which constitutes 7.02 per cent, and 401,176 non-workers which constitutes 51.77 per cent of the total population. In 1991 the proportion of the main workers is 42.29 per cent (511,497); the marginal workers are 0.39 per cent (4,740); and the non-workers are 57.32 per cent (693,309). In 2001 the proportion of the main workers has further decreased to 35.63 per cent (708,455); 7.12 per cent marginal workers (141,527); and the population of the non-workers is 57.26 per cent (1,138,654). The *non-workers* who are 401,176 in 1981 have increased to 1,138,654 in 2001 to an increased percentage of 183.83 per cent in two decades.

Table 6.5: Occupational Structure in the State (Nagaland)

Year	*Total Main Workers*					*Marginal Workers*	*Non-Workers*	*Total Population*
	i	*ii*	*iii*	*iv*	*Total*			
1981	266,241	2,979	1,461	97,640	368,321	5,433	401,176	774,930
1991	371,597	7,233	1,991	130,676	511,497	4,740	693,309	1,209,546
2001	—	—	—	—	708,455	141,527	1,138,65	1,988,636

Note: 1. (i) Cultivators, (ii) Agricultural Labourers, (iii) Household Industry, (iv) Other Workers

2. Census Department, Kohima.

From the point of view of absorption of the educated unemployed, it is necessary to understand the growth of employment. It is essential to understand the growth of main workers or the percentage expansion of the main workers. As given in Table 6.6, the total expansion of the main workers during 1981–1991 has been found to be slow, being only 38.87 per cent, which turns out to be a bare 3.89 per cent per annum. The total expansion of the main workers during 1991–2001 has shown similar slow growth, i.e. 38.51 per cent turning out to be a bare 3.85 per cent per annum.

On the other hand, the decadal population growth during 1981–1991 which is 56.08 per cent has increased to 64.41 per cent in 1991–2001 recording the highest decadal growth rate in India for two decades. At the same time we see the decreasing trend of the proportion of the main workers to the total population, say, 47.52 per cent in 1981 to 42.29 per cent in 1991 and further decreasing to 35.63 per cent in 2001.

Again the study shows that the maximum concentration of the main workers is cultivation, i.e. 72.29 per cent in 1981 and 72.65 per cent in 1991. The educated youth with their degrees do not opt for cultivation but desire jobs in the organized sector of the economy, which includes public sector and private sector jobs as discussed earlier. Public sector employment is divided into (i) Central government, (ii) State government, (iii) Quasi/semi government, and (iv) Local government. The educated youths aspire for government jobs because it promises stability, security of tenure with assured level of wages and salaries along with guaranteed retirement benefits.

The situation will further worsen if there is to be any negative growth of employment in the governmental departments. This picture can be supplemented by the closing down of industries like Tuli Paper Mill and Dimapur Sugar Mill. The state government has also come up with a new policy in the wake of the emerging fiscal crisis to downsize the employed population. The seriousness of job problem is visible. Take for instance the case of 3000 candidates fighting for a handful of jobs officered by the NPSC in every. In 2000, as against 37,090 registered job seekers, only 339 vacancies were notified and 73 placements were made through the Employment Exchanges, thus offering 508 persons for a single job. Consequently, the probability of a person getting a job through the Employment Exchanges is very iow. Now the question arises as to what will the 507 persons do to earn a living? Do they remain silent especially when the selection is not fair? Whom do they blame for not getting a job? Again the vacancies notified to the Employment Exchange and the vacancies filled-in vary widely indicating that candidates from the open market got the jobs. Thus the very purpose of the Exchanges for which it has been started get defeated and further discouraged the unemployed to do registration with the Exchanges. The employment scenario in the state is not healthy but gloomy for the rapidly expanding number of educated unemployed youth.

VII

To study the period of unemployment, the educated youths were asked a question, "How long have you remained unemployed?" The made period is (2–3) years and the mean period 2.63 years. In other words, the average educated youth have remained unemployed for 3 years. These educated youth have been unsuccessfully searching for remunerative jobs to earn their livelihood. One can get frustrated when he/she has to wait for many years to get a job; and a frustrated man is a diseased man which ultimately affects the family, the society and affects the nation at large. About 25.66 per cent of the youths have not mentioned the period of their unemployment, and it is possible that they have remained unemployed for more than the classificatory period which extends only up to 6 years.

The study implies that about 93.19 per cent of the youths are aware of the increasing trend of unemployment. In relation to the study of the unemployment period, another question "Whom do you blame most for not getting a job?" was asked with four choices: (i) self, (ii) your education, (iii) family, and (iv) government. Of which, more than one-half, i.e. 54.45 per cent has blamed 'the government' for not getting a job; though at the same time about 87.44 per cent of the youths indicates that the government won't be able to employ all of them. No doubt the government cannot generate employment for every educated person, yet these majorities expects the government to do better. The educated unemployed youths blame the government for not getting a job because the appointments are biased in favour of the rich and the bureaucrats. Corruption and favouritism in the process of selection are unanimously accepted by the unemployed youths. Generally presenting, 30.37 per cent regard themselves responsible for the unemployment; 13.09 per cent the education system, 0.52 per cent the family and 54.45 per cent blame the government for their unemployment.

The study shows that more than three-fourth (87.44 per cent) of the educated youths are worried about the prospect of employment while 12.57 per cent responded 'not worried'. The study shows that about 39.27 per cent of the youths are 'very much worried'. It is obvious that an educated unemployed will not only be frustrated but very much worried when he is unemployed and is without any earning job for a long period. He/she is not only worried about the prospect of getting a job, but also will blame oneself, the government and everybody. Firstly, an educated unemployed is worried, because he continues to be a parasite by depending on others for everything. Secondly, he cannot support the family, which is expected of him in completing his education. Many are also worried and under pressure to get a job immediately if they have to work in the government sector as the maximum age limit runs out. Some of the educated job seekers are frustrated for they have been denied the jobs, which they thought they are qualified for in spite of all their efforts. Many of them have seen failure after failure. They are also worried for they know about the limited availability of jobs.

The educated unemployed of 'not worried' category belong to two sections: (i) Those who have just completed their studies or the period of unemployment is small, and (ii) Those from richer families.

Many a time the fresh unemployed fails to understand the stiffness of competition to get a job in the state. It has also been conceived that the richer the youth's family the less likely he is to feel worried about his occupation. The family can permit him to be unemployed for a longer duration during which time he might be able to work out or grab jobs that are more satisfying. On the other hand, for the educated unemployed with limited means, the strategy is to find the job, satisfying or not, as soon as possible. The extent of concern for a job is also related to the perspective job market where for instance, medical graduates are not worried or little worried as the job market for them is comparatively still high. It is also quite natural that those who indicated that they are worried have spent much more time in thinking about their occupational prospects. And not surprisingly those who are not worried spent much less time thinking about their occupational prospects.

The educated youths' estimate of how long will it take them to obtain their first employment probably determines the extent of their worry. However, almost half of the youths are not certain how long it will take them for their first employment. This group appears confused and frustrated with no hope to get any suitable job. The study shows that the mean period of unemployment is 3 years, and the maximum respondents have estimated that it will take at least 5 or more years to get their first employment. And this is without restriction to any kind of job. Perhaps those uncertain youths must have purposively and intentionally omitted the question to save themselves from the embarrassment of their worry. Further the certainty of getting a job has become a big question and who is going to get a job is another issue. In relation to this, it is not surprising to hear a respondent answering "survival of the fittest" on being asked about his personal view regarding employment.

In order to understand the chief sources of information about jobs, five categories of choices were listed in a separate question. It includes (i) News media, (ii) Employment experience of educated who preceded you, (iii) Classroom discussion, friends, colleagues, (iv) Activities of guidance and employment bureau, and (v) Any other. News media or newspaper advertisements (53.93%) provide a major source of information about jobs. This is followed by activities of guidance and employment bureau (26.70%); employment experience of educated who preceded (10.99%); classroom discussion, friends and colleagues (5.76%); and the least (92.62%) has indicated 'any other' as the major source of information about the job market.

At the time of the study about 63.87 per cent has tried for a job at least once while the rest 36.13 per cent has not tried for any job even once. It is also worth noting that almost all the youths keep trying for jobs by themselves, without relying much on the Employment Exchange notification, for 52.88 per cent indicates that it is not necessary to get registered in an Employment Exchange to get a job. The highest frequency of job attempts is twice with 30.33 per cent but it is not known whether they have tried for the same job or few different jobs. There are cases of attempting even more than five times, and one could ask whether there is an employment opportunity for a person who has seen failure five times or more in trying for jobs.

VIII

More specifically, in the line of the above discussions, how do the educated youths view the job market? How do the unemployed youths estimate their probabilities of securing jobs? Which jobs do the unemployed feel, are likely to become available and which jobs will be hard to come by? These are some questions which need to be discussed diligently. The responses of the youths to such questions represent a realistic appraisal of the situation in the state, or perhaps a hope that in their chosen field jobs will be available, or perhaps could indicate the extent to which the unemployed youths are able to correctly interpret the changing market trends. Since the classification of occupations adopted in the questionnaire is more specific, the analysis represents the reactions of the youths to information they receive from different sources, rather than an accurate estimate of manpower needs.

The educated youths are asked to estimate the incidence of unemployment, of which 83.77 per cent estimated that more than 20 per cent of the educated youths must be unemployed. On a more personal level, the youth are asked about the present status of their three best friends who have completed studies in the recent past. They responded of these friends remain unemployed for long stretches of time. The picture therefore is gloomy, and the educated unemployed youths as discussed earlier, blame the government for their not getting a job. At the same time they are helpless for they are also aware that the government would not be able to generate employment for all. In spite of the gloomy picture, the youths have a mixed opinion. About 27.22 and 6.28 per cent respectively believe that the job opportunities would 'increase' and 'rapidly increase' in the next 10 years. These respondents perceive that the government will be able to create more job avenues in the near future. The attitude towards the government is positive. About 26.18 per cent of the youths believe that the job opportunities in the next 10 years will 'remain the same'. However about 26.18 and 14.14 per cent respectively believe that the job opportunities will 'somewhat decrease' and 'rapidly decrease' in the next 10 years. This group of the youths has lost confidence in the government and their attitude is negative towards the government.

The educated youths are asked to rank a given list of occupations (14 occupations as shown in Table 6.6) where they expected the job opportunities will increase the most and least in the next 10 years. As depicted in the table, the educated unemployed youth perceive that in the next 10 years business opportunities will increase more rapidly than any other occupation, while job opportunities will increase the least with the occupation category—Government Administrative, Executive Official. Then, one can ask the question why if job opportunities will be available in business, the youths still seek for government jobs. Perhaps these educated youths do not have sufficient capital to start business or it is the last option of them. Of the 14 occupations shown in Table 6.6, there are 8 government occupations. And quite a considerable percentage of the educated unemployed youths perceive that job opportunities will increase in 2 governmental occupations, i.e. police or military and as secondary school teachers. Job opportunities as teachers will increase because the rapid growth in the number of students necessarily demands more teachers. However, this is directly related to the financial position of the state government or the private proprietors. As far as police or military is concerned the educated youth might have observed the recent recruitments in the state (say IRB's). The youths on the other hand perceive that jobs in the other 6 governmental occupations will not increase. For that matter, almost half of the respondents argue that job opportunities in the government sector especially administrative and executive official level will increase the least.

Table: 6.6: Views of Job Opportunities

Sl. No.	*Occupations*	*Proportion of educated youth's indicating that the opportunities will*	
		i *Increase the most*	*ii* *Increase the least*
1.	Government Administrative, Executive Official	7.85	**43.47**
2.	University Teacher	4.71	3.66
3.	Secondary School Teacher	14.66	1.57
4.	Higher Research Worker	8.90	3.14
5.	Legal (Law) Practitioner	1.57	3.14
6.	Engineer	0.52	19.37
7.	Physician/Surgeon (Medicine)	5.24	1.57
8.	Salesman/Business	**26.70**	1.57
9.	Farming	3.14	12.57
10.	Political/Political Agents	2.62	5.24
11.	Clerk	0.52	3.66
12.	Editor/Journalist	2.62	0.52
13.	Police/Military	19.90	0.52
14.	Computer Jobs	1.05	0.00

IX

Thus to conclude, the aspirations of the educated youths are reflected in their preferences and desires for particular jobs. The unemployed wants a secure, stable and prosperous job. As discussed, the jobs most desired by the educated are the government jobs that promise stability and security of tenure with assured levels of wages and salaries along with guaranteed retirement benefits. Most educated job seekers do not like hard work, and prefer sedentary jobs and are inclined towards the desk job. Their first preferred choice is relatively for white-collar jobs. However, majority of them are ready for even manual jobs in case of other alternatives are not found. Therefore, though the educated prefer government jobs, yet the final aspiration is found to consist in getting any job in order to earn a livelihood.

The desire to 'acquire more knowledge' emerged as the primary reason for seeking education in all subjects, for all occupational groups and for all income groups. And the youths are satisfied with their education and subjects. There is a great discrepancy between the occupational preferences and the occupational expectations. In other words, there is no correspondence between the proportions indicating preferences for occupations and those indicating the occupations that the educated youths expect to get. The location of job is not the primary consideration for preferences when there is scope for interesting work, security and higher salary. Yet, preferences for urban locations are slightly greater than rural areas. The educated unemployed youths regard achievement criteria—education, hard work, and ability—to be the most important factors for getting satisfactory jobs.

However, the future of the educated unemployed is expected to be very bleak in view of the shrinking employment opportunities. The proportion of the main workers to the total population in the state is decreasing in spite of the increasing population and increasing literacy rate, resulting in increasing unemployment among the educated. There is no balance between the number of students produced and the number of jobs available. The study has revealed that the unemployed youths have remained without any remunerative job for many years and they blame the government for not getting a job. The average frequency of job attempts by these educated youth is twice and the maximum youths perceive that it will take another five or more years to get any job. As discussed, the prospects in the job market look gloomy, though many educated youths remain hopeful. Under these circumstances, the educated unemployed youth in the state are very much worried about the prospect of employment.

REFERENCES

Aggarwal, A.K. (1987). *Economic Problems and Planning in North-East India.* New Delhi, Sterling Publishers Pvt. Ltd.

Ahuja, Ram. (1997). *Social Problems in India (Second Edition).* New Delhi, Rawat Publications.

Bajpai, Pramod Kumar. (1992). *Youth, Education and Unemployment.* New Delhi, Ashish Publishing House.

Chadha, G.K. (2000). "Youth Unemployment in India: Past policy Gaps and Future Strategic Options" in *The Indian Journal of Labour Economics.* Vol. 43, No. 4, Oct–Dec., 2000.

Chakrapani, C. (1995). *Unemployment Stress—A Study of Educated Unemployed.* New Delhi, Vikas Publishing House Pvt. Ltd.

Chauhan, S.S. (ed.). (1990). *Advanced Educational Psychology.* New Delhi, Vikas Publishing House.

Das, B. (1992). *Unemployment in Assam, an Account of Human Error.* New Delhi, Cosmo Publications.

Dhar, T.N., A.S. Ilchman and W.F. Ilchman. (1976). *Education and Employment in India.* Calcutta, Minerva Associates (Publications) Pvt. Ltd.

Dholakia, J. (1977). *Unemployment and Employment Policy in India.* New Delhi, Sterling Publishers Pvt. Ltd.

Government of Nagaland, Directorate of Economics and Statistics. *Statistical Hand Book of Nagaland.* Kohima.

Government of Nagaland, Directorate of Economics and Statistics. *Basic Facts—2006.* Kohima.

Government of Nagaland, Directorate of Employment and Craftsmen Training.

Krishna, Raj. (1973). "Unemployment in India" in *Economic and Political Weekly.* Vol. VIII, No. 9, March 3.

Kuppuswammy, B. (ed.). (1984). *Advanced Educational Psychology.* New Delhi, Sterling Publishers Pvt. Ltd.

Puttaswamaiah, K. (1977). *Unemployment in India—Policy for Manpower.* New Delhi, Oxford and IBH Publishing Co.

Saraswathi, S. (1988). *Youth in India.* New Delhi, Indian Council of Social Science Research.

Sinclair, P. (1987). *Unemployment, Economic Theory and Evidence.* Oxford, Basil Blackwell Ltd.

Temsu, L. (1997). *Job Aspiration among Youth in Mokokchung Town, Nagaland.* Dissertation, M.Phil, Deptt. of Sociology, NEHU.

Thakur, D.S. (1985). *Poverty, Inequality and Unemployment in Rural India.* Delhi, B.R. Publishing Corporation.

7

HUMAN DEVELOPMENT IN NAGALAND
An Inter-District Analysis

SUBHENDU DUTTA

Introduction

Of late, economists have shifted their main focus from various developmental indicators to human beings as one of the forceful catalysts for attaining all-round development in a country or region. As we have grown and advanced, our perspectives towards life has also come under dramatic transformations. Depending on one major factor for defining economic development, i.e. income, has now been considered out of date. In fact, it is not the single factor for looking at a country's advancement. Apart from income we have some other factors which strongly influence the development of a region.

Humans are one of the very precious and powerful resources which can trigger all-round development of a country. "... diverse patterns of development were, of course, the product of a number of historical, cultural, and other circumstances peculiar to the various countries involved. Underlying these special circumstances, however, were certain forces that economists have found to be central to the growth process in general. These underlying forces have to do with the size, quality, and organization of a country's basic productive apparatus (Gill, 1992). One of these productive and valuable apparatuses is human beings, which needs to be converted into human capital for all-round development of a country. Development of human beings is one of the foremost criteria today, for speedy growth and development of a country. Their development encompasses various spheres of life that have to be moulded in accordance to our need for achieving the required growth rate.

The present paper attempts to study the state of human development in Nagaland by selecting some select indicators for each district. It tries to find the levels and disparity of human development in various districts of the state.

I

Human Development—Meaning and Measurement

Human development is a process of enlarging people's choices. The choices, among other things, are to lead a long and healthy life, to be educated and to enjoy a decent standard of living. "The basic objective of development", wrote Mahbub-ul-Haq in the first "Human Development Report" in 1990 is to create an enabling environment in which people can enjoy long, healthy and creative lives (UNDP). Still the vision retains a powerful significance.

'If these essential choices are not available, many other opportunities remain inaccessible. But human development does not end here. Additional choices, highly valued by many people, range from political, economic and social freedom to opportunities for being creative and productive, and enjoying personal self-respect and guaranteed human rights. Human development has two sides: the formation of human capabilities—such as improved health, knowledge and skills—and the use people make of their acquired capabilities—for leisure, productive purposes or being active in cultural, social and political affairs. If the scales of human development do not finely balance the two sides considerable human frustration may result' (HDR–1990, UNDP). It is, therefore, apparent that human development does not only mean increasing one's income and accumulating the same, but something more than that. Income is just a means for the satisfaction of our infinite ends. It does not always give us happiness—the happiness we sometimes look for.

Human development, according to UNDP, can be measured by including some variables as indicators. These indicators may together reflect the attainment of human development. Though, in reality, we may list a number of indicators for measuring human development of a region, but broadly, the following three indicators have been used to measure human development:

1. Longevity, i.e., life expectancy at birth;
2. Knowledge, i.e., literacy rate; and
3. Decent standard of living, i.e., GDP per capita.

The attainment of all these broad indicators can serve as a measurement of human development in a country.

II

A Profile of Nagaland

Nagaland stands out as a land of diverse tribes, systems of governance, cultures, sheer colour and variety. It is a sociological and anthropological gold mine as it is still scientifically unexplored. Indeed, in spite of its many constraints and challenges, Nagaland has continued to chart new developmental paths for itself and has shown a unique model for the country. It emerged as the 16th State of India in 1963. Statehood came as a result of a political agreement. One of the smaller hill states of India, Nagaland is known for its myriad tribes (officially 16 in numbers) with their rich culture and traditions. The State has a distinct character both in terms of its social composition as well as in its developmental history (NSHDR, 2004).

As regards to human development in Nagaland, in certain areas it has shown high levels of achievement. The HDI (2001) of Nagaland was 0.62, as compared to 0.472 (2001) for India, reflecting the State's good performance in terms of the constituents of the indices and the factors that influence them, including literacy, health status and income levels. The per capita income of Nagaland during 2000–01 was almost equal to the national average. The per capita income in the State increased from Rs. 1361 during 1980–81 to Rs. 5520 during 1990–91. During 2000–01, per capita income was Rs. 11,473 (at constant 1993–94 prices) as against Rs. 10,306 for the country as a whole. Among districts, Dimapur was having the highest per capita income Rs. 16,837 and Mon having the least Rs. 4,500. The literacy rate in the state has reached 67.11 per cent from a mere 20.40 per cent in 1961. Its sex ratio, CDR, IMR and MMR rates are better than the national average. Life expectancy is 73.4 years. (NSHDR, 2004).

Development in Nagaland started under very challenging circumstances. Besides near absolute lack of any infrastructure, its remoteness and inaccessibility, the State was also engulfed in protracted and violent insurgency, which disrupted development efforts at every stage. Nevertheless, in 40 years of statehood, Nagaland has made significant progress (NSHDR, 2004).

III

Objectives and Methodology of the Study

The study aims at analyzing the levels of human development in eight districts of Nagaland by taking into account some indicators and to find the level of disparity among these districts. The three newly created districts (Peren, Kiphire and Longleng) have been excluded due to the non-availability of data.

The inter-district HDI has been estimated by constructing a composite index for select indicators. The 'Deprivation Method' used here is adopted from the UNDP report on 'Concept and Measurement of Human Development, 1990'. The study is based on the secondary data that have been collected from Statistical Hand Book of Nagaland, 2001 and 2004; Nagaland State Human Development Report, 2004, Seventh All India Educational Survey, 2002—Ministry of Education, New Delhi and from various relevant websites.

The Human Development Index (HDI) is constructed in three steps. In the first step, a measure of deprivation is defined that a district suffers in each of the variables. For this purpose, a maximum and minimum value is determined for each of the variables given the actual values. The deprivation measure helps in placing a district in the range of zero to one as defined by the difference between the maximum and the minimum. Thus, I_{ij} is the deprivation indicator for the jth district with respect to the ith variable and it is defined as:

$$I_{ij} = \frac{(\max_j X_{ij} - X_{ij})}{(\max_j X_{ij} - \min_j X_{ij})} \quad \ldots\ldots\ldots\ldots\ldots\ldots\ldots\ (1)$$

In the second step an average deprivation indicator I_j is defined. This is done by taking a simple average of the indicators:

$$I_j = \sum_{i=1}^{n} I_{ij} \text{ ....(2)}$$

Where, n is the total number of indicators.

Finally, we have to measure HDI as one minus the average deprivation index:

$(HDI)_j = (1 - I_j)$.........................(3)

Using the above method, this paper attempts to analyze inter-district levels of human development. The indicators that have been used for assessing the phenomenon are:

X_1 = Percentage of literacy; X_2 = per capita DDP (Rs.); X_3 = Life expectancy; X_4 = Percentage of hospitals, dispensaries etc; X_5 = Percentage of habitations with drinking water facilities; X_6 = Percentage of primary and upper primary schools; X_7 = Percentage of secondary and higher secondary schools; X_8 = Percentage of colleges.

As stated, the scores for judging the status of human development in a district range between 0 and 1. Any district scoring less than 0.5 is termed as less developed or backward. Moderately developed districts are required to score between 0.5 and 0.8 (including 0.5 and excluding 0.8) and districts are called developed if they score between 0.8 and 1.00 (both inclusive).

IV

Measurement of Indices and HDI

In Table 7.1, we have shown the data pertaining to eight indicators for the state of Nagaland in various districts.

With the help of Table 7.2, the human development indices for various districts in Nagaland have been estimated (see page 159).

Table 7.2 shows that most of the districts (50%) are moderately developed as these (Dimapur, Kohima, Mokokchung and Tuensang) have scored between 0.5 and 0.8. None of the districts is developed in respect of human development dimensions, i.e., scoring between 0.8 and 1.00. About (50%) of the districts are less developed, which scored less than 0.5. The HDI values of Dimapur, Kohima, Mokokchung and Tuensang are 0.684, 0.670, 0.522 and 0.548 respectively. Among all districts, it is seen that, Dimapur scored the highest HDI value and therefore, ranked one in the table.

Table 7.1: Human Development Indicators in districts of Nagaland

District	X_1	X_2	X_3	X_4	X_5	X_6	X_7	X_8*
Dimapur	78.15	16837	74.0	11.63	11.26	13.54	15.29	40.81
Kohima	74.28	11906	73.2	10.59	18.30	15.57	23.13	32.65
Mokokchung	84.27	12305	72.3	13.19	9.85	12.98	13.33	8.16
Tuensang	51.30	8149	70.8	16.49	25.35	18.10	11.76	6.12
Phek	71.35	9880	74.2	13.36	9.85	10.17	13.72	2.04
Wokha	81.28	13647	68.6	10.24	14.08	7.81	7.05	4.08
Zuneheboto	69.73	8372	73.6	10.59	8.45	10.84	11.37	2.04
Mon	42.25	4500	75.0	13.88	2.81	10.96	4.31	4.08

* Does not include theological colleges.

Sources: Statistical Hand Book of Nagaland—2001, 2004; Nagaland State Human Development Report—2004, Govt. of Nagaland; Deptt. of Higher Education, Nagaland; Summary Report—2002, 7th All India Survey on Education—www. 7thsurvey.ncert.nic.in

Table 7.2: Human Development Indicators in districts of Nagaland (Estimated using Deprivation Method)

District	X_1	X_2	X_3	X_4	X_5	X_6	X_7	X_8	*Total*	*Avg. Dep. Index*	*HDI*	*Rank*
Dimapur	0.14	0.00	0.15	0.77	0.62	0.44	0.41	0.00	2.53	0.316	0.684	1(MD)
Kohima	0.24	0.40	0.30	0.94	0.31	0.24	0.00	0.21	2.64	0.330	0.670	2(MD)
Mokok-chung	0.00	0.36	0.42	0.52	0.68	0.49	0.52	0.84	3.83	0.478	0.522	4(MD)
Tuensang	0.78	0.70	0.65	0.00	0.00	0.00	0.60	0.89	3.62	0.452	0.548	3(MD)
Phek	0.31	0.56	0.13	0.50	0.68	0.77	0.50	1.00	4.45	0.556	0.444	5(LD)
Wokha	0.07	0.26	1.00	1.00	0.50	1.00	0.85	0.94	5.62	0.702	0.298	7(LD)
Zune-heboto	0.35	0.68	0.22	0.94	0.74	0.70	0.62	1.00	5.25	0.656	0.344	6(LD)
Mon	1.00	1.00	0.00	0.41	1.00	0.69	1.00	0.94	6.04	0.755	0.245	8(LD)

MD—Moderately Developed; LD—Less Developed

We know that the less the deprivation value for any indicator, the more the development. In this respect, we can also analyze independently each indicator for each district, though it cannot reflect all-round development of human beings. It is always better to have measured the levels of human development using a composite index. On examining independently each indicator, we find that in case of Dimapur X_2 and X_8 are efficient indicators, since deprivation values in respect of these two indicators are lowest among all districts. It means per capita of income earned by people residing in Dimapur is the highest among all districts. This is also true if we look at the official data for 2001. The number of colleges providing general and technical (theological colleges excluded) education is also highest in number there. In Kohima, the deprivation index for X_7 is found to be the lowest meaning that the district enjoys maximum number of secondary and higher secondary schools. Mokokchung has the highest percentage of literates i.e. 84.27 (2001) as the deprivation value for X_1 is the lowest among all districts. For Tuensang, the efficient indicators are X_4, X_5 and X_6. Thus, in Tuensang the health indicators i.e. number of hospitals, dispensaries etc. and percentage of villages/ habitations enjoying good drinking water are the highest. Percentage of primary and upper primary schools in the district is also the highest (18.10 %, 2002). The most economically backward district of Nagaland, i.e. Mon is better in X_3. It means life expectancy of people in the district is the highest (75 years, 1991). In Mon, it is revealed that people have high life expectancy whereas their per capita income is the lowest among all districts in the state.

One of the indicators to judge quality of life is longevity. It is evident from some studies that some countries with relatively higher per capita incomes perform poorly with respect to longevity while some with lower per capita incomes perform better in terms of health indicator. A study by Morris and McAlpin reveal that there is no correlation between per capita GNP and PQLI. For instance, Sri Lanka with per capita GNP of $179 has a PQLI equal to South Korea with per capita income of $ 464. As against this, Mexico with per capita GNP of $ 996 showed a lower PQLI as compared to South Korea (Morris and McAlpin, 1982). There is no doubt that per capita income is very important in the life of the people in a country, but it is not the sum total of their lives. Another similar study reveals that between 1965 and 1995 poorer countries gained more in terms of longevity than richer countries did. Thus, the change in inequality in income per capita actually underestimates the degree of convergence in welfare across countries (Gary Becker, Tomas Phillipson, and Rodrigo Soares). The first global Human Development Report (HDR), prepared by the United Nations Development Programme (UNDP) in 1990 under the leadership of Mahbub-ul-Haq and Amartya Sen, also argued that income alone does not capture all dimensions of human development and that a composite index of health, education and income is a much more comprehensive measure of development.

Theoretically, the case of Mon seems contradictory. We know that good things of life come with handsome earnings but we cannot also deny that people who live in urban regions are more prone to a number of diseases, particularly 'lifestyle diseases', which a rural dweller seldom experiences. Life expectancy depends upon a number of factors and not only on income. Our life is considerably influenced by the environment in which live. The intensity of pollution, climatic conditions etc; the food we eat—all have profound bearing on our life. Now-a-days we tolerate foods which are mostly grown using chemical fertilizers that are very hazardous for our health. Consumption of such foods gives rise to many diseases that tend to decrease our longevity. Rural people, on the other hand, are likely to take locally grown foods which are almost free from chemicals. Their life is full of physical activities which makes them sturdy than their counterpart living in urban areas and are less vulnerable to many diseases that are caused by over exposure to pollutants; stress of life and hectic but sedentary lifestyle. Probably these may be reasons for high life expectancy of people living in Mon although it has the lowest per capita income.

Conclusion

Measuring how good the quality of human beings in a country is not an easy task. Despite listing some indicators for finding whether we have developed ourselves in qualitative terms, it is really not easy to say what type of development we wish to attain. Human development not only means improving our standard of living and for that earning higher incomes but also the attainment of our basic rights, and living in an environment which is conducive for expressing our thoughts freely, walk without fear and capability to fight against evils endangering our society.

REFERENCES

Concepts and Measurement of Human Development, HDR–1990, UNDP.

Gill, Richard T, (1992) *Economic Development: Past and Present,* 3rd Edition, Prentice-Hall of India, New Delhi, p. 3.

Morris David Morris, Michelle B. McAlpin, (1982) *Measuring the Condition of India's Poor, The Physical Quality of Life Index,* Promilla and Co., New Delhi, pp. 24–28.

Nagaland State Human Development Report, (2004) Department of Planning and Coordination, Government of Nagaland.

7th All India Educational Survey, Planning Commission, www. 7th survey.ncert.nic.in

The Quantity and Quality of Life and the Evolution of World Inequality, co-authors Gary Becker, Tomas Phillipson, and Rodrigo Soares, http:/www.nber.org/digest/nov03/NBER Working Paper No. 9765.

SECTION III

Infrastructure and Bio-Resource Conservation

8

INFRASTRUCTURE DEVELOPMENT IN NORTH-EAST INDIA
A Case Study of Mizoram

R.K.P.G. SINGHA and K.C. KABRA

Introduction

Infrastructure may be defined as the base (foundation) of a world system (i.e. economy, society, organization). It is an equipment required for a particular system to function[1] and represents the basic facilities, services and installations[2] that must be in place in order for a community or a country (region) to function as a state including the capital needed for supporting day to day economic activities of public transportation (airports, ports, railways, roads, highways, bridges, sewers), communication network (telephone), and provision of water and power (electricity), and the public utility institutions needed for security, health (hospitals), education (schools), and post offices[3]. It is the human-made[4] permanent resources serving society's needs[5] to support residential development[6] in the form of improvements made to an area[7] that provide any or all of the normal public services (e.g. water supply, sewage, utilities, traffic control). While there is no universally recognised definition of infrastructure, there is broad agreement about what it is and is not. Thus, the MacMillan Dictionary of Modern Economics (1996) defines infrastructure as "The structural elements of an economy that facilitate the flow of goods and services between buyers and sellers". The Routledge Dictionary of Economics (1995) broadens the definition to include "the basic services or social capital of a country, or part of it, which make economic and social activities possible by providing transportation... [and other facilities]... in which community activities can take place." Infrastructure has traditionally been provided and maintained by the government. However, some nations are currently experimenting with privatization of some elements of it as they seek to cut their expenditures[8]. Larimer (1994) speaks of the underlying foundation or framework of basic services, facilities and institutions upon which the growth and development of an area, community or a system depend. Slootweg and Verhoef (1999) defined it as a large-scale technological system, consisting of immovable physical facilities and delivering (an) essential public or private service(s) through the storage, conversion and/or transportation of certain commodities. It also includes those parts and subsystems necessary for fulfilling the primary storage, transportation and/or conversion function(s) as well as those supporting a proper execution of the primary function(s). The Merriam Webster Dictionary gives the following definitions for infrastructure:

(i) The underlying foundation (basic framework) of a system or organization,
(ii) The permanent installations required for military purposes,
(iii) The system of public works including waste management of a country, state, or region based on a specific type of physical structure for providing the goods or services,
(iv) The resources such as personnel, buildings, or equipment required for an activity.

Infrastructure, therefore, is the set of interconnected structural elements that provide the framework for supporting the entire structure and includes a broad spectrum of services, institutions and facilities that ranges from transportation systems and public utilities to finance systems, laws and law enforcement, and education and research. The timing with which infrastructure can adjust to changing demands, the capability to respond to changes both predicted and unexpected and the long term risk implications of long gestation times are fundamental characteristics of infrastructure. Many definitions of infrastructure throughout the literature show common features of infrastructure, such as:

- It is a large-scale system,
- It has a strong technological dimension,
- It consist of immovable physical components,
- It delivers an essential service (where essential means necessary and hardly replaceable),
- It offers significant economies of scale in production, reflected in high initial fixed costs and relatively low variable costs of operation,
- It works as a common carrier offering economies in supplying diverse consumers jointly rather than stand-alone facility,
- Owing to high fixed costs and declining marginal costs, it causes natural monopoly making it difficult for new entrants to compete with an incumbent supplier,
- Because of natural monopoly, it has witnessed, historically, a high level of government intervention directly or more recently through regulation of prices and supply arrangements.

Chart 8.1 depicts few basic items that are considered as the part of infrastructure (see page 168).

It is clear from the above description that infrastructure plays a key role in society and is crucial for economic growth of a country (region). Infrastructure investment and consumption of its services have significant implications for achievement of sustainable development objectives, as these services underpin many aspects of economic and social activity and, as a consequence, infrastructure failures can have widespread impacts across the community. Infrastructure is considered as social overhead capital in Economics to distinguish it from directly productive capital. It is in this sense a part of the capital stock of a country (Mishra and Puri, 2003). Growth in agriculture, industry and now the service sector is increasingly depending upon infrastructure development. Agriculture requires credit for investment, power for irrigation, transportation (railway and well-connected roads) for distribution of agricultural produce. Similarly, industry requires finance for technology upgradation, power for production, transportation for both production and distribution activities and a reliable communication system for co-ordinating

Chart 8.1: Items Considered under Infrastructure

Category	*Items*	*Lumpiness*	*FC:VC ratio*	*Sunk Cost*	*Multiple-users*	*Exter-nalities*	*Long lead time*
Transport: Air	Airport runways	High	High	High	Moderate	Moderate	High
	Terminal facilities	Moderate	Moderate	Moderate	Moderate	Low	Moderate
	Air Navigation Assets	Low	Low	Moderate	Moderate	Low	Moderate
Transport: Sea	Dock facilities	High	Moderate	Moderate	Low	Moderate	Moderate
	Accessibility	Low	Moderate	Moderate	Low	Moderate	Low
	Harbour approaches	Low	Low	Moderate	Moderate	Moderate	Moderate
	Navigation aids	Low	Low	Moderate	Moderate	Low	Moderate
Transport: Rail	Tracks	Moderate	Moderate	Moderate	Low	Low	Moderate
	Signalling	Low	Low	Low	Low	Low	Low
	Interchange	Moderate	Moderate	Moderate	Moderate	Moderate	Low
	Rolling stock	Low	Low	Low	Low	Low	Low
Transport: Road	Road carriageways	Moderate	Moderate	High	High	Moderate	Moderate
	Interchanges	Moderate	Moderate	Moderate	Moderate	Moderate	Low
Tele-communications	Non-local transmission	Moderate	Moderate	Moderate	Low	Low	Low
	Cellular towers	Moderate	Moderate	Moderate	Low	Moderate	Moderate
	Local loops	Moderate	Moderate	Moderate	Moderate	Low	Low
	International cables, satellite connections etc.	Moderate	Moderate	Moderate	Low	Moderate	Moderate
Energy: Gas	Resource availability	High	Moderate	High	Low	Low	Moderate
	Extraction assets	Moderate	High	Moderate	Low	Moderate	High
	Processing assets	Moderate	Moderate	Moderate	Moderate	Low	Moderate
	Bulk distribution	High	High	High	Moderate	Moderate	Moderate
	Local reticulation	Moderate	Moderate	Moderate	Low	Moderate	Moderate

(contd.)

(contd. Chart 8.1)

Category	*Items*	*Lumpiness*	*FC:VC ratio*	*Sunk Cost*	*Multiple-users*	*Exter-nalities*	*Long lead time*
Energy: Electricity	Primary energy	High	Moderate	Moderate	Moderate	Low	Moderate
	Generation assets	High	High	High	Low	High	High
	Transmission	High	Moderate	Moderate	Low	Moderate	High
	Local reticulation	Moderate	Moderate	Moderate	Low	Moderate	Moderate
	Retailing	Low	Low	Low	Moderate	Low	Low
Energy: Petroleum	Importing	Low	Low	Low	Low	Moderate	Moderate
	Refining	Moderate	Moderate	Moderate	Moderate	Moderate	Moderate
	Bulk Storage	Moderate	Moderate	Moderate	Moderate	Moderate	Moderate
	Distribution (by road)	Low	Low	Low	Moderate	Low	Low
	Retail outlets	Moderate	Low	Moderate	Low	Moderate	Moderate
Water	Water capture	High	High	High	Moderate	Moderate	Moderate
	Treatment	High	Moderate	Moderate	Low	Moderate	Moderate
	Bulk Distribution	High	High	High	Moderate	Moderate	Moderate
	Local reticulation	Moderate	Moderate	Moderate	Low	Moderate	Moderate
	Irrigation	Moderate	Moderate	Moderate	Moderate	Moderate	Moderate

various activities at distant places, etc. The port facilities are of immense importance for international trade (Rajaram and Singh, 2005).

Chart 2: Relationship of infrastructure services with output

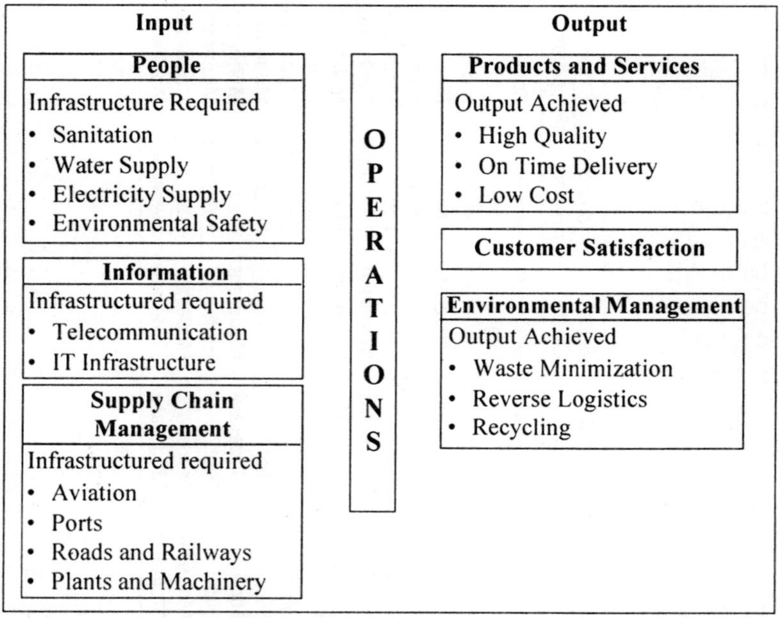

Physical infrastructure covering transportation, power and communication through its backward and forward linkages facilitates growth; social infrastructure including water supply, sanitation, sewage disposal, education and health, which are in the nature of primary services, has a direct impact on the quality of life. The visible signs of shortfalls in capacity and inefficiencies include increasingly congested roads, power failures, long-waiting lists for installation of telephones and shortage of drinking water. They illustrate the widening gap between demand and supply of infrastructure and also raise questions concerning the sustainability of economic growth in future. The above figure shows the influence of various infrastructural factors on operations of a project. The output of the well managed operations creates better services and products which are the assets of any country. Manufacturing of the products adds value to the Nation's economy and delivering of high quality service raises the standard of living of the country contributing to its development. The above mentioned chart explains the relationship of infrastructure services with output (goods and services).

Infrastructure Development in India

In India infrastructure development has been accorded high priority since the reforms of 1991. India scored 9.4 per cent GDP growth in 2006–07 in which there is contribution of nearly 51% from services and 16% from manufacturing sector and there is a need for proper alignment of resources. But in many respect India is far behind China. Among them infrastructure is a vital area where India is lagging far behind than China. In 2006, China produced 2830 billion kilowatt hours (kWh) of power and, for the first time, had a power surplus. In contrast, India produced 664 billion kWh with a 14.5 per cent peak power deficit. China already has around 45,000 km. of barrier, restricted access, and multi-lane dual carriageways. Let's forget barriers and restricted access, as on 31 May 2007, we had 6989 km. of four or six lane dual carriage national highways. Telecom is an Indian success story. In 2006–07, we had 166 million mobile subscribers. By March 2007, the number of mobile subscribers in China was 463 million. China's exports are eight times that of India's; and imports four times greater. In 2006, China's total value of exports and import was $1,761 billion (or 69 per cent of its GDP). India's was not even a fifth at $307 billion, or 37 per cent of GDP (Goswami, 2007).

India's economic performance in recent years has been among the best in the world, leading to a decline in *poverty*. But, Infrastructure development is a major constraint on the industrial growth in India and high transaction costs arising from inadequate and inefficient infrastructure preventing the economy from realizing its full growth potential regardless of the progress on other fronts. Infrastructure development has a crucial role to play if India is to sustain its high growth, which must become more inclusive as the country matures, Haruhiko Kuroda, President of ADB at its 39th Annual Meeting said, "Despite these improvements, most poverty-related education and health indicators continue to show disturbing gender gaps, large rural-urban differences, and wide variation across the states." India is aiming to achieve 10 per cent annual GDP growth by the year 2011–12, but the country needs over $300 billion to upgrade its infrastructure over the next five years according to the Prime Minister Dr. Manmohan Singh. The new economic policies aimed at stepping up economic growth, improving market efficiency and competitiveness, and integrating the Indian economy with global markets have already placed a heavy demand on all types of urban infrastructure services. The resulting bottlenecks are beginning to pose serious impediments to enhancing productivity. Urban infrastructure includes water supply and sanitation which are important basic needs for improvement of the quality of life and enhancement of the productive efficiency of citizens. There has been a steady increase in the urban population on account of rapid industrialization, natural growth and migration from rural areas. This has prompted the working out of alternative ways of meeting the increasing transport demand given the constraints of land and capital, and the need to control energy consumption, pollution and accidents. So there is a need for development of infrastructure in the Indian context to compete with other countries for the growth of overall economic development.

The Asian Develcpment Bank (ADB) and AMP Capital Investors, (the funds management arm of the $70 billion Australian financial services group), making initial contribution of US$ 15 million and US$ 30 million respectively, announced the launch of a US$ 125 million fund to promote investment in infrastructure development in the country through the Infrastructure Fund of India (TIFI) which is to invest in non-listed securities of companies that develop, own or operate infrastructure projects such as power, transport (toll roads, railways, ports, and airports), telecommunications (wire-line and wireless networks), and urban facilities (water and sewage networks) in India. It will help the private sector in India meet its infrastructure financing needs for commercially viable projects, raise the efficiency of infrastructure projects, and mobilize long-term capital from international institutional investors. ADB's participation is critical in helping introduce best environmental and corporate governance practices. ADB has consistently assigned high importance to India's infrastructure sector reforms and has provided a number of facilities aimed at helping the development of the infrastructure sector (Louis de Jonghe, Country Director, India Resident Mission, 9 February 2004).

In this paper, an attempt has been made to highlight the present status of infrastructure development in the North-Eastern Region as well as in Mizoram. The paper also tries to focus on the problems confronting development of infrastructure in Mizoram.

Infrastructure in North-East India

If one is really keen to analyze the socio-economic development scenario of the eight North-Eastern States, one could easily find out that Mizoram is ahead of other North-Eastern States in many respects. According to the Eleventh Finance Commission's Index of Economic and Social Infrastructure, Mizoram ranks first among the North-Eastern States getting 82% points followed by Assam which gets 77.7%. Weightage given in this index includes infrastructures available in agriculture, banking, electricity, transport, communications, education, health and civil administration.

North-East India (NEI) comprises eight States at present. The states are Assam, Arunachal Pradesh, Manipur, Meghalaya, Mizoram, Nagaland, Tripura and Sikkim which was included in the recent past. Focusing on North-East India, it is observed that barring Assam, most of the states are late comers to the process of development as they were created subsequently to the first decade of planning. In the hill states, majority of the population is tribal, ranging from around 70% in Arunachal Pradesh to 94% in Mizoram. In the hill areas the population density is very low, infrastructure very weak and production technology is primitive. Imbalances have been rising despite the treatment of the North-Eastern States as special category states for plan finance, launching of the subsidy schemes like capital and transport subsidy, concessional finance, etc. The major problem is the problem of infrastructure development due to the typical land structure of this region which is considered as the backbone for any economy.

In terms of hydro power potential NEI can be termed as a power house. If exploited fully NEI can be a power exporter region in our country and can earn a lot of revenue which can be utilized for other infrastructure development as well for overall development of the economy of this region. Table 8.1 exhibits the state-wise Mega, Major and medium hydro power potential in NEI. Arunachal Pradesh has the highest potential followed by Mizoram and Sikkim.

Table 8.1: State-wise Mega, Major and Medium Hydro Power Potential in NEI

State	*Potential (MW)*	*Unexploited (MW)*	*Exploitable (%)*
Arunachal Pradesh	26,765.00	26,631.17	99.53
Assam	351.00	148.50	42.31
Manipur	1176.00	1006.50	85.59
Meghalaya	1070.00	948.33	88.63
Mizoram	1455.00	1448.00	99.52
Nagaland	1040.00	958.12	92.13
Sikkim	1283.00	1225.50	95.52
Tripura	9.00	0.50	5.56
Total NEI	**33,140.00**	**32,366.62**	**97.67%**

Source: *Yojana,* December 2005, p.46.

Table 8.2 shows the State-wise Small, Mini and Micro Hydro Power potential in NEI. It also disclosed that Arunachal Pradesh has the highest potential with 452 sites and potential of 1243.47 MW. Likewise the other NEI States have high potential except Tripura with 10 sites and potential of 30.85 MW only comparing to other states in this region.

Table 8.2: State-wise Small, Mini and Micro Hydro-Power Potential in NEI.

State	*No of Sites*	*Potential*
Arunachal Pradesh	452	1243.47
Assam	40	119.54
Manipur	99	91.75
Meghalaya	90	197.32
Mizoram	53	135.93
Nagaland	84	149.31
Sikkim	70	214.33
Tripura	10	30.85
Total NEI	**898**	**2182.50**

Source: Yojana December 2005, p.46.

Infrastructure in Mizoram

On analysing the socio-economic development of the NER, Mizoram ranks first (82% points) followed by Assam 77.7%[9]. This index is measured after giving due weightage to infrastructure available in the respective state for agriculture, banking, electricity, transport, communications, education, health and civil administration.

Mizoram attained amazing literacy rate (88.8%) i.e., second highest in the country and the next to Kerala (Census, 2001) especially when it got its first High School only in 1944 and first Under-Graduate College in 1958. Women's literacy in Mizoram (86.13%) is again highest in the entire NE region. The gender difference in work participation is as low as 9 in Mizoram as against the national average of 26 (Economic Survey, 2002–03). As regards the Educational Development Index (EDI) of 1995 (developed after considering investment in education, literacy achievement, universalization of elementary education and availability of educational facilities), Mizoram found the place at the top of the list at the national level. This is surely an indicative of an all-round improvement in educational infrastructure both at the elementary and secondary educational levels.

As regards poverty eradication (one of the socio-economic indicators of development), Mizoram among the all North-Eastern States recorded least number of families living below poverty line (BPL) with further declining trend as is evident from the figure of 25.66 in 1993–94 to 19.47 in 1999–2000 as against the corresponding figure of 35.97 and 26.10 respectively at the national level (The Ministry of Food and Civil Supplies, Government of India). In spite of Mizoram being land-locked and inaccessible as compared to other States of the North-East, a big achievement for the state is to register the highest per capita income at current prices of Rs. 13,479 in 1998–99 which increased to Rs. 22,207 in 2002–03 (Economic Survey, 2002–03). The Human Development Index of 1991 placed Mizoram at the 7th position at the National level, as against Manipur (9th), Nagaland (11th), Tripura (22nd), Meghalaya (24th), Assam (26th) and Arunachal Pradesh (29th), (Economic Survey 2002–03). As regards agricultural food grain production (rice), Mizoram stands third in the rank amongst the NE States and recorded the output at 1,624 kg./hectare for 1997–98 as against the regional average at 1,427 kg./hectare. The landmark development in the history of Mizoram is the commissioning of Lengpui Airport (one of the best airports in the NER) which since 1998–99 is increasingly easing out the communication problems of the state. Till recently, Mizoram had air linkage with the rest of India for three days a week and that too from one service provider. But, now it has increased to 7 days a week with two service providers (Indian Airline and Air Deccan).

Mizoram has good potential for economic growth in the areas of Agriculture, Horticulture, Tourism, Handicraft, etc. Universally, the development of infrastructure, particularly transport infrastructure, is a key prerequisite for economic development. In Mizoram, the lack of adequate transport infrastructure has been the major inhibiting factor on its economic growth and development. Being a hilly state with difficult terrain and climatic conditions, transport infrastructure in Mizoram is essentially road based. The initiatives of the State Government to promote various developmental activities and thus alleviate the poverty of the people are largely dependent on the capability of the road network to carry passengers and goods efficiently and economically. A well laid out and well maintained road network is, therefore, essential for cost effective movement of people and materials, without which trade and industry also cannot maintain a competitive edge.

In Mizoram the only reliable transportation system is road transport. National Highway 54 is the lifeline of the state and the only main road of Mizoram state which connects with the rest of the country *via* Silchar, Asom. Railway transport is also connected to Mizoram at Bhairabi bordering Hailakandi, Asom which is just for name sake and there is a possibility to extend it up to Sairang near Aizawl town, the capital city of Mizoram. If it is extended up to this point really Mizoram will benefit to a great extent but so far it is a dream only. Air services have improved to a great extent at present and connect the state with Kolkata—Guwahati—Imphal.

Table 8.3 shows the category-wise road length up to 31 March 2006 in Mizoram. The total length of road is 5948.15 kms. consisting of 3526.76 kms. of surfaced and 2421.37 kms. of unsurfaced roads in Mizoram. In 1991 the road length was 3708 kms., 1268 kms. surfaced and 2440 kms. unsurfaced which shows a great improvement during this period. Border Roads Organization (BRO) has greatly contributed in terms of National Highway Road construction in Mizoram.

Passenger vehicles (buses, cars, jeeps, two-wheelers) constituted about 88% of the total vehicle population in the year 2000. Amongst the passenger vehicles, cars, jeeps, etc. have the highest share of passenger transport constituting 44%, with two-wheelers as the second highest at 41%, while buses represent only about 3% of the total number of vehicles. The low proportion of goods vehicles—about 10% of the total vehicle population—is indicative of the relatively low economic activity within the state. Most truck and bus traffic in Mizoram involves inter-state movement of vehicles registered outside Mizoram.

Table 8.3: Category-wise Length of Roads in Mizoram Up to 31-3-2006

(in kms.)

Sl.No.	*Type of Roads*	*Surfaced*	*Unsurfaced*	*Total*
1.	National Highway (PWD)	301.00	27.00	328.00
2.	State Highway	51.95	109.02	160.97
3.	Major District Road	857.53	644.71	1502.24
4.	Other District Road	613.27	597.94	1211.21
5.	Town Road	186.90	102.59	290.49
6.	Village Road	147.68	807.75	955.43
7.	National Highway (BRO)	1368.45	131.36	1499.81
	Total	**3526.76**	**2421.37**	**5948.15**

Source: Statistical Handbook of Mizoram 2006.

Most of Mizoram's bitumen-surfaced roads are in very poor condition, with potholes, ruts, cracks and other signs of pavement distress showing at many places, reflecting lack of sustained maintenance. The terrain is hilly and the roads have to negotiate steep gradients and sharp curves. Given the poor road conditions and generally bad geometry, the travel on the roads in Mizoram is not only inefficient and uneconomical but also hazardous and unsafe, resulting sometimes in serious accidents.

Considering the importance of the roads to the State's socio-economic development, major road rehabilitation, maintenance and up gradation efforts are needed in Mizoram. This will require significantly increased road funding commitments, well beyond the State's normal budgetary allocations for the road sector as well as upgraded road maintenance strategies and practices. The following table shows the mismatch between the proposed and actual expenditure which shows that actual expenditure is much less than the proposed expenditure.

Table 8.4: Plan Allocation

(Rs. in Lakhs)

	Five Year Plan	*Period*	*Proposed Expenditure*	*Actual Expenditure*
1.	7th	1985–90	5,018.23	—
2.	8th	1992–97	13,970.00	8,767.09
3.	9th	1997–02	18,972.00	15,098.65
4.	10th	2002–07	20,205.00	—

Source: Document on Road Development Policy, Government of Mizoram.

Table 8.5 discloses the statistics of Tele Communication connection in Mizoram up to 31 March 2006. Up to the end of 2006 there are 76 Telephone Exchanges, 782 PCOs, 55222 landline connections and 33955 mobile users (BSNL) in the state. It is a big achievement for the state. But the interesting fact is that the mobile connections are highly concentrated in Aizawl District and only few private players have entered in the state such as Airtel, Reliance, and Air Cell.

Table 8.5: Statistics of Tele Communication in Mizoram upto 31 March 2006

Sl.No.	*Particulars*	*Nos.*
1.	Number of Telephone Exchanges	76
2.	Number of PCOs	782
3.	Number of Landline Connections	55222
4.	Number of Mobile Phone Users (BSNL)	33955

Source: Statistical Handbook of Mizoram, 2006.

The energy supply (a crucial infrastructure sector) must be described as the "mother of all sectors of developments." Mizoram came on the Grid Map of India in 1997 with the construction of a 140 km. long 66 KV line from Dulabcherra to Aizawl. The current position regarding the consumption and supply of electricity is 72 MW as against the requirement of 120 MW, whereas the State's own generation of electricity stands at 22 MW only (Diesel: 16 MW and Mini/Micro Hydel: 6 MW) for the rest it depends on neighbouring States (50 MW). As regards rural electrification, 691 villages could be electrified by 31st March 2002. It is the highest in the North-East. Recently, the 80 MW Bairabi Hydro Electric Project and the 12 MW

Serlui 'B' Hydel Projects have been approved by the Government of India. A State with 40 % short of electricity requirement is unlikely to be able to make much headway in development. Other sectors of infrastructure do not seem to fare better be it a human resource development, or public health services or the transport system, Mizoram faces a daunting task of quality upgradation.

Table 8.6 gives information about installed capacity for generation of electricity in Mizoram during 2004–05 to 2005–06. There has been a little improvement in terms of electricity generation which rose from 386.435 MW in 2004–05 to 2005–06 being 400.314 MW.

Table-8.6: Electricity Generation in Mizoram in MW

Years	*Diesel*		*Hydel*		*Thermal*		*Import*	*Total*	
	Inst	Genr.	Inst.	Genr.	Inst.	Genr.	Gen.	Inst	Genr.
2004–05	9.92	0.065	14.25	5.75	22.92	0.59	380.0	47.09	386.44
2005–06	9.92	#	14.25	8.65	22.92	2.40	389.26	47.09	400.31

Source: Statistical Handbook of Mizoram 2006.

Table 8.7 discloses the category-wise consumption of electricity in Mizoram from 2002–03 to 2005–06. The domestic consumption is quite high and the commercial and industrial consumption is just marginal which shows that Mizoram is an industrially undeveloped state.

Table 8.7: Category-wise Consumption of Electricity in Mizoram

Sl. No.	*Category*	*2002–03 MKWH*	*2003–04 MKWH*	*2004–05 M.U.*	*2005–06 M.U.*
1.	Domestic	68.801	82.002	84.45	91.01
2.	Commercial	6.541	7.085	6.53	6.94
3.	Industrial	0.992	1.673	1.93	2.26
4.	Bulk Supply	5.846	8.51	8.65	11.08
5.	Public Lighting	3.76	4.933	5.60	5.28
6.	Public Water Works	8.587	18.789	18.03	17.94
7.	Outside State	N.A	N.A	181.38	191.82
	Total	**91.144**	**122.99**	**306.57**	**326.33**
8.	Per Capita	—	—	KWH141.44	KWH151.64

Source: Statistical Handbook of Mizoram 2006.

The unsystematic approach to infrastructure development has now resulted cumulatively in the distortion of the whole development process. In such a situation as this, no sector of the economy can be expected to make any significant progress.

As noted earlier, Mizoram is critically deficient in *infrastructure* building. Take the example of Bairabi Thermal Power Plant with a capacity to produce 22 MW of electricity, which was set up at the cost of Rs. 105 crores and was inaugurated early this year. It is now lying idle, not for want of fuel as claimed by the authorities, but because the estimated unit cost is too high to be introduced to public consumers. Around Rs. 9 crores of compensation has recently been awarded for land and properties to be affected by a 12 MW Hydel Project at Tuirial, making it almost certain that this mini project will also become cost-ineffective. The post-accord governments have not been able to produce even one cost-effective infrastructure project so far. Agriculture, the main stay of rural economy, has remained stagnant. The bulk of essential items of food continue to come from outside the state. *Private sector* is unable to take off, thereby failing to play its important role of generating jobs. Instead, government service becomes the main stable source of employment, leading to surplus staffing of the government departments The income gap between urban and rural dwellers is steadily widening. Critical drinking water problem in dry season continues unabated. There continues a decline in per capita success rate of young graduates in the national level competitions for jobs owing to lack of quality education. A random illustration of the economic situation, as is given here, is perhaps enough to show that the development process in the state is in alarming disarray.

Problems for Infrastructure Development in Mizoram

It is observed that the scenario of infrastructure in Mizoram at present is at a very infant stage. But at the same time development of infrastructure is an uphill task in this part of the country. The problem may be discussed as hereunder.

Transport and Communication: It is considered that the whole structure of industry and commerce depends on the good foundation of efficient transport and communication. In spite of road planning and development for more than 50 years, Mizoram is experiencing deficiencies in matters of transport and communication. It is not an easy job to construct roads in the hills of Mizoram.

Power: Power is another important infrastructure for economic development of any country or region. At present power availability is satisfactory through import from other neighbouring states as the major use is for non-commercial purpose. Mizoram has ample scope to develop hydel power generation. But so far nothing big could be achieved. In the near future Mizoram has to develop its own generation of power to support the business and industry in the state.

Problem of Landslides: The problem of landslides is very common in Mizoam. During the rainy season most of the roads in the state often face the problem of landslides and roads are damaged to a great extent. This requires huge costs to maintain and the life span of the roads is also curtailed which is also an extra burden on the Government.

Long Rainy Season: Mizoram experiences a long rainy season and it is almost half of a calendar year and continuously disturbs the life style of the Mizo People. During this period Mizoram faces severe landslides, road jams, traffic problems, communication problems etc. Due to this the construction work is being hampered to a considerable extent.

Hilly Terrain: Mizoram being a hilly state no flat land is available in the real sense. Construction of roads in the state is a very difficult job because of the nature of the terrain. The hills are very steep and it is difficult to negotiate. Due to this road construction is a costly and time taking affair in this region.

Problem of Finance: Finance is the life blood of any economy. Development of infrastructure needs huge funds. Government is the only funding agency for development of infrastructure in the state. Private participation is a far cry so far. Government spent most of the budget allocation for salary and allowances and other unproductive expenditure. So, a very limited portion of the allocated funds is utilized for infrastructure development.

Measures for meeting challenges of Infrastructural Development

Good infrastructure management ensures that all the components required to deliver quality performance are performing at optimum levels. Following are some of the measures for achieving better infrastructure management:

- Increase productivity by automating manual processes,
- Reduce complexity through more accurate and efficient data collection, and manage diverse platforms by sharing common tools and services.
- Reduce costs by building the system with application-focused products that cross all platforms with the ability to deploy infrastructure management solutions only as needed,
- Maximize the existing infrastructure investment by effectively centralizing existing and new environments,
- Deliver a common communications infrastructure through a central GUI and by providing a common presentation interface with the ability to view all components of infrastructure,
- Keep track of all IT infrastructure assets and make strategies to utilize them optimally to derive best value out of it,
- Implementing Quality of Service (QoS) measures for interconnection.

Conclusion

Infrastructure facilities are most vital and are the backbone of all round development of an economy. But in the case of the North Eastern Region, especially of Mizoram, the standard of infrastructure is very poor level at this juncture. Lack of transport, power, communication, banking and finance, along with other social overheads are the major hurdles for development of this region. The Government as well as the public has given high priority to create the necessary infrastructures for the development of the state. But, unfortunately the money allocated for this purpose is mainly spent to meet the expenditure on salaries, office expenses, dearness allowances, medical expenses, and other unproductive expenses of the employees, and the development of the state including infrastructure remains at a low level which is also a matter of great concern as it is linked with the development of this region.

With the current GDP growth of 8%, in which there is contribution of nearly 51% from services and 16% from manufacturing sector there is a need for proper alignment of resources. To sustain this growth India needs to develop sound infrastructure so that the right input of skilled, qualified and socially contented labour visible and reliable supply chains prompt and accurate information for decision making and efficient process and updated technology. There is a potential for public private partnership (PPPs) to help bridge the infrastructure gap in India. There has been considerable progress in the last ten years in attracting private investment into the infrastructure sectors; first in telecommunications, then in ports and roads, and in individual projects in other sectors.

In this connection, the Government needs proper planning of the state budget for the development of infrastructure such as transport and communication, power, water supply etc. It is also the need of the hour for various organizations such as the NEC and DONER to give more emphasis and allocate funds for infrastructural development in NEI as well as in Mizoram for their overall economic development.

NOTES

1. envision.ca/templates/profile.asp
2. www.southampton.gov.uk/environment/development-control/planning-terms.asp
3. www-personal.umich.edu/~alandear/glossary/i.html
4. www.extension.umn.edu/distribution/naturalresources/components DD6097hr.html
5. www.haltonkelly.co.uk/glossary.shtml
6. www.ohiofinancialgroup.com/glossary.html
7. www.realestateagent-listings.com/terminology/terminology_i.htm
8. www.icons.umd.edu/pls/reslib/display_glossary
9. The Eleventh Finance Commission's Index of Economic and Social Infrastructure.

REFERENCES

Agarwal, A.K, Infrastructure for Development—A Case of Mizoram, In: *Modernization of the Mizo Society,* Prasad, R.N. and Agarwal, A.K. (eds.). Mittal Publication, New Delhi, 2003.

Basic Statistics of NER 2002, NEC. Ministry of Home Affairs, Shillong.

Goswami, Omkar, Comparing China and India, *Business World,* Vol.27 Issue 7, 9 July 2007, p. 44.

Misra, S.K. and Puri, V.K., *Economic Environment of Business,* Himalaya Publishing House, New Delhi, 2003.

Rajaram, Kalpana and Singh, Satish Nandan, *Indian Economy,* Spectrum Books Private Limited, New Delhi, 2005.

Sorokhaibam, Robita, Development of Infrastructure for Industries in the North-East India with Special Reference to Manipur, *Kangleipak Business Review Journal,* Department of Commerce, Manipur University, Imphal, Vol.1. 1996

Statistical Handbook Mizoram 2006.

9

EXISTING SCENARIO OF INFRASTRUCTURE IN NORTH-EAST INDIA
An Overview

GAUTAM PATIKAR and P. K. DEKA

Introduction

North-East India comprises eight states, namely Arunachal Pradesh, Assam, Meghalaya, Manipur, Mizoram, Nagaland, Sikkim and Tripura is situated to the North-Eastern part of India having foreign boundary with Bangladesh on the west, Myammar in the East and the Tibet region of China in the North. The region has a total population of about 3.90 crores (as per 2001 census), characterized by ethnic diversity with higher literacy rate over the national average of 68.77% and accounts for 7.97% of India's total land surface. The region is connected with the rest of India by a narrow strip of land through the State of West Bengal.

The region is still backward as compared to other parts of the country and could not develop much industrially despite having vast natural resources. This may be due to shortage of investments in infrastructure as well as in direct productive activities. Investments in infrastructure are not directly productive of consumable goods. It is, therefore, desirable to maintain, as far as practicable, a balance between investments in infrastructure and investments in directly productive activities. In the case of North-East India the infrastructure needed for Industrial Venture Capital is very less, if not non-existent. Here any investment in a directly productive activity will have to be preceded by or synchronized with investments in social overhead capital. Therefore, the problem of infrastructure assumes immense importance in the study of the economic development in the North-Eastern region, which is one of the most backward areas of the country.

Infrastructure is an economy's capital in the form of roads, railways, water supply, electric power and public services. Sometimes it is called social overhead capital. The term is thus widened to include health, skills, education and other qualities of the people. Infrastructure is an essential pre-condition for economic development and the nature and degree of development of infrastructure in an economy determines to a large extent the pattern and the rate of growth of the economy. Therefore, any study on regional development such as ours must make it a point to examine the existing status of infrastructure in the region with the primary object of suggesting lines of development in the future. Among the several constituents of the infrastructure of the economy of the region, we propose to discuss here the existing position of infrastructure facilities like transport and communication, power supply, financial and credit institutions and facilities of education and public health.

Transport and Communication

Transport and communication constitute the core of infrastructural facilities. In this backward region, the transport and communication facilities are far below the desired level and thereby retard growth. These facilities include railways, road transport. Post and telegraph, and telecommunication; information technology (IT) has also been considered recently.

Railways

The whole North-East Region does not appear in the railway map of India. The State of Assam, Arunachal Pradesh, Nagaland, Tripura, and Manipur are connected by railways. Of the total railway length in this region Assam shares about 97.47% and 2.53% is available for Nagaland, Manipur, Mizoram, Tripura and Arunachal Pradesh, whereas the State of Meghalaya is yet to be connected by railways.

The following table reflects the position of Railway Network in the region:

Table 9.1: Railway Network in NER

(As on: 31. 3. 2003)

States	*Aruna-chal Pra-desh*	*Assam*	*Mani pur*	*Megha-laya*	*Mizo-ram*	*Naga-land*	*Tripura*	*Total*
Total Length (in kms.)	1.26	2517.23	1.35	NIL	1.50	12.85	64.42	2598.61

Sources: Basic Statistic of North-Eastern Region (2006).

Of the total railway length of 2598.61 kms. in the region only about 1238.83 kms. have been converted to Broad Gauge so far and the remaining 1359.78 kms. are still in Meter Gauge (as on: 31-03-03).

Road Transport

The inadequacy of raiiways in the region necessitated the emphasis on road and road transport. The road transport network in the region plays a vital role for the movement of people and goods, although, the road transport system is not adequate and often suffers from bottlenecks due to the peculiar terrain and climatic condition in the region. Yet it is the major life line for the people here. After independence steps were taken to improve the existing road network and construction of new roads and bridges in the region both by the Central Government as well as State Government. Particularly major initiatives were started in the 2nd Five-Year Plan onwards. At present, the region has a total road length of 173261 kms. of which 44261 kms. are surfaced and the remaining is unsurfaced. The Prime Minister's "Gram Sadak Yojana" is definitely a major effort in improving the road transport system in their region. Under this scheme a village having a population of 500 and more is to be connected to the nearest urban area with *pucca* road. Though National Highways are the major arterial roads in the country, state and village roads along its border roads are playing a predominant role in this region. This includes both—two wheelers, three wheelers and four wheelers. The road network was principally meant for connecting the main administrative centres, townships and suburban areas with the villages.

Table 9.2 : Road Length in NE

(In km. as on 31-03-02)

State	Total	Surfaced length	Un-surfaced length	Road/ 100 Sq. Km.	Road/ .000 Population	% of Surfaced Road to total length
Arunachal Pradesh	18365	5689	12676	21.93	16.70	30.98
Assam	89486	12882	76604	114.09	3.29	114.40
Manipur	11434	3863	7571	51.21	4.76	33.79
Meghalaya	9565	6560	3005	42.65	3.98	68.58
Mizoram	5075	2877	2198	24.07	5.64	56.69
Nagaland	21021	6451	14570	126.79	10.51	30.69
Tripura	16296	4393	11903	155.41	5.09	26.96
Sikkim	2019	1546	473	28.45	3.36	76.57
Total	173261	44261	129000	65.83	4.46	25.55
All India	**2456647***	**1420489**	**1036158**	**74.73**	**2.39**	**57.82**

* Excludes 26697 km. (in 2002) of PMGSY Road.
Source: Basic Statistic of North Eastern Region (2006).

Post and Telegraphs

The region is almost isolated and lagging behind as compared to other parts of the country especially in the field of communication. Post and Telegraph services were deemed to be the only modes of communication in the region till recently. But the quality of the existing post and telegraph facilities is poor and does not meet the requirements fully. As per 1991 census the population per post office in the region was 3552 as against 5502 at the national level, about 64.6% of the all India figures. It has increased dramatically to 7132 in 2003. This means North-eastern India accounts for 4.35% of the total post offices of the country. Except Assam, the population of NE is better served by Post Office. For example (Table 9.3), one post office serves 6595 people in the all India level, whereas the NE (except Assam) is much lesser than the national level.

Table 9.3: Post Office in NER

(As on 31-03-03)

State	Total No. of Post Office	* Population/ P.O.	** Area/P.O.
Arunachal Pradesh	305	3574	274.43
Assam	3993	6672	19.63
Manipur	694	3444	32.13
Meghalaya	491	4705	45.62
Mizoram	403	2208	52.36
Nagaland	324	6142	50.93
Tripura	714	4468	14.57
Sikkim	208	2596	34.13
All India	**155618**	**6594**	**21.12**

* Based on 2001 Census population
** *Area in sq. km.*

Communication

There has been a phenomenal growth in the telecommunication sector in the last decades. But the North-eastern Region could not make significant headway in this direction. Only recently steps have been taken to provide telecommunication facilities to all the villages in the region. The modern communication systems like cellular telephone and WLL are proposed to be provided in all the NE states. The region had a total of 721 telephone exchanges and 703278 sub-stations as on 31 October 99. On an average 40–50% of the total population is availing of telephone facilities in the region today.

Another most vibrant communication facility available today relates to Information Technology (IT). The information explosion has necessitated the use of modern and sophisticated means of communication. Accordingly, internet has emerged as a quick two-way communication medium. There has been some progress in this field even in this remotest area of our Country. Under the union budget for 2000–2001, the total number of 446 Community Information Centres was proposed to be set up in the North-East Region under the Ministry of Information Technology. One Software Technology Park of India (STPI) has already been set up at Guwahati (Assam). Similarly, efforts are being taken to develop STPI in other states of the region.

Power

A very important component of infrastructure is power. Power increases the productivity capacity of the economy by several times. There is an acute power shortage in the whole of the North-eastern Region. Agriculture and industry cannot make headway in the region if the present power situation is allowed to continue. Henceforth, greater emphasis is required in the development of power generation. Up to the end of 1997–98 the net generation of electricity in the region was 3933.71 MW, which was far below the required level. The per capita consumption of electricity in the North-eastern Region during 1995–96 was about 103 KWH as against 335.42 KWH at the national level. The installed capacity of power generation in North-east India is 2520.3 MW as on 31 December 2006. On an average 78.24 per cent of the villages are electrified in this region up to the end of March 2000. Of the eight states, Tripura records the highest coverage of electrification in 94.02 per cent of the villages and Meghalaya has the lowest record of 50.05 per cent. The power generation in this region in addition to few thermal power generation units is basically hydro based and gas based. Loktak in Manipur and Kopili HER and Meghalaya Electricity Board are hydro based whereas Agartala Gas Turbine Power Project and Assam Gas Based Power Project are gas based.

Table 9.4 : Actual Power Supply Position in NE

(As on 31-12-2006)

State	*Peak Demand*	*Peak Met*	** Peak -/+ in MW*	*Energy Requirement*	*Energy Availability*	** Energy -/+ in MW*
Assam	771	688	–83	3278	3046	–232
Arunachal Pradesh	77	76	–1	188	181	–7
Meghalaya	343	198	–145	1054	839	–215
Tripura	169	142	–27	639	581	–58
Manipur	106	101	–5	363	347	–16
Nagaland	79	79	0	264	254	–10
Mizoram	70	68	–2	171	163	–8
Sikkim	40	40	0	156	153	–3
Total (NER)	**1407**	**1166**	**–241**	**5957**	**5411**	**–546**

* *Shortage or Surplus*

Source: Yojana, Dec. 2007, pp. 66.

Table 9.5: Installed Capacity of Power in NER in MW

(As on 31-12-06)

State	*Hydro*	*Thermal*	*Renewable*	*Total*
Assam	333.0	797.7	0.2	1130.9
Arunachal Pradesh	116.5	36.9	26.0	179.4
Meghalaya	258.6	28.1	1.5	288.2
Tripura	78.0	165.3	1.1	144.5
Manipur	82.5	71.4	4.0	157.9
Nagaland	78.5	21.0	3.2	102.7
Mizoram	38.0	67.9	10.0	116.8
Central Unallocated	128.0	55.9	0.0	183.9
Total NER	1113.1	1244.2	46.9	2404.2
Sikkim	40.0	67.0	9.1	116.1
Total (Sikkim+Ner)	**1153.1**	**1311.2**	**56.0**	**2520.3**

Source: *Yojana*, December 2007, p. 66.

Financial and Credit Institutions

Although in the early stages of human civilization, the economic systems were non-monetised, it is anachronistic today to think of a totally non-monetised economy. Indeed, money is the life blood of economic development and the degree of monetization of an economy is a direct indication of the level of development attained by it. Now principal test of the degree of monetization of the economy of a particular country or region is the structure and efficiency of the financial and credit institutions operating therein. Thus, the types and the nature of organization of the financial and credit institutions in a country and the level of their operational efficiency provide a fairly dependable measuring rod of the degree of economic development of the country or region in question. Coming to the specific area of our study, it pains to observe that the North-eastern Region has not yet given birth to many of the types of financial and credit institutions, which one commonly finds in the more developed regions of our country and those financial institutions, which have seen the light of day are in a stage of infancy, requiring as they do sympathetic and careful nursing. The region has a total number of 2133 Bank Branches as on March 1999. Besides, there is only one Industrial Development Bank located at Guwahati (Assam) called NEIDBI (North Eastern Industrial Development Bank of India) along with branches of SIDBI (Small Industrial Development Bank of India) in all the seven states. North-eastern Development Finance Corporation Limited (NEDFC) at Guwahati has been recently set up to provide financial assistance and consultancy services to entrepreneurs of the region. The State Financial Corporations are also giving loans and concessional assistance to small and medium size units and in turn get refinance from the IDBI and SIDBI. To encourage the small entrepreneurs of the region, IFCI has constituted a 'Technical Assistance for Small Entrepreneurs' scheme and under this scheme technical consultancy facility to new and existing small entrepreneurs are provided through North-eastern Industrial and Technical Consultancy Organisation Limited (NEITCO). The following table gives some ideas about the pattern of bank advances in this region upto 31 March 1999:

Table 9.6: Credit Extended in the Selected Sectors in NE

(Rs. in lakhs)

Sl. No.	*Sector*	*Commercial Bank (Rs.)*	*Regional Rural Bank (Rs.)*	*Co-operative Bank (Rs.)*
1.	Agriculture	32635.53	10433.89	8559.22
2.	Women Beneficiary	11716.39	3709.85	9928.40
3.	Minority Communities	25583.46	7497.48	2863.41

Source: Basic Statistics of North-eastern Region (2000).

The economy of the region is predominantly agricultural and thus the bulk of bank advances goes to priority sector including agriculture. Thus total advances provided to priority sector upto 31 March 1999 was Rs. 201712.40 lakhs of which Rs. 147245.45 lakhs were by Commercial Banks, Rs. 30526.66 by Regional Rural Banks and Rs. 83714.79 lakhs were by Co-operative Banks.

So long we have been discussing those aspects or ingredients of infrastructure, which are purely economic. Now we have to take up another component of infrastructure, which is extra-economic component but which has got such a fundamental economic significance that economic development can hardly be thought of without it. This particular component comprises the social overheads like education and public health. Today, the fundamental problem of economic development is not creation of wealth but rather capacity to create wealth. This capacity to create wealth lies in the quality of the people. It consists of their brain power and physical health. Thus, education and public health measures help to develop the brainpower and physical heath of the people. Here, we examine these aspects of social overheads in North-East India.

Education

Education plays a distinct role in the economic development of a backward region and provides adequate quantum of manpower. In this region the growth of general education especially at the primary level has been phenomenal. While in 1991 only 58.26% of the populations of North-eastern were literate, the percentage of literacy rose to 68.38% in 2001. This growth rate compares quite favourably with the all India rate which rose from 52.21% in 1991 to 65.37% in 2001.

Table 9.7: Number of Education Institutions in NE

(as on 2004–05)

States	*Primary School*	*Upper Primary*	*Secondary School*	*Hr. Sec. School*	*Engineering College*	*Medical College*	*ITIs, Polytechnics*
Assam	30068	8143	4692	745	4	3	35
	(107.86)	(29.21)	(16.60)	(2.87)	(0.01)	(0.01)	(0.13)
Arunachal	1371	495	136	78	1	0	3
Pradesh	(120.16)	(43.38)	(11.92)	(6.84)	(0.09)	(0.00)	(0.26)
Naga-	1520	480)	336	43	0	0	6
land	(73.50)	(23.21	(16.25)	(2.08)	(0.00)	(0.00)	(0.29)
Manipur	2552	831	588	118	1	1	8
	(113.37)	(36.92)	(26.12)	(5.24)	(0.04)	(0.04)	(0.36)
Megha-	5851	1759	631	80	0	0	3
laya	(242.78)	(72.99)	(26.18)	(3.32)	(0.00)	(0.00)	(0.32)
Mizoram	1481	939	445	67	0	0	3
	(160.28)	(101.62)	(48.16)	(7.25)	(0.00)	(0.00)	(0.53)
Sikkim	684	185	111	50	1	1	3
	(121.93)	(32.98)	(19.79)	(8.91)	(0.18)	(0.18)	(0.53)
Tripura	1776	1001	409	243	1	1	5
	(53.41)	(30.11)	(12.30)	(7.31)	(0.03)	(0.03)	(0.15)
All India	767520	274731	101777	50272	1302	817	6285
	(71.12)	(25.46)	(9.43)	(4.66)	(0.12)	(0.08)	(0.58)

Note: Figures in brackets are the No. of institutes per 1 lakh population.
Source: *Yojana,* December 2007. p. 21.

Public Health

Public Health is yet another important component of infrastructure. In terms of resources for economic development, nothing is more important than the health of the people which measures their energy and capacity to work. It goes without saying that in determining worker's efficiency in agriculture, industry and other occupations. People's health is an essential condition. But there should exits a right relationship between the size of the population and economic development so as to optimize the per capita income. Towards this end, efforts should be taken for increasing hospital facilities, control of debilitating diseases, ensure urban and rural water supply, and effective family planning. Attempts to control debilitating diseases have been fairly successful. Because of increase of general hospital facilities and planned eradicating common disease, epidemics like cholera, small poxes etc. have become things of the past. As on 1st January 1996 there were 645 hospitals in this region of which 71.72% were in the rural areas. Out of the 2782 numbers of hospital beds about 32% are available in the rural areas. As per 1991 Census population served per doctor in this region was 1:4935 and it has improved tremendously in 2001 Census (*see* Table 9.8). In all the eight states there exists family welfare department for providing general awareness among the people about the significance of family planning.

Table 9.8: Doctor-Population Ratio

State	*No. of Doctors*	*Population per Doctor*	*As on*
Arunachal Pradesh	464	1:2352	2002–03
Assam	2160	1:11980	1-1-1999
Manipur	945	1:2427	2002–03
Meghalaya	389	1:5411	1998
Mizoram	89	1:10360	1-1-1999
Nagaland	367	1:5422	2002
Sikkim	174	1:3108	2001–02
Tripura	860	1:3720	2003–04

Source: Basic Statistics of NER 2006.

The drinking water requirement of the people here is 70 litres per capita per day in rural areas and 200 litres per capita per day in urban areas. The Public Health Engineering (PHE) provides the water supply facilities in the region. The services rendered by PHE are inadequate and thus people depend on natural sources, especially in the dry season. Now-a-days even Urban Area Water Supply Organization under HUDCO is providing water supply facilities in some parts of the region.

Table 9.9: Percentage of Households having Safe Drinking Water (in 2001)

State	*Rural*	*Urban*	*Total*
Arunachal Pradesh	73.7	90.7	77.5
Assam	56.8	70.4	58.8
Manipur	29.3	59.4	37.0
Meghalaya	29.5	73.5	39.0
Mizoram	23.8	47.8	36.0
Nagaland	47.5	42.3	46.5
Sikkim	67.0	97.1	70.7
Tripura	45.0	85.8	52.5
All India	**73.2**	**90.0**	**77.9**

Source: Basic Statistics of NER 2006.

Conclusion

Thus, to conclude, it must be noted that the present scenario of infrastructure in North-East India is unsatisfactory excepting the area of education, because of several problems that retard infrastructure development. The problems are social, economic or political in nature. The geographical location is also a hurdle for infrastructure development. On the other hand, the region is rich in natural resources and ideal for the growth of industries. As a result, there is imperative need for basic infrastructure development on a more liberal scale so as to ensure smooth and sustained industrial growth. The development of such basic infrastructure should be in a time bound manner. The Government must provide funds and roads in core areas. Toll free roads and express highways, called the Malayasian Model, will have to be developed for strengthening the infrastructural base. The Prime Ministers *Gram Sadak Yojana* is definitely a positive step in this direction.

REFERENCES

A. Bannerjee, (1999), *Economic Planning and Development of North-eastern States,* EKTA Distributors, New Delhi-110059.

Basic Statistics of North-eastern Region 2000, North-eastern Council, Government of India, Shillong-793001.

B.K. Sarma, (1993), *Industrial Landscape of North-east India,* Mittal Publications, New Delhi-110059.

Economic Survey (1991–92), (2000–2001), Government of India, Economic Division, New Delhi.

Swabera Islam Saleh, (1989), *Nagaland's Economy in transition since 1964,* Omsons Publications, New Delhi.

10

APPLICATION OF BIO-TECHNOLOGICAL TOOLS

For the Conservation, Sustainable Use and Genetic Enhancement of Bio-resources in the Indo-Burma Biodiversity Hotspot

ROBERT THANGJAM and U.K. SAHOO

Introduction

Due to human activities such as energy generation from fossil fuels and deforestation atmospheric concentrations of greenhouse gases has been increasing beyond their natural levels, resulting in an enhanced greenhouse effect, causing increase in global temperatures, a phenomenon known as global warming. This warming can be amplified through increases in water vapour, or reduced through increases in stratospheric aerosols. The sum of all these potential changes is referred to as climate change.

Loss of biological diversity may be seen as one of the likely consequences of climate change. The geographical distribution of different ecosystems and their structure are likely to be altered as temperature and rainfall patterns change, and these ecosystems are subjected to different environmental stresses. There are enormous scientific concerns about the effects of global warming on the narrowing of genetic variations within species. The success of the Green revolution was because the availability of genetic diversity which the plant breeders could manipulate. Plant genetic resource is a term used to describe the total genetic diversity of cultivated species and their wild relatives, landraces or primitive forms which are races or populations, often collected from remote areas where the new, highly bred cultivars have not been introduced. They are highly diverse genetically, and have often been grown as mixtures of species, as well as diverse populations of one species. They may often originate from the old Vavilovian centres of diversity. Now-a-days nearly all major crops that we grow have narrow genetic bases and it contributes to their genetic vulnerability.

"Biodiversity" is often defined as the variety of all forms of life, from genes to species, through to the broad scale of ecosystems (Gaston, 1996). "Biodiversity" was coined as a contraction of "biological diversity" in 1985, but the new term arguably has taken on a meaning and imports all of its own. A symposium in 1986 and the follow-up book Biodiversity (Wilson, 1988), edited by biologist E.O. Wilson, heralded the popularity of this concept. Ten years later, Takacs (1996) described its ascent. Overall, the major issue for biodiversity is how its conservation may be integrated with other needs of society.

British ecologist Norman Myers defined the biodiversity hotspot concept in 1988 to address the dilemma that conservationists face: what areas are the most immediately important for conserving biodiversity? The biodiversity hotspots hold especially high numbers of endemic species, yet their combined area of remaining habitat covers only 2.3 per cent of the Earth's land surface. Each hotspot faces extreme threats and has already lost at least 70 per cent of its original natural vegetation. Over 50 per cent of the world's plant species and 42 per cent of all terrestrial vertebrate species are endemic to the 34 biodiversity hotspots. A seminal paper by Norman Myers in 1988 first identified ten tropical forest "hotspots" characterized both by exceptional levels of plant endemism and by serious levels of habitat loss. In 1990, Myers added a further eight hotspots, including four Mediterranean-type ecosystems. Conservation International adopted Myers' hotspots as its institutional blueprint in 1989, and in 1996, the organization made the decision to undertake a reassessment of the hotspots concept, including an examination of whether key areas had been overlooked. Three years later an extensive global review was undertaken, which introduced quantitative thresholds for the designation of biodiversity hotspots: ***To qualify as a hotspot, a region must meet two strict criteria: it must contain at least 1,500***

species of vascular plants (> 0.5 per cent of the world's total) as endemics, and it has to have lost at least 70 per cent of its original habitat. In the 1999 analysis, published in the book *Hotspots: Earth's Biologically Richest and Most Endangered Terrestrial Ecoregions*, and a year later in the scientific journal Nature (Myers *et al.*, 2000), 25 biodiversity hotspots were identified. Collectively, these areas held as endemics no less than 44 per cent of the world's plants and 35 per cent of terrestrial vertebrates in an area that formerly covered only 11.8 per cent of the planet's land surface. The habitat extent of this land area had been reduced by 87.8 per cent of its original extent, such that this wealth of biodiversity was restricted to only 1.4 per cent of Earth's land surface.

The Indo-Burma hotspot encompasses 2,373,000 km^2 of tropical Asia east of the Ganges-Brahmaputra lowlands. Formerly including the Himalaya chain and the associated foothills in Nepal, Bhutan and India, the Indo-Burma hotspot has now been more narrowly redefined as the Indo-Chinese sub-region. The hotspot contains the Lower Mekong catchments. It begins in eastern Bangladesh and then extends across North-eastern India, south of the Brahmaputra River, to encompass nearly all of Myanmar, part of southern and western Yunnan Province in China, all of the Lao People's Democratic Republic, Cambodia and Vietnam, the vast majority of Thailand and a small part of Peninsular Malaysia. In addition, the hotspot covers the coastal lowlands of southern China (in southern Guangxi and Guangdong), as well as several offshore islands, such as Hainan Island (of China) in the South China Sea and the Andaman Islands (of India) in the Andaman Sea. The hotspot contains the Lower Mekong catchments. The transition to the Sundaland Hotspot in the south occurs on the Thai-Malay Peninsula, the boundary between the two hotspots is represented by the Kangar-Pattani Line, which cuts across the Thailand-Malaysia border, though some analyses indicate that the phytogeographical and zoogeographical transition between the Sundaland and Indo-Burma biotas may lie just to the north of the Isthmus of Kra, associated with a gradual change from wet seasonal evergreen dipterocarp rainforest to mixed moist deciduous forest. Much of Indo-Burma is characterized by distinct seasonal weather patterns. During the northern winter months, dry, cool winds blow from the stable continental Asian high-pressure system, resulting in a dry period under clear skies across much of the south, centre, and west of the hotspot (the dry, North east monsoon). As the continental system weakens in spring, the wind direction reverses and air masses forming the southwest monsoon pick up moisture from the seas to the southwest and bring abundant rains as they rise over the hills and mountains. A wide diversity of ecosystems is represented in this hotspot, including mixed wet evergreen, dry evergreen, deciduous, and montane forests. There are also patches of shrublands and woodlands on karst limestone outcrops and, in some coastal areas, scattered heath forests. In addition, a wide variety of distinctive, localized vegetation formations occur in Indo-Burma, including lowland floodplain swamps, mangroves, and seasonally inundated grasslands.

Indo-Burma is one of the most threatened biodiversity hotspots, due to the rate of resource exploitation and habitat loss. Only about five per cent of natural habitats remain in relatively pristine condition, with another 10 to 25 per cent of the land in damaged, but ecologically functional, condition. Indo-Burma was one of the first places where humans developed agriculture, and has a long history of using fire to clear land for agriculture and other needs. The need for agricultural products has only increased in recent years, with the expansion of both human populations and markets. This has contributed to widespread forest destruction; tree plantations (teak, rubber, oil palm) have replaced large areas of lowland forest, while coffee, tea, vegetable crops and sugarcane plantations threaten montane and hill forests. Other threats to forests include logging, mining for gems and ore, firewood collection, and charcoal production. Aquatic ecosystems are also under intense development pressure in many areas. Draining for wet rice cultivation, particularly in Thailand, Myanmar and Vietnam, destroys freshwater floodplain swamps and wetlands. Rivers have been dammed in order to store water to generate electricity for the countries' economic growth, or for export to neighbouring countries to generate foreign exchange earnings. Damming a river section not only transforms that section into a large pond, but also reduces the temperature and oxygen content, and increases riverbed erosion and water turbidity downriver. Reservoir operation procedures result in occasional or regular flooding of sandbars, sandbanks, stretches of channel mosaic, and other habitats that would normally be exposed during the dry season, with severe impacts on nesting bird and turtle species. Mangroves have been converted to shrimp aquacultural ponds, while intertidal mudflats have been extensively afforested with mangrove or intensely fished by lines of stack nets, which severely impact their value as feeding habitat for migratory waterbirds and other species. Moreover, sand dune ecosystems are severely threatened by afforestation, for instance, with the Australian exotic *Casuarina equisetifolia*. Finally, over fishing and the increasing use of destructive fishing techniques are a significant problem in both coastal and offshore marine ecosystems. The combinations of rapid population growth and economic development have also caused overexploitation of natural resources to reach critical levels in the hotspot. As in the other hotspots of Southeast Asia, the wildlife trade, particularly for the food and traditional medicine markets in China, is an enormous problem for biodiversity conservation. The increasingly high value of products derived from some species has put them at risk even within strictly protected areas. The Chinese demand for turtles, snakes, tigers, and other species has depleted populations to the brink of extinction in just a few years. The volume of trade in turtles is astounding, with over ten million individuals exported to China from Southeast Asia each year. Adults, juveniles, and eggs of all species are harvested. The threat to plants through international and domestic trade could be just as great, but there is far less accurate information; timber species, orchids, and other high value plants are particularly at risk. Commercial logging has been particularly intense in lowland evergreen forests, to the point where few intact tracts remain and stocks of some species have been exhausted commercially.

Bio-resources refers to the total biological variation manifested as individual plants, animals or their genes, which could be taken by man for use as drugs, food, livestock feed, construction materials for shelter, environmental protection, etc. or in the development of improved crops and animals for higher yield and tolerance to biotic and abiotic stresses (Eneobong, 1997). Man depends on these bio-resources for his continued existence and, therefore, he must use and preserve them for future generations. The concept of sustainable development indicates that economic development and environmental protection are inextricably linked and that the quality of present and future life rests in meeting basic human needs without destroying the environment on which life depends. Since we cannot do without exploiting the available bio-resources to our advantage, there has to be a balance between uses of resources and their conservation. In this way, we would preserve an ecosystem, which although altered would still be rich in bio-resources and at the same time would provide food and other needs as well as perform vital environmental functions on a long-term basis. It is necessary to conserve these naturally endowed resources, which apart from their direct usage by man also serve several ecological functions such as the control of flood, soil erosion, landslides and hurricanes, maintenance of water quality, climate amelioration and checking desersification (Okoro, 1994). A 1982 El Salvador landslide that killed more than 1000 people was attributed to deforestation. The hurricane Mitch that occurred in Central America in 1998 was compounded by about 30% deforestation. The endangered species and threatened crops deserve urgent and special attention. Biotechnology can be defined as any technique that uses living organisms or parts thereof to make or modify a product, improve plants or animals or develop micro-organisms for specific uses. It is invaluable in research on conservation of bio-resources. Although modern biotechnology is a newly introduced science (less than 50 years old) its impact has greatly excited the imagination and provoked the concern of almost every part of the society worldwide. Developments such as the tomato that can be frozen, and the cassava and other agricultural crops that has been genetically engineered for insect and virus resistance and which are in or near commercial release is simply spectacular by any standard. The richness of plant and animal diversity in developing countries is a major asset in agricultural development and, therefore, the conservation of such resources is fundamental to the progress and usefulness of biotechnology.

Conservation of Genetic Resources

Plant Genetic Resources

Efficient conservation of plant genetic resources can best be achieved through an appropriate combination of *in situ* (in natural or original areas) and *ex situ* (in artificial habitat or habitat different from the original one) methods (IPGRI, 2001). The choice of conservation methods and techniques will depend on the objectives of the particular conservation effort, the breeding system and seed behaviour of the species in question as well as on the available resources including funds, infrastructure and technologies (Perrino, 1990; Eneobong, 1997). Generally plants with orthodox seeds (high tolerance of low temperature storage conditions) are best preserved *ex situ*, under medium or long-term conditions as comparatively dry seeds stored at low temperatures. Plants that produce recalcitrant seeds (intolerant of desiccation and low temperatures) could be preserved as *ex situ* live-gene banks (or gene libraries) or by *in vitro* conservation methods of enforced reduced growth storage. Plant resources are also routinely preserved *in situ* in parks, reserve areas and rangelands. This section of the paper will discuss in vitro methods for storage as well as the cryopreservation of embryos, seeds, protoplasts and other materials in long-term liquid nitrogen base-storage systems. Many plants, especially forest plants, are extremely difficult to propagate through conventional means since they are frequently polyploids and aneuploids or produce seeds with little or defective endosperms. However in the Indo-Burma hotspot there is the risk of losing some of these plants due to industrialization and urbanization, characterized by rapid deforestation, uncontrolled logging, burning and uncontrolled search for food and other non-timber forest products. Many of these plants constitute an important component of local diet in this region (e.g. Rice varieties, zingibers, pulses, tree legumes, etc.). Plant tissue culture provides a method for the mass clonal propagation of such materials, as well as serving as a tool for their germplasm conservation.

Micropropagation

This refers to *in vitro* mass production of plant propagules from any plant part or cell. Such propagules are used to raise whole plants. The principal approaches are:

(a) *Axillary budding*: The induction of adventitious buds on non-meristematic tissue (that is, inducing a shoot where one should normally not exist).

(b) *Somatic embryogenesis*: Where individual cultured cells or small groups of cells undergo development resembling that of the zygotic embryo (Thangjam and Singh, 2006). The embryoids produced can be used to produce whole plants.

The attraction of micropropagation, as an alternative to other propagation methods, lies in its ability to multiply elite clonal material very rapidly. More than 1000 plant species have been micropropagated, including more than 100 forest tree species (FAO, 2001). Work done with some crop species indicates the possibility of encapsulating somatic embryos to form artificial seeds, which can then be handled like conventional seeds. Such propagules may be used in forest plantation establishments. Micropropagation exploits the "totipotency" nature of plant cells and tissues. The explants are made to form callus under appropriate nutrient environments. Numerous clonal plants can be obtained from sub-cultured callus or from embryoids, which are then hardened and transferred into potted soil in nurseries. In this way planting propagules can be provided for rare or threatened plant species as well as for plants with inviable or difficult to germinate seeds. Furthermore, tissue culture techniques can serve as an enhancing tool in plant breeding for the rescue of defective hybrid embryos, caused by post zygotic incompatibility during crossing (Enebong and Okonkwo, 1994). Nutrients provided in the culture medium will perform the function of the malformed endosperm. Embryo cultures also adopt the nutritional and physical requirements for embryonic development to bypass seed dormancy (thus shortening the breeding cycle) and seed sterility and to provide micro-cloning material (Hu and Wang, 1986).

***In vitro* conservation**: Germplasm conservation of vegetatively propagated crops (e.g. banana, plantain, yam, cassava etc.), forest species especially those with recalcitrant (hard to store) seeds (e.g. mango, cocoa, *Symphonia globulifera, Irvingia gabonensis*) in live gene banks in fields poses tremendous problems in terms of required land space and labour input during annual or perennial replanting, testing and documentation. Biotic and abiotic stress agents also expose such collections to threats. Consequently, *in vitro* conservation is recommended, at least as a supplement to field collections, as long as an adequate protocol for micropropagation has been worked out for the species. The advantages of *in vitro* or reduced growth storage include little space necessary in growth rooms for maintaining thousands of genotypes and the absence of diseases and pest attack in culture vessels. Furthermore, in vitro storage eliminates the need for long and frustrating quarantine procedures during movement and exchange of germplasm. Virtually any part of the plant could be used as explants in establishing cultures for storage, although the best results have been obtained using apical meristems, axillary buds, embryos and gametes. Normal in vitro cultures use media like Murashige and Skoog and Arnold and Eriksson. Frequent subcultures into fresh media are necessary. Excised plant tissues, organs, or cells are usually cultured on these media. The culture medium could be liquid or solidified using agar. Under these conditions the cultures rarely last longer than a few months, requiring transfers into fresh media to maintain optimal growth. During in vitro storage the growth of the culture is slowed down through one or a combination of several methods namely:

(a) Reducing the concentrations of the minerals or by using media with lower salt concentrations (Ng and Ng, 1991).
(b) Using low incubation temperatures (Dale, 1980; Henshaw *et al.*, 1985; Ruredzo and Hanson, 1991).
(c) By the addition of osmotica (Ng and Ng, 1991; Ruredzo and Hanson, 1991).
(d) Reduction of the gas pressure in culture vessels (Bridgen and Staby, 1981).
(e) By varying the light regime (Mullin and Schelegel, 1976).

***Cryopreservation*:** Collected plants are normally stored either in active gene banks containing material that is kept ready for distribution, evaluation or exchange; or as base collections containing duplicates that are kept for future use (long term) or "emergency" material in case of loss from the active gene banks. Base collections can be maintained under very cold conditions in high tech ultra low temperature freezers. Cryopreservation is an attractive alternative for the storage of base collections and involves the freezing of plant material, usually to the temperature of liquid nitrogen (–196°C), at which point cell division and consequently growth and all other biological activities are completely arrested. This must be done in a manner that viability of the stored material is retained and biological functions and growth can be reactivated after thawing (Towill, 1991). Liquid nitrogen storage is useful for the preservation of various types of plant material including whole seeds, embryos, suspension cells, callus, protoplast cultures, gametes and meristems. Although the techniques of freeze-preservation in liquid nitrogen have been modified in several ways to minimize freeze damage, there are three major steps involved.

(i) The material to be frozen needs to be cryoprotected from freeze-damage by treatment with cryoprotectants. The commonly used chemicals for this purpose include dimethyl sulphoxide (DMSO), ethylene glycol, glycerol and proline, used at concentrations usually less than 10% (w/v), to enhance the survival of hydrated tissues or cells during freezing. These chemicals cause changes in cell permeability, freezing point and responses to stresses of freezing and thawing. Cryoprotectants can be added before freezing or even at lower temperatures during the freezing process. For the former, incubation for a few hours may be necessary before initiating the freezing process. Some pretreatment methods, which have been found to be successful in some species when used with cryoprotectants, include:

   (a) Cold treatment for callus or cell suspension cultures (Chen *et al.,* 1984),
   (b) Pre-culture of shoot tips with 0.25–0.75 M sucrose and 5% DMSO (Dereuddre *et al.,* 1987), and
   (c) Cooling under osmotic stress induced with mannitol or sorbitol (Towill, 1991).

(ii) A two-step process of cooling is recommended for most plant material, since continuous slow cooling below –33°C to –40°C leads to considerable loss of viability in many plants (Towill, 1991). In practice, the initial cooling down to –40°C may be fast (several hundred °C/min) or slow (0.5–2°C/min) depending on plant genotype, before the storage in liquid nitrogen (Ng, 1991). Freezing may be initiated by the induction of a nucleation with a small ice crystal achieved by briefly touching the outside of the cryotube with LN-cooled forceps (Towill, 1991) or, as in bananas and plantains by plunging the cryotube for a few seconds in liquid nitrogen at temperatures near zero and then slow cooling to –40°C (De Smet, 1995).

(iii) Rapid warming is necessary during the thawing process and the tube containing the cryopreserved material can be dipped directly into warm water (30–40°C) for a few seconds to melt the ice. In the cases of cultured cells, callus and meristems, the samples are then diluted with liquid culture medium to remove the cryoprotectants and the viability of the cryopreserved material can be tested through regeneration or germination in the case of seeds.

Animal Genetic Resources

Animal Genetic Resources, like plant genetic resources need to be conserved for future generations. The use of artificial reproduction is a very useful tool in conservation of endangered species. It should, however, be made to complement the conventional methods of breeding. Some of the biotechnological methods used for production and conservation of animal genetic resources are summarized below:

(i) *Cryopreservation* : The procedure is similar to what has been described already for plants. Materials such as cells, tissues, gametes, oocytes, DNA samples etc. are stored in a genetic databank for future use.

(ii) *In vitro production embryos*: Methods used in the production of embryos *in vitro* include splitting and cloning of embryos, marker-assisted selection, sexing of embryos and transfer of new genes into an embryo (First, 1992). Cloning in animals is enhanced by nuclear transplantation, a method used to produce a large number of viable identical embryos and offspring of desirable genotype in cattle, sheep, rabbits and swine. The procedure involves the separation and transfer of nuclei of a valuable embryo at a multicultural stage into enucleated oocytes at metaphase II followed by serial cloning (First, 1992).

(iii) *Embryo Culture and Transfer*: This technique is used to introduce fertilized embryos into surrogate mothers. Sometimes closely related species can be used to produce the offspring of an endangered species. The great majority of commercial embryo transfer is done with cattle for strictly economic reasons since the economic value of production per head is much higher for cattle (and buffaloes) than for other farm animal species (Seidel and Seidel, 1992).

(iv) *Artificial insemination*: This technique is useful in livestock farming. Cryopreserved sperm from selected males are thawed and introduced into ovulating females.

(v) *Intracytoplasmic sperm injection*: Here sperm from selected males are microinjected directly into the oocyte. These biotechnological methods offer many advantages to conventional captive breeding procedures. Firstly, less stress is experienced since the animals do not have to be moved around. Secondly, the problem of space for keeping the animals is also solved since samples can be taken in the wild. Thirdly, storage of genetic resources will help to preserve biodiversity and counter the effect of genetic drift on small populations. Fourthly, even if an animal dies, its genes will still be available for future breeding work. Also gametes can be extracted from animals that have been dead for up to 24 h and cryopreserved for future use. The main disadvantage is that sometimes preserving only the DNA samples may not be enough to conserve the entire animals as many animals need to learn about behaviour (which may not be in the genes) in order to survive. Moreover, the use of biotechnological tools for endangered species is still at a very early stage and is very expensive.

Sustainable use of Bio-resources

Wrong utilization or exploitation of bio-resources has led to genetic erosion, desertification and a general threat to the survival of man. Sustainable use of bio-resources demands that while utilizing the resources so generously placed by nature at our disposal, we should try not to be cruel to the environment and our children yet unborn. Biotechnology provides methods through which a balance between the economic exploitation of bio-resources and their conservation for the future can be achieved. Some of the techniques of bio-technology and their applications for the sustainable use of bio-resources are summarized below:

(a) *Plant Cell Tissue Culture*: This refers to the culture of explants usually embryos, seeds, cells (virtually any part of the plant on specific media composed of major and minor mineral salts, iron, vitamin and a carbohydrate source (usually sucrose) and subsequently regeneration of whole plants there from. It has found applications in:

  (i) Mass clonal propagation; disease elimination (mainly viral); germplasm exchange; in vitro conservation and cryopreservation of seeds, embryos, suspension cells, meristerms and other suitable plant parts. It is especially useful for threatened plants, and crops with recalcitrant seeds and seedless polyploids,
  (ii) Embryo culture for overcoming postzygotic incompatibilities,
  (iii) Anther/pollen and ovary cultures for fast production of homozygous plants through embryogenesis and chromosome doubling. Haploids could be useful for isolation of desirable recessives,
  (iv) *In vitro* production of plant secondary metabolites,
  (v) Generation of variability in somaclones, and
  (vi) Somatic embryogenesis.

(b) *Protoplast isolation, fusion and culture*: This is useful in overcoming prezygotic incompatibilities in crossing.

(c) *Biological Nitrogen fixation*: Used for development of bio-fertilizers; improvement of the capability of free-living N-fixing bacteria and development of farming systems using green algae and Azolla.

(d) *Use of Molecular Markers*: Plant and animal breeders use markers to aid selection for desirable/beneficial genotypes. These molecular markers are based on DNA variation and can be grouped into two:

(i) Those based on restriction and hybridization techniques and include restriction fragment length polymorphism (RFLP), which is costly, cumbersome and use isotopes in blotting and is thus avoided by many laboratories.

(ii) Those based on the polymerase chain reaction (PCR) is used for gene amplification and include: -

(a) *Random amplified polymorphic DNA (RAPD)*, otherwise called Arbitrary Primed PCR (APPCR). Here, a pair of DNA primers are designed to hybridize to opposite strands of the genomic DNA, acting as primers for the *in vitro* synthesis of the intercalated DNA sequence (Thangjam *et al.*, 2003).

(b) *DNA amplification finger printing (DAF)*. It uses DNA primers to generate amplified products through the PCR. Such products can be stained in mercury during gel electrophoresis. The method is useful in germplasm and phylogenetic studies (Eneobong, 2003).

(c) *Amplified Fragment Length Polymorphism (AFLP)*. This is a genetic fingerprinting technique based on detection of selected genome restriction fragment by PCR amplification. The method is useful for detection of genetic variation *in vitro* (Ubi *et al.*, 2003).

(e) *Gene Transfers/Genetic Transformation*: The modern techniques for gene transfer are based on the natural process of transformation. They are mainly recombinant DNA technology plus tissue culture, aided by several molecular biology tools such as gene isolation, cloning and vector construction. The technique is used for production of transgenic organisms. Examples include:

(i) *Agrobacterium-mediated transfer,* which is quite successful for dicots but not monocots (Eneobong, 2003).

(ii) *Direct DNA uptake.* This has found application more in animals than in plants. The first attempt to transfer foreign DNA in animals was done in mice by microinjection. The first transgenic sheep and pigs were reported in 1985 when a mouse metallothionin growth hormone (mMThGH) fusion gene was transferred into sheep. Since then, many transgenic farm animals have been produced on a routine basis. Examples are transgenic fish that grows 2–3 times faster than normal and is cold-tolerant was produced by microinjection of desired DNA into oocytes, transgenic cattle, sheep, swine and rabbits produced by microinjection of desirable gene into zygote to produce faster-growing animals with better meat quality, transgenic goats and sheep which produce human milk because of the transfer of human genes into such animals, and to viral diseases because of the transfer of growth hormone gene as well as a gene that increases viral resistance based on interference (Bazer, 1992; Fox, 1992; Forano and Flind, 2000).

(iii) *Particle mediated gene transfer,* using gene gun.

REFERENCES

Bazer, F.W. (1992). Reproductive biology of domestic animal: Linkages with veterinary and human medicine. Pages 102–113 *In:* JF Macdonald, (ed.) *Animal Biotechnology, opportunities and challenges.* NABC report No. 4, National Agricultural Biotechnology Council, Ithaca, New York.

Bridgen, M.P., Staby, G.L. (1981). Low pressure and low oxygen storage of *Nicotiana tabacum* and *Chrysanthemum folium* tissue cultures. *Plant Sci. Lett.* 22: 177–186.

Chen THH, Kartha, K.K., Constabel, F., Gusta, L.V. (1984). Freezing characteristics of cultured Catharanthus *roseus* (L) cells treated with dimethylsulfoxide and sorbitol in relation to cryopreservation. Plant Coombs J, Campbell P.N. (1991) *Biotechnology worldwide.* CPL Scientific Ltd., Berkshire, U.K.

Dale P.J. (1980) A method for *in vitro* storage of *in vivo* apple shoots. *Hort. Science* 14: 514.

Dereuddre, J., Fabre J., Bassagha, C. (1987). Resistance to freezing in liquid nitrogen of carnation (*Dianthus caryophyllus* L. var. Eolo) apical and axillary shoot tips excised from differentaged *in vivo* plants. *Plant Cell Rep.* 7: 170–173.

De Smet, K. (1995). Germplasm conservation in banana and plantain. *In:* Lectures on plant tissue culture and biotechnology. *African Biosciences Network* (ABN) International Training Course, University of Nigeria, Nsukka.

Eneobong E.E. (1997). Biotechnological techniques for the conservation and use of plant genetic resources. Pages 72–75 *In:* EE Eneobong, (ed.) *Biological conservation for sustainable agricultural production,* Federal University of Agriculture, Umudike, Nigeria.

Eneobong, E.E. (2003). Current tissues in agricultural biotechnology. Quarterly public lecture, Nigerian Academy of Science.

Eneobong, E.E, Okonkwo SNC (1994). Embryogenic callus and plantlet regeneration from inter-specific seeds of Solanum. pp. 123e–128 In AT Ba, (ed.) Biotechnology for rapid development in Africa, *African Biosciences Network,* Dakar, Senegal.

First, N.L. (1992). Animal biotechnologies: Potential impact on animal products and their production. In: Animal Biotechnology, opportunities and challenges (ed. Macdonald, J. F.) *NABC report No. 4,* pp. 37–47. National Agricultural Biotechnology Council, Ithaca, NY.

Food and Agricultural Organization (2001). Biotechnologies and tree improvement (review of the current status of biotechnology). Biotechnologies and tree improvement (Review of the current of biotechnology and applications in tree developments). www.fao.org/DOCREP/003/X3910E/X3910E08.htm.

Forano, E., Flind, HJ (2000). Genetically modified organisms. Consequencies for ruminant health and nutrition. *Ann. Zootech.* 49: 255–271.

Fox M.W. (1992). The new creation: An update on animal genetic engineering. *In:* Animal Biotechnology, opportunities and challenges (ed. Macdonald, J. F.) *NABC report No. 4,* pp. 49–61. National Agricultural Biotechnology Council, Ithaca, New York.

Gaston, K.J. (1996). *Biodiversity: a biology of numbers and difference,* Blackwell Publishing Company, New York.

Henshaw, G.G., O'Hara, J.F., Stamp J.A. (1985). *In*: K.K. Kartha, ed. *Cryopreservation of plant cells and organs.* CRC Press, Boca Raton, FL.

Hu, C.Y., Wang, P.J. (1986). Techniques for propagation and breeding. *In* : DA Evans, WR Sharp, PV Ammirato, Y Yamada, (eds.), *Handbook of plant cell culture,* Vol. 1, Macmillan, NY.

International Plant Genetic Resources Institute (IPGRI) (2001). *Forest genetic resources.* www.ipgri.cigiar.org/programmes/grst/FGR/activities.htm.

Mullin, R.H., Schlegel, DE (1976). Cold storage maintenance of strawberry meristem plantlets. *Hort. Sci.* 11: 100–101.

Myers, N., Mittermeler, RA, Mittermeler, CG, da Fonseca, GAB, Kent, J (2000). Biodiversity hotspots for conservation priorities. *Nature.* 403: 853–858.

Ng, S.Y.C., Ng, N.Q. (1991). Reduced growth storage of germplasm. *In* : J.H. Dodds, (ed.) *In vitro methods for conservation of plant genetic resources,* Chapman and Hall, London.

Ng, S.Y.C. (1991). *In vitro* conservation and distribution of root and tuber crop germplasm. *In:* N.Q. Ng, P. Perrino, P. Attere, H. Zedan, (eds.) *Crop genetic resources of Africa,* Vol 2, IITA, IBPGR and UNEP Trinity Press, U.K.

Okoro, O.O. (1994). Application of biotechnology in Nigerian forestry practice. In A.T. Ba, (ed.) Biotechnology for rapid development in Africa, *African Biosciences Network,* Dakar, Senegal.

Perrino, P. (1990). Germplasm e ambiente. Biologi Italiani 7–8: 19–30.

Ruredzo, T.J., Hanson, J. (1991). *In vitro* conservation. In: F. Attere, E. Zedan, N.Q. Ng, P. Perrino, (eds.) *Crop genetic resources of Africa,* Vol. 1, Trinity Press, U.K.

Seidel, G.E., Seidel S.M. (1992). Analysis of applications of embryo transfer in developing countries. *In:* Potentials and limitations of biotechnology in livestock production in developing countries. Part 1: Animal reproduction and breeding. Proceedings of a symposium held at FAL in cooperation with the Council for Tropical and Subtropical Agricultural Research (ATSAF).

Takacs, D. (1996). *The idea of biodiversity: philosophies of paradise,* Baltimore: The Johns Hopkins University Press.

Thangjam, R., Singh, M.R.K. (2006) Induction of callus and somatic embryogenesis of cotyledonary exlants of *Parkia timoriana* (DC.) Merr., a multipurpose leguminous tree. *J. Food Agric. Env.* 4: in press

Thangjam, R., Maibam, D., Sharma, G.J. (2003) Detection of genetic diversity in *Parkia timoriana* (DC.) Merr. Using randomly amplified polymorphic DNA analysis. *J. Food Agric. Env.* 3 and 4: 46–49.

Towill, L.E. (1991). *Cryopreservation: In vitro methods for conservation of plant genetic resources* (ed. Dodds J.H.) Chapman and Hall, London.

Ubi, B.E., Kolliker, R., Fujimori, M., Komatsu, T. (2003). Genetic diversity in diploid cultivars of Rhodesgrass determined on the basis of amplified fragment length polymorphism markers. *Crop Sci.* 43: 1516–1522.

Wilson, E.O. (1988). *Biodiversity* (Washington: National Academy of Sciences/ Smithsonian Institution).

SECTION IV

Micro Finance and Rural Development

11

MICRO FINANCE AND ITS IMPACT ON RURAL DEVELOPMENT OF MANIPUR

A. RAJMANI SINGH

Introduction

Development of India is possible only when rural India is developed. Despite massive development efforts undertaken by the Central Government and State Governments in different five year plan periods through different schemes such as IRDP, DWCRA, ICDP and TRYSEM, the problem of mass poverty, malignant growth of unemployed youth and large scale migration of people to urban areas persist in rural areas. Unless we improve the rural economy, we cannot lessen the burden of poverty nor can we solve the problem of unemployment. About 37 per cent of the rural population still lives below the poverty line (estimation of the planning commission report). The problem of unemployment cannot be tackled by creating more jobs in the public sector and other various government departments. There must be development of micro and small entrepreneurship for self-employment and expansion of job opportunities. For this the educated youth of the region must be trained and involved in entrepreneurship oriented vocations through different Entrepreneurship Development Programmes.

Manipur, a small state situated in North-eastern corner of India with a total population of 23,88,634 as per 2001 census. Out of the total population, 74.89 per cent lives in the villages and the remaining 25.11 per cent of total population lives in urban areas. Thus, 74.89 per cent of the population inhabiting 99.38 per cent of the geographical area which makes up the rural areas of the state, cannot be taken lightly in undertaking any strategy of rural development. The distribution of population in the nine districts of the state is very much heterogeneous in nature showing a heavy concentration of the population in one district and very thinly spreading population in other districts such as Imphal West district with 18.40 per cent of population and Tamenglong district with 4.67 per cent of the total population. Manipur continues to be one of the most backward states due to inadequate infrastructure, low level of industrialization, high level of unemployment (26.5 per cent) and pressure of population on land resources. The per capita income at current prices and constant prices for the year 2001–02 was estimated to be at Rs. 15,032 and Rs. 9,102 respectively. The share of the Primary, Secondary and Tertiary sectors in the Gross Domestic Product amounts to 29.57 per cent, 23.10 per cent and 47.33 per cent respectively.

The following Table given below shows the district-wise demographic status of Manipur. Among the nine districts, Imphal West district has the highest rate of unemployment followed by Thoubal district. Further, among the five hilly districts, Churachandpur district has the highest rate of unemployment. Senapati district has the lowest literacy rate among all the districts and Imphal West has the highest literacy district.

Table 11.1: District-wise Demographic Status of Manipur

Districts	*Area Sq. km.*	*Population as per 2001*			*Literacy Percentage*	*Density*	*Sex Ratio*	*Sub Division*	*Unemployment as on 31st Dec.'06*
		Total	*Male*	*Female*					
1	*2*	*3*	*4*	*5*	*6*	*7*	*8*	*9*	*10*
Imphal West	519	439532	218947	220585	80.61	847	1007	4	201712
Imphal East	709	393780	197710	196070	76.38	555	992	4	80530
Thoubal	514	366341	183338	183003	67.90	713	998	3	83285
Bishenpur	496	205907	102772	103135	71.59	415	1004	3	53700
Churachandpur	4570	228707	114740	113967	74.67	50	993	5	52172
Ukhrul	4544	140946	73413	67553	68.96	31	920	5	23044
Senapati	3271	379214	196646	182568	50.47	116	928	6	42026
Chandel	3313	122714	61778	60936	57.38	37	986	4	20035
Tamenglong	4391	111493	57994	53499	58.46	25	922	4	16828
Total	**22327**	**2388634**	**1207388**	**1181296**	**68.87**	**107**	**978**	**38**	**573,332**

Source: 1. Census of India, Series Manipur, 2001.
2. Manipur General Knowledge, 2007.
3. Directorate of Employment Service, Manipur, 2007.

Centrally Sponsored Schemes for Rural Development in Manipur

Despite the planned economic and social development initiatives undertaken by the Government and NGOs over the past 50 years in India, the problem of poverty continues to pose a serious threat to India. More than 30 per cent of the population in Manipur still lives in abject poverty. In order to improve the quality of life of the economically weaker sections of the society and for alleviation of poverty, the Central Government has been initiating various centrally sponsored schemes of area based and beneficiary oriented programmes over the last few five year plans such as Command Area Development Programmes (CADP) 1974, Integrated Rural Development Programme (IRDP) 1980, District Rural Development Agency (DRDA), Council for People's Action and Rural Technology (CPART) 1986, National Rural Employment Programme (NREP), Rural Landless Employment Guarantee Programme (RLEGP) 1983, Jawahar Rojgar Yojana (JRY) 1989, Training of Rural Youth for Self Employment (TRYSEM) 1979, Development of Women and Children in Rural Areas (DWCRA) 1982, Prime Minister Rojgar Yojana (PMRY) 1993 and so on.

After successfully implementing all of the above centrally sponsored schemes for the upliftment of rural economy in the state, the pace of rural development of the state in particular and the region in general is very slow. Few of the schemes have already been closed and some of the schemes have been merged with the newly launched rural development programmes. One of the main reasons behind the slow pace of rural development in North-eastern region in general and the state in particular is lack of effective and efficient utilization of funds allocated for development, lack of transparency from the policy makers and also lack of people's participation at the grass-roots level.

The first effort was taken up by NABARD in 1986–87 when it supported and funded an action research project on "savings and credit management of SHGs" of Mysore Resettlement and Development Agency (MYRADA). Then NABARD launched a pilot project to provide Micro credit by linking SHGs with banks in 1991–92. As in March 2005, 1.62 million SHGs comprising 22 million poor households were accessing credit through 41,082 branches of 573 commercial and co-operative banks under the SHG-Bank Linkage Programme. The cumulative disbursement of loans by the SHGs has been Rs. 68.98 billion.

Self Help Groups (SHGs)

Self Help Groups are fast emerging as powerful tool of socio-economic empowerment of the poor in our rural areas. The Self Help Group is a small body formed by the people for meeting their specific objectives, particularly credit. It is managed by the rules and regulations formed by them and functions on democratic principles. They are extremely useful in generating savings, ensuring successful delivery of credit to individual women and effecting recovery and also gradually removing the exploitation by local money lenders. In addition, they serve as an ideal mechanism for bringing women out of their homes, making them more articulate and enhancing their leadership qualities and their skills as motivators.

Self Help Groups (SHGs) are usually informal groups whose members have a common perception of need and importance of collective action. These groups promote savings among members and use the pooled resources to meet the emergent needs of their members, including the consumption needs. The number of members in SHGs normally ranges from 10 to 20. It is expected that, within the group, there should be a true democratic culture in which all the members must participate actively in the decision making process by taking part in the debate or discussion. The basic objective of SHGs is to develop saving capability among the poorest sections of the society which in turn reduces dependence on financial institutions and develop self-reliance.

Thus, the benefits of SHGs have a multi dimensional approach. Through this group a beggar on the street can also avail the benefit; poor people who do not have collateral guarantees can also get loan from the bank through the group; the members have access to large quantum of resources; provide a window for better technology and skill upgradation; have access to various promotion assistance and assurance of freedom; experience self reliance and empowerment. All these benefits can be attained through collectively. Little drops of water make an Ocean!

Table 11.2: Growth of Micro Finance and SHGs in Manipur As on 31st March 2007

(Amount in Rs. Lakhs)

Banks	*Deposit Linkage*		*Credit Linkage*					
			Under SGSY		*Direct SHGs*		*Total*	
	No.	*Amount*	*No.*	*Amount*	*No.*	*Amount*	*No.*	*Amount*
SBI	5,217	560.5	962	727.43	1,251	728.80	2,213	1,456.23
UBI	2,227	36.17	497	141.61	32	9.13	529	150.74
Other CBs	478	158.02	120	105.25	130	82.24	240	187.49
RRBs	3,689	111.85	—	—	2,771	558.35	2,771	558.35
Co-op.	170	2.20	—	—	16	8.00	16	8.00
Grand total	11,781	868.74	1,569	974.29	4,200	1,386.50	5,769	2,360.81
Current year's performance	5,581	575.3	672	269.51	1,666	613.29	2,338	882.8

Source: SLBC, Manipur March 2007.

For the last few years it has been observed that a large number of Self Help Groups are setup in Manipur through different NGOs and other social organizations under the sponsorship of technical and financial support from NABARD, SIDBI and other Self Help Promotion Institutions and agencies. As on 31st March 2007, there were 11,781 SHG units formed in the state. Out of this 5,769 SHGs were directly linked to different commercial and regional rural banks under NABARD. The performances of these SHGs were quite encouraging as well as discouraging, looking at their performance appraisal. To promote the micro enterprise units, a micro finance scheme has been introduced in the state to undertake income generating activities through SHGs.

To uplift the rural poor the Rural Development Organization (RDO) Lamsang, Manipur has initiated a Bangladesh Grameen Bank model called **Loyalam Bank Project** with financial assistance from NABARD under a Revolving Fund Assistance (RFA) since 1992 in Manipur with the support from Grameen Trust, Bangladesh, NABARD and Rashtriya Mahila Kosh. Through this project RDO Lamsang has opened its five functioning branches at Moirang, Wangoi, Lamsang, Sagolmang and Thoubal. As on 31st October 2006 there are 3,302 SHGs comprising 5 self-chosen members drawn from similar socio-economic background under 547 centres covering 16,920 outreached members under Loyalam Bank project of RDO providing micro credit and micro finance to them. All borrowers are women. Loan disbursed under the MFI model stood, under the Loyalam Bank at Rs. 4.47 crores and savings stood at Rs. 2.76 crores. The goal of the project is to contribute in the reduction of poverty through Micro credit by expanding the outreach to 50,000 poor families by the year 2015 in rural areas of four valley districts of Manipur.

In the hill areas, special packages for rural development programmes were undertaken by the International Fund for Agricultural Development (IFAD) and Central Government sponsored programme of National Rural Employment Guarantee Schemes (NREGS). The International Fund for Agricultural Development (IFAD) assisted North-Eastern Region Community Resource Management Project (NERCRMP) since 1998 in two districts each of Assam (Karbi Anglong and North Cachar Hills), Manipur (Senapati and Ukhrul) and Meghalaya (West Garo Hills and West Khasi Hills). The project, costing Rs. 159.36 crore covers 39,203 families (2,53,000 persons) in 862 villages of 6 selected districts. 2443 SHGs and 990 Natural Resources Management Groups have been set up with its help.

Under IFAD-NERCRMP in the Ukhrul district of Manipur, altogether 83 project villages were covered out of the 230 villages in the district. Further the 83 project villages were managed and controlled under 128 Natural Resource Management Groups (NRMG) and 502 SHGs with financial assistance from the IFAD. The same project was also started simultaneously in the Senapati district of Manipur covering 108 project villages with 427 SHGs and 148 Natural Resource Management Groups with financial assistance from the IFAD. Construction of road, community hall, safe drinking water facilities, agro-processing units, plantation of banana, orange, pineapple, passion fruits, piggery, fishery are some of the important activities undertaken by the SHGs and NRMG with the financial assistance from the IFAD.

National Rural Employment Guarantee Scheme (NREGS) was launched on February 2, 2006. The two rural development programmes of Sampoorna Grameen Rojgar Yojana (SGRY) and National Food for Work Programme (NFWP) are being subsumed within the NREGS in 200 districts identified in the initial stage. Tamenglong district of Manipur was covered in the first phase and two more districts, i.e., Churachandpur and Chandel districts have been included in the second phase of 130 more districts of the country and works have started recently.

The NREGS is way behind yielding desired results. Not only could the scheme not provide employment to all eligible persons but in many cases the labourer did not get the stipulated rate of wages too. According to a recent survey, in 2006–07, only 6 per cent of households registered in the scheme in the country got 100 days of employment as prescribed by law. NREGS was initially applicable to only 200 districts in the first phase and it was extended to 330 districts in the second phase and now it is proposed that it will be applicable to all the 595 districts of the country which are classified as rural, (Prime Minister Dr. Manmohan Singh, 28th September 2007). The allocation for the NREGS for 2006–07 was Rs. 11,300 crore (200 districts) and Rs. 12,000 for 2007–08 (330 districts) and Rs. 20,000 crore for 595 districts from April 1, 2008. However, against this allocation, only Rs. 8,800 crore was actually spent in 2006–07 and this year the expenditure is likely to touch Rs. 10,000 crore at the most. "The programme is an Act that has legal backing, so whatever money is required for the demand-driven NREGS will be provided by the government" Singh said. It will provide an employment to 2.10 crore rural households in 200 districts in 2006–07, creating 90.5 crore man-days. Of this, over 60 per cent are belonging to Scheduled Castes and Scheduled Tribes. Also, 40 per cent of those employed were women.

Role of NABARD for Rural Development in Manipur

In order to improve the access by the poor to the formal credit institutions and their social empowerment NABARD has taken various initiatives for direct linkages of SHGs with banks, enlisting support from NGOs, training and sensitization of a large number of bank personnel and NGOs, capacity building of NGOs and providing 100 per cent refinance facilities to the credit institutions. Few selected activities undertaken by the NABARD are:

- As on 31st January 2004, 689 SHGs have been given direct credit linkage with banks of which 250 have been linked to refinance assistance of Rs. 21.69 lakh through the Manipur Rural Bank.

- Sanctioned Revolving Fund Assistance (RFA) of Rs. 562.50 lakh to Rural Development Organization (RDO) Lamsang for up-scaling their Loyalam Bank Project to provide micro credit of Rs. 2500 each to 10,000 families over a period of 5 years on the pattern of Bangladesh Grameen Bank (BGB) Model. A grant of assistance of Rs. 18.38 lakh was also sanctioned to create necessary infrastructure after BGB model.
- Provided Rs. 5.10 lakh to Women's Education Development Association (WEDA) for lending to 200 women members on the pattern of BGB model.
- Rs. 7.50 lakh soft loan assistance to Craft Society of Manipur (CSM) for development of 700 craftsmen.
- Manipur Rural Bank has been provided with a grant assistance of Rs. 2.35 lakh to promote 200 SHGs.
- Provides guidance to banks/NGOs by conducting orientation workshops, visit to NGOs/SHGs, arranging exchange meets of SHGs and providing refinance to banks.
- Sanctioned Rs. 1.71 lakh for conducting EDPs on agro-processing industries to Association of Food Scientists and Technologists (AFST).

Micro Finance has come to mean the provision of credit and other financial services to the poor so that they can reduce their poverty and raise their living standards. Micro finance has the potential to become an important component of a successful and sustainable poverty alleviation programme. Micro finance provides credit access to poor with no collateral Obligations. It encourages savings and promotes income generating activities. Loans are provided at the market driven rates of interest and peer pressure is used in repayment. Micro finance is carried out through Self Help Groups where poor come together in the range of 10–20 by weekly, fortnightly and monthly meetings. It is hoped that through such interventions hitherto uncovered groups are covered with credit and in the process get empowered.

NABARD has defined microfinance as "provision of thrift, credit and other financial services and products of very small amount to the poor in rural, semi-urban and urban areas for enabling them to raise their income levels and to improve living standards". The success of micro finance has dispelled many doubts and change many paradigms. The earlier proverbs always taught one to stay away from credit, and advised bankers not to let the poor come near them. But most of the studies conducted on micro credit operations through SHGs have shown a much higher repayment rate of over 90 per cent to 100 per cent than experienced in case of larger loans to non poor, who paradoxically, do not repay so faithfully (Gibbons, in Basu and Jindal, 2000:152)

Micro finance has become a worldwide movement. By the end of 2003, about 80 million clients across the world were being serviced by approximately 2,900 microfinance institutions (MFIs). India's share in this global micro credit market is quite impressive. In India, micro finance is being pursued through SHG-Bank linkage model and Micro finance institutions model. Recent compilations of support provided by major financial institutions show that the outstanding micro finance credit of domestic financial institutions (including non-regulated NGO-MFIs) did not exceed Rs. 3,500 crore (US$ 804 million) by March 2005 with an outreach of less than 15 million families—at best less than 25 per cent of the 60–70 million poor families in the country. This includes the NABARD scheme for linking Self Help Groups (SHGs) directly with banks. The available data indicates that progress and outreach in the latter scheme were around Rs. 2,000 crore (US$ 460 million) outstanding and covering, at most, 10 million families at the end of March 2005.

At the same time, the involvement of commercial banks in micro finance is negligible both in relation to the current volume of micro finance and (even more so) to their broader engagement in rural areas. The total credit from the scheduled commercial banks to the "weaker sections"[1] is estimated at Rs. 32,300 core (US$ 7.5 billion) at the end of March 2004 compared to the total rural deposits of Rs. 176,000 crore (US$ 41 billion).

A Micro Enterprise is a type of small business. A micro enterprise is defined as a business having 5 or fewer employees and a seed capital of not more than $ 35,000. Typically, micro enterprises have no access to the commercial banking sector. Micro finance institutions have become common sources of funding for micro-enterprises, particularly in the Third World. Even though micro financing made significant progress after 2000—mostly through various Self Help Groups, whose number increased from 255 in 1992-93 to 2.24 million in March 2006, disbursing Rs. 11,398 crore against Rs. 29 lakh in 1992–93 as micro-credit—this minimum gap between demand and supply reflects the dismal situation of a majority of unorganized micro enterprises, which contribute nearly 30 per cent to the GDP and provide employment to 104 million.

Micro Enterprises play a critical role in the economic development of any economy, but particularly so of those economies which are undergoing a transition from the traditional subsistence to a modern industrial economy. In India, the micro and small industries sector has a long historical tradition and since independence has contributed significantly to the overall economic development of the country. Given its employment pattern, growth, geographical dispersion and contribution to total industrial output, the micro enterprise sector will continue to play a significant role in eradicating poverty and promoting higher levels of gainful employment. Development organizations have begun playing a very crucial role in promoting micro enterprises. Hence skills pertaining to development of micro-enterprises must be acquired by them.

Today, the idea is being taken one step further. According to the World Employment Report (2004–05) Employment, Productivity and Poverty Reduction by the International Labour Organizations, 50 per cent of the world's labour force is unemployed or underemployed. Micro enterprise, defined as businesses with up to 10 employees, with minimal start up costs are the biggest sources of job globally. However, micro enterprise growth is constrained by **lack of competitiveness, low productivity and low skill level of owners and workers.** The micro enterprise model is particularly relevant to societies such as China and India, faced with a large number of unemployed university and college graduates.

Significance of Microfinance and Micro-enterprise: Following are the important findings about the significance of Micro finance and Micro enterprise:

- Micro finance has reduced the incidence of poverty through increase in income, enabled the poor to build assets and thereby reduce their vulnerability.

- It has enabled households that have access to it to spend more on education than non client households. Families participating in the programme have reported better school attendance and lower drop-out rates.
- It has empowered women by enhancing their contribution to household income, increasing the value of their assets and generally by giving them better control over decisions that affect their lives.
- In certain areas it has reduced mortality, improved maternal health and the ability of the poor to combat disease through better nutrition, housing and health-especially among women and children.
- It has contributed to a reduced dependency on informal money lenders and other non-institutional sources.
- It has facilitated significant research into the provision of financial services for the poor and helped in building capacity at the SHG level.
- Finally, it has offered space for different stakeholders to innovate, learn and replicate. As a result, some NGOs have added **micro insurance** products to their portfolios, a couple of federations have experimented with undertaking **livelihood activities** and **grain banks, yarn banks,** etc. have been successfully built into the SHG model in the eastern region. SHGs in some areas have employed **local accountants** for keeping their books of account and **IT applications** are now being explored by almost all for better **MIS, accounting and internal controls**.

Conclusion

Thus, it is concluded that when older SHGs became experienced and more exposed then Micro credit grew into **Micro finance** or the provision of a range of financial services to the poor. This includes **savings, micro insurance and other financial innovations**. The success of micro credit and micro finance in helping break the cycles of extreme poverty and unemployment and slowly building wealth through engagement of self-employment projects has been phenomenal. With time, micro credit has even begun to gain credibility among the mainstream finance industry and larger development organizations.

The increased involvement of commercial banks in micro financing is absolutely essential for a sustainable micro financing programme in the country. It also suggested that support should be provided for building assets to run enterprises, increase in the product mix by adding insurance, and money transfer, along with credit and thrift and provision of livelihood, financed to take care of essential infrastructural requirements and capacity addition of SHGs, micro financing institutions and NGOs, so that entrepreneurs can make value additions in existing projects.

Therefore, it is suggested that the micro credit or micro finance provided by the Central Government through NABARD, Commercial Banks, MFIs, SHGPI, and NGOs, individuals through SHGs, IFAD's financial assistance for the upliftment of rural poor in the hilly areas through NARMG, and SHGs towards poor families, NREGS for providing income etc. should give more emphasis on establishment of Micro Enterprise in the prospective and potential areas like Bakery, Floriculture, Garment making, Knitting and Embroidery, Tailoring, Masala Grinding, Papad Making, Toy Making, Vermi Composting, Beautician Training, Food Processing, Handicraft Making, Mushroom Cultivation, Screen Printing, Typing Institutes, Handloom Weaving Units, Call Centre and PCO Booths, Designing, Animal rearing activities, Bamboo based industries and Fish farming and fishing.

Various rural development agencies such as SHGPI, MFI, and NGOs should take the parental role for the development of micro enterprise through micro finance in the rural villages of the state and an area and need based approach is highly essential. To encourage this, the financial, technical and managerial support of the SIDBI, NABARD, IFAD, SISI, IIE, NEC, State Government and Central Government is the need of the hour. Further, a firm commitment, transparency, and sincere effort of the people and good governance will help to alleviate rural poverty on the one hand and the upliftment of rural economy through generation of more employment avenues on the other.

SELECTED READINGS

A Microfinance Banking of Loyalam Bank Project, (2007) Rural Development Organization, Lamsang Bazar, Manipur-146.

Biren Okram, (2007) *Performance of Micro Finance Delivery under the Grameen Model,* RDO Lamsang, Manipur.

Basic Statistics of North-eastern Region (2006) North-eastern Council, Shillong-3.

Basu, *et al.* (2000) *Micro-finance: Emerging Challenges,* Tata McGraw Hill Publishing Co. New Delhi-8.

Handbook for NGOs, (2005) A Nabhi Publication, New Delhi-1.

Jerinabi, U. (2006) *Micro Credit Management by Women's Self Help Groups,* Discovery Publishing House, New Delhi-2.

Mishra, Indira, (2005) *Micro-credit for Micro Impact on Poverty,* National Publishing House, New Delhi-2.

N.E. Newsletter, (2002) Ministry of Home Affairs, Government of India. Vol. 4 No.3 March.

Singh, Rajmani (2007), 'SHG and Micro finance for Micro Enterprise in Manipur', Paper presented as resource person at "One Day Women SHG Sensitization Programme" organized by Manipur Rural Bank and Human Resource Development Organization at Imphal on 23rd November.

State Focus Paper 2007–08, Manipur, National Bank for Agriculture and Rural Development, Regional Office Imphal.

11th State Level Banker's Committee Meeting, Manipur. Agenda-*cum*-background paper (Meeting for June 2007).

Status Report (2004) Ukhrul District Community Resource Management Society (UDCRMS) A project report of IFAD.

Towards a Sustainable Microfinance Outreach in India: Experiences and Perspectives. (2006), Published by NABARD, GTZ and SDC.

Yambem, Sanamani (2007), 'Microfinance and Economic Development', Key note speech delivered on inaugural function of 7 days training programme on financial management and accounting practices for Micro and Small enterprises of Manipur and organized by Department of Commerce, Manipur University from 10th–17th December.

12

MICRO FINANCE AND ECONOMIC BACKWARDNESS

W. C. SINGH

Introduction

Improving access to the financial services is one of the effective tools to tackle poverty and for broad basing the economic growth. More than 43 per cent of the world's population lives in an economically poor condition. In 2001, approximately 2.7 billion people were living on less than $ 2.15 per day. Of that, a little more than 1 billion survived on $ 1.08 or less. The poor remains poor in spite of democracy being there for them. Since India got independence, we have succeeded some how in saving political democracy in our country, but we are yet to taste the fruits of inclusive growth and economic democracy. Such unbalanced growth is quite prominent especially in the eastern part of the country. Manipur and other tribal dominated states are still struggling for a square of meal in a day. These backward communities are facing the problem of inaccessibility to the proper developmental infrastructures. In fact, no single sector alone can solve these problems and bring them up.

Micro finance, micro enterprises and Self Help Groups are playing major role in bringing up such communities. With the help of micro finance institutions, they are entering the mainstream of economic development.

Growth of Micro Finance

During 1990s, Micro Finance Programmes have emerged as a mainstream development intervention for addressing poverty alleviation and women's empowerment. These programmes have become a much favoured intervention among international development agencies providing a new paradigm for remodelling economic and social development. The growth of micro finance is visible in many aspects. There are more than 2000 Non-Government Organizations (NGOs) involve in the National Bank for Agriculture and Rural Development (NABARD) Self Help Group (SHG), Bank linkage programme. Out of these, approximately 800 NGOs are involved in some form of financial intermediation. Further, there are 350 new generation of co-operatives providing thrift and credit services. In March 1999, about 0.56 families engaged in micro enterprises were financed under the scheme through 33,000 Self Help Groups, and out of which 84 per cent were women SHGs. In all, 202 banks consisting of 129 (64 per cent) Regional Rural Banks, 38 (19 per cent) Commercial Banks, and 35 (17 per cent) Co-operative Banks were participated in the programme. In the year 1991–92, NABARD introduced SHG bank Linkage Programme, as a pilot project to reach the banking services to the unreached rural poor through the medium of SHGs. It is a cost effective credit delivery mechanism. The SHG bank Linkage programme has now become hugely popular all over India, particularly in the South. Since its inception, the linkage programme has been increasingly accepted by the various partners of the programme, viz. Banks, NGOs and other Self Help Promoting Institutions (SHPIs) and general public. It has been proved to be a very good tool for providing micro finance to the rural poor in the country.

Taking its effective credit delivery potentials, Reserve Bank of India had, in 1996, advised all banks to treat the SHG lending as a normal business activity under priority sector. The progress of SHG bank linkage programme in the country is very encouraging at present. As on 31 March 2002, a cumulative number of 4,61,478 SHGs were credit linked with 444 banks (44 commercial banks, 191 RRB, and 209 co-operative banks) covering 78 lakhs rural poor families. About 90 per cent of the Self Help Group (SHG) Bank linkage programmes are exclusively women groups. The programme is implemented in all the States and Union Territories spread over 488 districts. As many as 2155 NGOs/SHPIs are involved in the promotion and linkage of SHGs with banks. As on 31 March 2002, a total amount of Rs. 1026 crore was provided as bank loan to the SHGs against which NABARD has provided refinance assistance of Rs. 797 crore to banks. The goal of NABARD is to credit link to10 (ten) lakh SHGs with bank covering 10 crore rural body by 31 March 2008.

In the light of practical effectiveness of SHG bank Linkage Programme launched by NABARD, the Government of India borrowed its concept and introduced 'Swarnjayanti Gram Swarozgar Yojna' (SGSY) programme as an alternative to Integrated Rural Development Programme (IRDP) and other allied programmes for poverty eradication in the country. Under SGSY the beneficiaries are known as Swarozgaries. The Swarozgaries can be either individual or group. The concept and the scope of micro finance, micro credit, and the SHGs are very limited in the North-eastern States of India (NEI). This problem lies with the State Government and the implementing agencies. Most of the officials are yet to understand the concept and the scheme thoroughly to implement it effectively.

How does Micro Finance help?

Micro Finance as defined by the Task Force of NABARD, RBI (2000), is the provision of thrift, credit and other financial services and products of very small amount to the poor in the rural, semi urban or urban areas for enabling them to raise their income levels and improving standard of living. Micro Finance has enabled the poor specially women to generate income for themselves and their families. The concept of Grameen Bank is the brain child of Dr. Muhammad Yunus of Chittagong University who felt the concern at the pittance earned by landless women after a long arduous day's work labouring for other people. He reasoned that if these women could work for themselves instead of working for others they could retain much of the surplus generated by their labour, currently enjoyed by others. Prof. Mohammad Yunus, popularly known as father of modern Micro Finance system started a research project in Bangladesh in 1979 and came out the idea of micro credit that resulted the establishment of Grameen Bank in 1983 (*Kurushetra* August 2003). Today, the (Micro Finance Institutions (MFIs) are the world's largest innovation system. In India, the first initiative was taken up by NABARD in 1986–87 when it was supported and funded an action research project on saving and credit management of SHGs of Mysore Settlement and Development Agency (MYRADA). Micro Finance movement was then formally lunched in 1992 with NABARD starting a SHG Bank Linkage Programme on a pilot basis in1992 and in right earnest in 1996. As on March 2004, 17953 SHGs were given access to bank under SHG Bank linkage Programme of NABARD as compared to 16 lakh SHGs in all over India which is only about 1 per cent. In 1996–97, Rashtrya Gramin Vikas Nidhi (RGVN) started Credit Support Programme (CSP) and began working in various clusters in Assam and Meghalaya by providing revolving fund to many groups.

Micro Finance as a strategic tool for poverty alleviation has become increasingly popular in the rural, semi-urban and urban areas of Manipur as other parts of country for enabling them to raise their income levels and improving the standard of living. But the condition of Micro Finance in Manipur is still in the nascent stage and the main concern is about its sustainability. The SHG Bank linkage programme and RGVN's Credit Support Programme failed to stimulate growth of Micro Finance activities in Manipur as compared to other parts.

Experience shows that micro finance can help the poor and backward community to increase income, build viable businesses, and reduce their vulnerability to external shocks. It can also be a powerful instrument for self-empowerment by enabling the poor and underprivileged community, specially the women, to become economic agents of change. By providing access to financial services, micro finance plays an important role to fight against many aspects of poverty. For instance, income generation from a business helps not only in expanding business itself, but also contributes to household income and its attendant benefits on food security, children's education, etc. Moreover, for women, who, in many contexts, are secluded from public space, transacting with formal institutions can also build confidence and empowerment. In the rural areas, as seen in the Israel, the farmers are getting rural finance instead of agricultural finance. They receive credit to finance three major activities: long term investment, production cost, and living standard.

Challenges of MFIs

Micro Finance has become the common talk of the people these days. Every nook and corner we hear about the SHGs but the real meaning of SHG and micro finance has not yet been convinced fully to the minds of the people especially in the hill areas of Manipur. When the concept of micro finance and its long term benefits to the people comes up as a priority, MFIs would need a focus more on the development of micro enterprises. In fact, the micro enterprises are going to move ahead the functioning of microfinance. Some of the challenges in achieving these objectives are given below:

- High lending risk,
- No clear blueprint to follow for microfinance by the SHGs,
- Clear Vision of Promoting Agency,
- Proper Business Planning,
- Start up Capital,
- Properly designed skill training,
- Proper hand-holding,
- Withdrawal strategy,
- Promoting micro enterprise programmes to develop specific strategies,
- Expand Target Groups to inciude the sizes and types of enterprise,
- Expanding support to a broader range of organization.

In order to facilitate in participating women and backward communities in micro and small enterprise, we need to face great challenges. It becomes more difficult for women in micro enterprises to make a profit because of:

- Lack of proper knowledge of market and potential profitability makes difficult in the choice of business,
- Inadequate book keeping,
- Employment of too many relatives which leads to diminishing returns to scale,
- Lack of pricing policy,

- Lack of capital,
- Inadequate credit regulatory policies.

Micro Finance and Micro Enterprises and SHGs are the core requirement for the upgradation of economically backward communities especially womenfolk. In fact, Micro Finance can never remain in the society for a foreseeable future period of time without a proper headway into the establishment of Micro Enterprises. This compels the MFIs to emphasize more on capacity building programmes for organizations in order to develop Micro Enterprise.

REFERENCES

Basu, K. and Jindal, K. (2003), *Microfinance Emerging Challenges*, Tata McGraw Hill, New Delhi.

Sa Dhan (2006), Newsletter, Volume 1, Issue 2, September, Association of Community Development Finance Institutions, B-4/3133, Vasant Kunj, New Delhi.

Wendt, H. and Eichfeld, R. (2006), *Building on Success: The Next Challenges for Microfinance*, American Enterprise Institute for Public Policy Research, No. 2. September, Washington, D.C.

13

SOCIO-ECONOMIC DEVELOPMENT IN RURAL ASSAM
Problems and Prospects

P.C. DUTTA and A. DEBNATH

"Development of India's rural economy is vital for growth than urban economy. It is a foregone Conclusion that there will never be a growth unless rural economy develops.........."

—Vinod Khosla

Even after 60 years of independence and completion of Tenth Five Year Plan, India remains predominantly a rural society with bulk of her huge population living in the villages under conditions of grinding poverty. Mass unemployment, widespread illiteracy, use of primitive technology, low rates of savings and investment, social backwardness, gross inter-regional and intra-regional inequalities of income and wealth, and mounting inflationary pressures still continues.

Rural means, a society or specific areas marked off by villages which are lying outside the jurisdiction of municipal area or committees. The economic structure of rural areas consists mainly with the system of production and consumption that are closely interlinked with the social structure. Development is a comprehensive term and multi-disciplinary in nature. It is a continuous process that tends to positively change the entire social, economic, technological, cultural, psychological, organisational and political aspects of a human society.

Thus "Rural Development" is used to denote the actions and initiatives which are undertaken to bring about sustained positive changes in socio-economic life of the people living in non-urban neighbourhoods, countryside, and remote villages. According to World Bank, rural development is a strategy designed to improve the economic and social life of a specific group of people—the rural poor. It involves extending the benefits of development to the poorest among those who seek a livelihood in the rural areas. Programmes meant for rural development are usually top-down from the local or regional authorities, regional development agencies, NGOs, National Governments or International development organizations. But then, local populations can also bring about endogenous initiatives for development.

Rural life is an integrated whole, with strength and weaknesses intermeshed. The impact of rural development on society is a subject of extreme importance. At the same time, this subject is very intricate and not susceptible to easy or quick analysis. The process of development inevitably affects, in varying ways and intensities, the existing social and economic arrangements and discord is built into the process. A typical village in India has traditionally been an extremely integrated unit where social stratification is based on religion, caste and economic power.

Development of social sectors such as health, education and nutrition etc, increase the productivity of labour time—the main asset of the poor, employment opportunities and contribute to reducing poverty. Education helps people not only in raising their own skill but also in raising the efficiency of other factors like capital, by making their use in a more efficient manner. It is a basic fact that without economic growth social sector development cannot be sustained for long and it is also more basic fact that healthy and well educated people make an economy more productive. Rural development is too important for the Nation, as a whole, to be treated in this routine fashion. Indeed, a prerequisite of urban development in India is rural development. The poor and unemployed of the villages will make up the city slums of tomorrow. Rural development is inescapable in India if the rural-urban relationship is to be corrected. Institutions created for rural development and empowering the poor, such as co-operatives, Panchayati Raj Institutions are completely politicized and bureaucratized. These institutions have become the stepping stone for potential political leaders and the handmaid of official machinery. The misfortune of Panchayati Raj has been that it did not receive fair treatment from the higher level of leadership.

· India has emerged as one of the richest economies in the developing world during the reform period. But the performance of any economic policy should not be judged by looking merely at its national level performance. Its impacts should also be evaluated by looking its performance at the sub-national or state-levels and in a backward state like Assam where more than 88 per cent of the population live in rural areas; an analysis of the impact of the policy on the rural development assumes an additional significance. In this context, a study meant to analyse the performance of income generating institutions in the rural areas of Assam will be an important issue to deal with. The agrarian rural structure is the predominant character of most of the Third World developing economies. Rural development in these countries is an inescapable prerequisite of National development. In India, commitment to development of rural areas has been one of the abiding concerns of successive five year plans.

The rural sub-system of the North-Eastern Region (NER) economy consists of some 35 thousand villages inhabited by over 32 million people who constitute about 85 per cent of the total population in the region. Of approximately 10.6 million main workers in the NER economy, about eight million workers are directly engaged as cultivators or agricultural labourers.

The state of Assam is predominantly a rural based and hilly in some areas. The topography of the region has largely shaped its economy. The State comprises of 27 districts and is situated in the North-east corner of India. Except for a narrow corridor running through the foothills of the Himalayas that connects the state with West Bengal, Assam is almost entirely isolated from India. According to 2001 census the state has a total population of 26,638,407 with a density of 340 persons per sq. km. The literacy rate is comparatively high at 64.28 per cent with males constituting 71.93 per cent and females comprising 56.03 per cent. The sex ratio is 932 females per thousand males. The state economy is primarily based on agriculture and oil. The state produces a significant part of the total tea production of the world and more than half of India's petroleum. It is ranked

14th in the Human Development Index which is the lowest among all the sub-project states.

Since the majority of population of Assam lives in the rural areas, development of rural areas must receive much attention in the schemes designed for the development of State's economy. More precisely, economic policies of the state must be evaluated on their capacity to raise the economic condition of rural Assam.

As stated by various scholars such as Myrdal (1970), Atkinson (1970), Adelman and Morris (1973) at the earlier stage of development socio-structural and institutional dimensions are more important, after that economic growth and improvement in per capita income may be important. Again, Hooda (1997) remarked that the rural development involves all agents of change and policy makers to activise the passive majority of rural people, to assist them by providing schemes, funds, skill, training, technology and opportunities to participate in the process of development and to raise their share in production and wealth. It is wrong to suggest that more investment in social sector development is anti-growth and it is more wrong to say that economic growth is unnecessary for social and human development.

According to Ghose (1993), 'Our real problem is not so much of economic restructuring to look outward—but restructuring of social, political, judicial and administrative—to look inward'. Rampant corruption can not be checked and rural or national development cannot be sustained without such institutional changes. Otherwise the declining political morality will lead to the deprivation of the poor from power and capabilities to participate, growing loss of faith in the system and break down of the social order (Kothari, 1988).

Arthur Lewis (1965) emphasised that developing of human resources is an urgent need in the developing countries since it has potential to produce according to the needs of people and viewed that an enquiry into the differences in the human behaviour among the countries having roughly equal resources is necessary. Schultz (1960) first time identified the impact of human capital formation on the economic growth. He emphasised that education is an important form of investment, which ensures skills and capabilities that produces future earnings, and productivity of labour.

In the changing *socio-politico* milieu, the concept of development has undergone a paradigm shift. The growth of the country measured in quantitative terms especially as a percentage growth of GDP lost its relevance in the context of sustainable economic development. The volume growth of GDP, till date, is, however, put on at par with increasing welfare or well-being of the society.

Donald Rutherford (2002) opined that the social welfare of a country is "often measured by the total volume of goods and services becoming available to it over a given period, i.e. real income". Martha Nussbaum and Amartya Sen (2003) pointed out that measure like Per Capita Gross National Product (GNP), in spite of their well-known shortcomings, "continue to be widely used when public policy is made".

Sharma (2006) concluded that cultivation is the major source of income of indebted farmer households in the state of Assam along with other states of India and 70 per cent of such households are marginal farmers. The amount of outstanding debt has positive and statistically significant relationship with size class of land possessed and per capita monthly expenditure in the state.

Woman has been an equal economic partner to man, besides her biological and social roles through history (Gengaje and Setty, 1992). The contribution of female labour in agriculture is quite high and well documented by many scholars (Rani and Raju, 1991; Bala, 1992; Dutta and Pradhan, 2004, 2006, 2007). As per the world economic profile they form 50 per cent of the world population, contributing 60 per cent of the working hours, make up 30 per cent of the official labour force and 50 per cent of the food production (Desai and Mohiuddin, 1992).

Keeping in view, the importance of the subjects discussed above, the broad objective of the present study aims at examining the socio-economic condition of rural regions of the state of Assam and its impact on over all socio-economic development of the state .The study takes a special look at the development experiences of the various sectors of the rural economy of Assam. Issues like people's participation, rural industrialization, marketing, entrepreneurship, tourism, technology, co-operation, education, gender and poverty are analysed in the light of development experiences of the state. However, special thrust has been given to Barak Valley region of the state which is its most backward region. The study deserves the attention of the researchers, policy makers and above all those who concern for the development of the state. The study is being made on the basis of published and unpublished statistical data and completed with viable suggestions.

Economic Development of Assam and Rural Economy

Development is a process, which improves the quality of life. It requires a balanced human resource development in the country. According to latest Human Development Index Report (HDIR), India's position is 96 out of 120. The impact of developmental activities cannot be evaluated fully by any single indicator because it is a multi-dimensional process. Hence there is a need of combining the effect of different indicators for assessing the level of development. The development of an area is best reflected in the quality of basic needs of life of its people.

The most striking fact of Assam's economic development is that, it is falling behind the rest of the country. At the beginning of the post independence era, Assam was ranked among the prosperous States of the country. In 1950–51, Assam's per-capita income was 4.1 per cent higher than the average for the country. By 1980–81, Assam's per capita income was 27 per cent lower than the national average, and by 1998–99, the gap had widened to 45.5 per cent. What is even more alarming is that the gap is widening. Nobel Prize winning economist Robert Lucas had uttered that *once you start thinking about economic growth, it is hard to think of any thing else*. What are the causes of economic growth and how can the process be enabled is a question that has obsessively occupied some of the best minds in the world of economics and commerce. The question takes on an unparallel urgency and importance when applied to the rural economy of Assam because it presents an enormous challenge, and consequently, presents an equally great opportunity for making a difference in the lives of hundreds of millions of people. Economic development of Assam is predicated upon rural development of Assam because nearly 90 per cent of the total population lives in rural Assam (Table13.1).

Table 13.1 : Percentage of Rural-Urban composition of population in Assam and India

	1971		*1991*		*2001*	
	Rural	*Urban*	*Rural*	Urban	Rural	Urban
Assam	91.1	8.9	88.8	11.2	88.9	12.72
India	**80.1**	**19.9**	**73.3**	**25.7**	**73.87**	**27.78**

Source: Census of India, 1971, 1991, and 2001.

Without rural economic development, Assam has little chance of achieving growth rates required to become a developed state. Furthermore, economic development is both a cause and a consequence of urbanization. Clearly, in the context Assam economy, urbanization through further rural to urban migration is both unsustainable and socially disruptive. Therefore, urbanization of the rural population will have to be achieved in the rural areas.

India's total cultivable area is 1,269,219 sq. km (56.78 per cent of total land area), which is decreasing due to constant pressure from an ever growing population and increased urbanisation. Although Assam is more industrially developed than the other North-Eastern states, it is primarily an agrarian economy with 74 per cent of its population engaged in agriculture and allied activities. As per 2001 census, 53 per cent of total work force are engaged in agricultural activities. But during the period 2000–05, the overall scenario of agriculture is not praiseworthy. The contribution of agriculture to Net State Domestic Product of the state is only 31.19 per cent in 2003–04. The production of winter rice steadily decreased from 2713 thousand tonnes in 2001–02 to 1800 thousand tonnes in 2004–05. Same trends are observed in case of Autumn rice, Summer rice, cotton, Jute etc. As per the report of livestock census 2003, the total livestock population in Assam was 140.23 lakh as against 134.67 lakh in 1997. The livestock products as milk, egg and meat are playing a vital role in the economy of Assam. As per the State Directorate of Fisheries, present level of annual fish production is 1.86 lakh metric tonnes (2004–05) which increased by 15.41 per cent in comparison to 2001–02. Agriculture not only supplies raw materials for industries outside the State such as Cotton, Jute, Ginger etc. but also provides inputs to other few small agro-based industries in the State such as turmeric, paddy, maize etc.

Agriculture and allied activities have overriding importance as a source of livelihood to the people of Assam in general and rural areas in particular. It is the agricultural prosperity which boosts up the economic conditions of the rural people directly by raising their income levels and indirectly by putting a sound base for rural industrialisation. It is not that rural development alone necessitates agricultural development, in fact economic progress of the state as a whole depends to a large extant on the blessing of this sector and this is well backed by the fact that agriculture still contributes more than one-third (31.2 per cent in 2003–04) of Assam's NSDP and supports about 70 per cent of its population, though the percentage is even higher in rural Assam. Though agricultural productivity has increased in the recent past, but the rate of increase is very slow. Table 13.2 shows the fact that throughout the period (1980–81 to 2005–06), the yield per hectare of various crops in the state of Assam are very low in comparison to all India level.

Table 13.2 : Yield Rate of Certain Crops in Assam and India (in Kg/Ha)

Name of Crop	*1980–81*		*2000–01*		*2005–06*	
	India	*Assam*	*India*	*Assam*	*India*	*Assam*
Rice	1,336	1,109	1,901	1,483	2,093	1,475
Wheat	1,630	1,158	2,708	1,279	2,607	1,066
Pulses	473	416	544	540	585	543
Maize	1,159	593	1822	722	1953	721
Cotton (lakh bales)	152	—	190	77	375	79
Jute (lakh bales)	1245	1463	2026	1605	2290	1274

Source: Economic Survey, 1980–81, 2000–01 and 2005–06.

In case of *Small Scale Industries (SSI), Handicrafts and Handloom industry* has the potential to promote income and employment generation in a big way. The high quality traditional handicrafts and handloom products enjoy a good market, both nationally and internationally. For providing employment opportunities in the rural areas and strengthening the rural economy, Khadi and Village Industries have play an important role. Development of SSI sector, therefore, is the only alternative to the economic backwardness of a state lies in its significance for generation of employment with low capital cost. The whole of NER contributes

79.58 per cent Nagaland positioned the first rank with highest production (in value) as 45.19 per cent followed by Assam with 37.35 per cent only amongst the states of NER. However, marketing of the product depends on growth of tourism promotion outside the State by the Government and adequate supply of input and infrastructure support.

Village and Khadi industries are an integral part of the economic life of an agriculturally-based poor state like Assam. As small industries take root, they go deeper in the life of people, extend work opportunities, raise income and standard of living of the people and bring about technical changes and a balanced and integrated rural economy. The Assam Khadi and Villages Industries Board has been given the responsibility to promote Village and Khadi Industries in the state with a view to generate rural employment and to uplift the rural economy of the State. For this purpose the board is financially supported by the Khadi and Village Industries Commission (KVIC), Government of India. As per information made available by the Khadi and Village Industries Board, Assam, a total of 56 bee-keeping centres, 521 oil extraction centres, 2184 pottery centres, 219 hand pounding centres and 1283 khandasari centres, 57 khadi production centres, 26 soap making centres, 5 cottage match factories, 189 footwear unit, 15 hand made paper unit, 832 cane and bamboo centres and 44 gobar gas plants were in operation in the state during 2002–03. These Khadi and Village industries have always been a great source of employment, especially for the rural people in the state. But, during the last few years, downward trends have been observed in case of production and employment generation of these industries (Fig. 13.1 and Fig.13.2).

Sericulture is yet another important agro-based labour intensive traditional rural industry of the State comprising culture of different varieties of silkworm. Rearing of Eri, Muga and Mulbery silkworm are playing an important role in the economic development of a large section of rural population of the State. There are 9,173 sericulture villages in Assam. Families involved in rearing of eri, muga, and mulberry during 2004 were132033, 23543 and 29715 respectively. During 2001–03, the state produced 599 MTs eri cut cotton. The figures for muga and mulberry were 92 MTs and 12 MTs respectively.

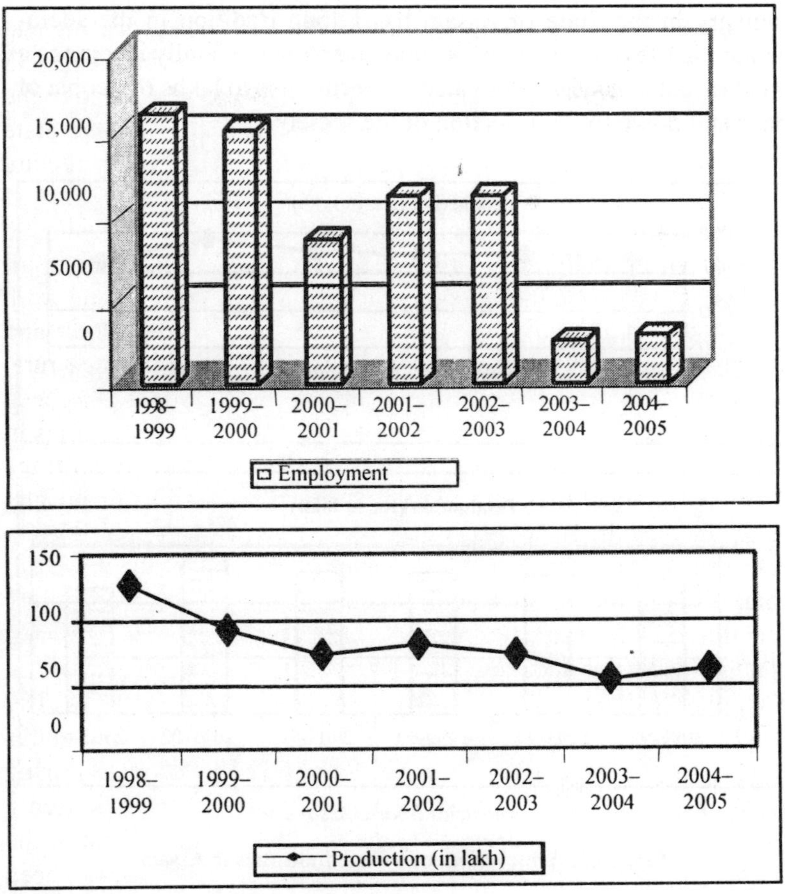

Source: Economic Survey of Assam, 2006–07.

Fig 13.1: Khadi Production and Employment in Assam (1998–2005)

In recognition of the importance of traditional industries, since the era of planning in the country a series of measures were adopted. An industry which received highest official patronage all along these years is handloom industry as it is the oldest and largest traditional industry.Even in this era of liberalisation, the need to develop the industry is being articulated. The study is with reference to the handloom industry of Assam as the said industry in the state exhibits a high order performance compared to the rest of India. The Handloom

Industry in the State of Assam has a long tradition in the socio-economic life of the people for supplementing the family income to a great extent and self-employment opportunities to lakhs of people of poor and down trodden section of the society.

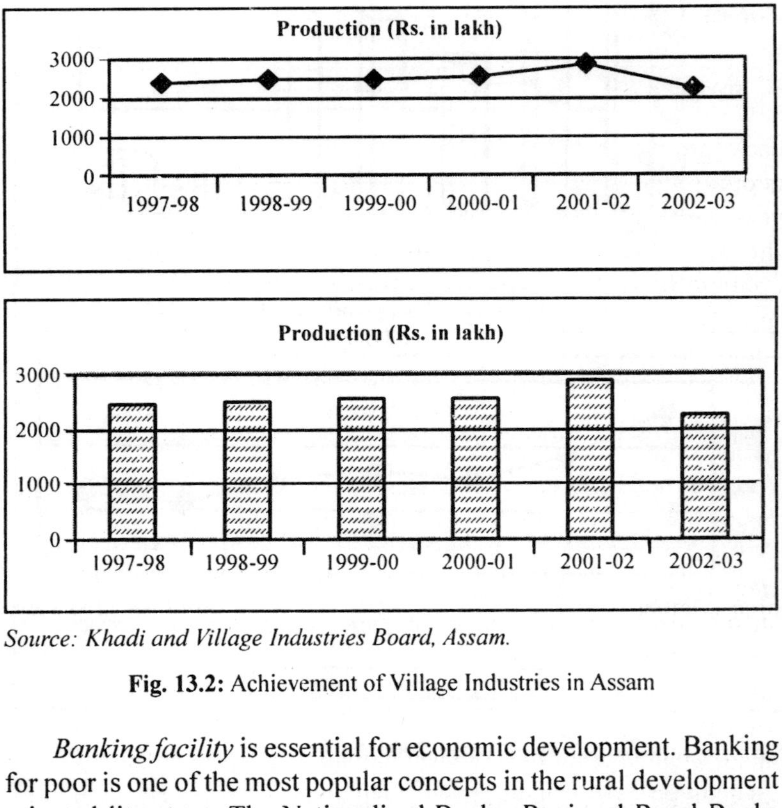

Source: Khadi and Village Industries Board, Assam.

Fig. 13.2: Achievement of Village Industries in Assam

Banking facility is essential for economic development. Banking for poor is one of the most popular concepts in the rural development oriented literature. The Nationalised Banks, Regional Rural Banks and other financial institutions have been playing proactive role in providing credit to SHGs/JLGs during the last 5 years for undertaking productive income generation activities.

The Banking facilities for the rural people are being served by a network of five Regional Rural Banks in Assam with a total number of 399 reporting branch Offices as on March, 2003. The aggregate deposits with these Banks was Rs.1364.85 crore at the end of March, 2003 against Rs.1217.37 crore at the end of March, 2002 thereby registering an increase of 12.11 per cent. The volume of Credit disbursed by these Banks increased to Rs. 465.64 crore at the end of March, 2003 from Rs. 358.53 crore at the end of March, 2002, thus showing an increase of 29.87 per cent. The Credit Deposit ratio of this Bank is 34.12 per cent during March, 2002 as against 29.5 per cent during the same period of the previous

Constraints to Rural Development

Development of infrastructural facilities opens the path of economic development of a particular region. The state largely remains backward in respect of infrastructural system. Due to its peculiar geographical features the entire state was neglected from the very early period. The states of the region were lagging behind the other states of the country in respect of *transportation, communication, electrification, credit facilities etc.* Due to infrastructural backwardness, industrialisation was either absent in some part or started very belatedly in some other parts of the region.

The transportation system of the state was very backward from the very beginning. The surface transport facilities of the region which includes Road transport, Railways and waterways along with the links with the neighbouring states and the rest of the country are totally inadequate and subject to severe hardships during monsoons.

Rural Assam, like rural India, is caught in what is called a *development trap*. Because of lack of economic opportunities, incomes are low. Therefore, they are unable to pay for goods and services that would enable them to increase their incomes. This leads to low demand for goods and services. Consequently, firms did not find it profitable to do business in rural India. This leads to the inadequate provision of infrastructure; which in turn led to the lack of economic opportunities, and so on.

Agricultural sector suffers from several weaknesses as dominance of low value crop, low value addition per hectare, declining factor productivity and declining cost-benefit ratio mainly due to inefficient use of resources such as irrigation water, fertiliser, etc. Besides, indiscriminate use of natural resources leading to environmental degradation (nearly half the agriculture land is severely affected by soil erosion, water logging, formation of gullies and ravines) and deterioration of village institutions have been other responsible factors for this process (Vyas, 1993). The agricultural growth is constrained by non-availability and low adoption of improved technology, poor access to international market, lack of adequate development of infrastructure, and lack of competitiveness in the domestic as well as international market, due to sub-standard and poor quality of product, weak agriculture research and extension system, poor infrastructure like road, market and credit, rapid urbanisation, inappropriate agricultural policies, unfavourable prices, and declining capital formation in agriculture sector, etc. Besides, in the changing economic scenario, globalisation has opened both new opportunities and challenges to the agriculture sector (Singh, 2000).

Floods in the Brahmaputra and Barak valleys of Assam cause "serious erosion, loss of life and livestock and heavy damage to infrastructure and property, retarding agricultural production on account of risk avoidance and sand casting, disrupting communications, education and posing health hazards. The floods damage to crops, cattle, houses and utilities in Assam alone between 1953 and 1995 was estimated at Rs. 4400 crore with a peak of Rs. 664 crore in a single bad year" (Shukla Commission, 1997). The assessed flood prone area in the state is estimated at 3.15 m. ha. (million hectares) or 92.6 per cent of the cultivated land as in 1992–93, almost half of which (1.63 m. ha.) do not have any flood management structures. Even the limited flood management structures that exist are poorly maintained. Floods have been an impediment to the technological transformation of agriculture in Assam. For farmers do not apply costly inputs such as fertilizers and HYV seeds for the fear of their being washed away by floods.

One serious problem faced by the silk industry of the state and other north-eastern region is the problem of exploitation by the village money lenders. "There is no escape route for vast majority of weavers in the state from the cocoon of exploitation from village moneylenders. As credit facilities to the small weavers are not easily available, it facilitates exploitation of weavers by local money lenders and middlemen" (Goswami, 2006). Ignorance, conservative attitude of the workers, lack of education etc. also aggravated the situation .These resulted in poor innovativeness, which is again having a link to inadequate training facilities common in north-east India. In the absence of formal training institution, the workers are mostly self-trained and work as unskilled workers. This poses a bigger challenge for the industry to live up to its business potential. Moreover, the inadequate training facilities for the workers to improve their skills deprive them from availing higher salary, social status, etc. This blocks the entrance for other new unskilled labour to join into the industry as ordinary labourers, and thus limit employment opportunities in the industry.

Inequality is a very complex and multidimensional concept. Quantitative inequality refers to economic inequality measurable in terms of income, wealth, goods and services enjoyed. Qualitative inequality refers to power and prestige, not measurable in physical form. Food security connotes livelihood security at household level and involves ensuring both physical and economic access to balanced diet, safe drinking water, environmental sanitation, primary education and basic healthcare. Basically it implies that entire population in a community has access to enough food at all times for leading an active and healthy life (World Bank, 1986; Parikh, 1998).

One of the important problems that the state of Assam has been facing is the problem of mass poverty. Though the Planning Commission Report (2007) shows a drastic fall in incidence of poverty (55.77 lakh i.e. 19.7%) still now a large section of rural population of Assam is living under poverty (22.3%) and there is no doubt that the incidence is more among the females.

A close look at the historical trend in the incidence of poverty, it is observed that the concentration of poverty in rural area is much higher than in urban areas. Along with these trends if we consider the fact that bulk (almost 90%) of the population lives in rural areas we could say that poverty in Assam is predominantly a rural phenomenon. Again, the incidence of rural poverty is the highest among agricultural and other labour (as high as 76% and 80% respectively), followed by self-employed in agriculture and self-employed in non-agriculture in that order. Among the social groups incidence of poverty is higher among the Scheduled Castes as compared to that among Scheduled Tribes. An important feature of poverty of Assam is that there exists a wide degree of variability in the incidence of rural poverty at the district level. The available data show that Kokrajhar ranks highest (75.92%) and Tinsukia ranks lowest (11.45%) regarding the incidence of rural poverty. The picture of rural poverty in case of Barak Valley is also frustrating (Table 13.3). It is obvious from the table that the incidence of rural poverty in Barak Valley region is greater/less than average.

Anyone who has ever struggled with *poverty* knows how extremely expensive it is to be poor (James Baldwin, 1961). One of the important problems that the state of Assam has been facing is the problem of mass poverty. Though the Planning Commission Report (2007) shows a drastic fall in incidence of poverty of the tune of 55.77 lakh (19.7%) still now a large section of rural population of Assam is living under poverty (22.3%) and there is no doubt that the incidence is more among the females. A minute look at the historical trend in the incidence of poverty, it is observed that the concentration of poverty in rural area is much higher than in urban areas. Along with these trends, by considering the fact that bulk of the population (almost 90%) lives in rural areas it can be remark that the poverty in Assam is predominantly a rural phenomenon. Again, the incidence of rural poverty is the highest among agricultural and other labour (76% and 80% respectively), followed by self-employed in agriculture and self-employed in non-agriculture in that order. Considering the social groups, it is observed that incidence of poverty is higher among the Scheduled Castes as compared to that of Scheduled Tribes (Table 13.3).

Table 13.3: Number of poor in Assam (per cent of total and in lakh)

Years	*Rural head count ratio*	*Urban head count ratio*	*Combined head count ratio*	*Rural poor (lakh)*	*Urban poor (lakh)*	*Total poor (lakh)*
1973–74	52.67	37.16	51.23	76.37	5.50	81.87
1977–78	59.82	37.58	57.63	97.55	6.70	104.25
1983	42.60	26.38	40.86	81.28	6.06	87.35
1987–88	39.35	9.94	36.21	73.53	2.22	75.75
1993–94	45.01	7.73	40.86	94.33	2.03	96.36
1999–2000 (30 day recall)	40.04	7.47	36.09	92.17	2.38	94.55

Source: http://www.indiastat.com (Planning Commission estimates based on Expert Group methodology).

An important feature of poverty of Assam is that there exists a wide degree of variability in the incidence of rural poverty at the district level. The available data show that Kokrajhar ranks highest (75.92%) and Tinsukia ranks lowest (11.45%) regarding the incidence of rural poverty. The picture of rural poverty in the districts of Barak Valley (44.34%) are also frustrating (Table 13.4). It is obvious from the table that the incidence of rural poverty in Barak Valley region is only marginally less than the total average but much higher than that of Tinsukia.

Table 13.4: Incidence of rural poverty

District	*Rural poverty (per cent below poverty line)*	*Rural poverty (Number of poor)*
Cachar	41.01	449862
Hailakandi	43.79	181694
Karimganj	48.23	369773
Kokrajhar	75.92	569322
Tinsukia	11.45	89160
All Assam	45.06	8758051

Source: Dubey and Gangopadhyay (1998).

Energy plays a crucial role in the socio-economic development of a country as growth in energy consumption is intrinsically linked to growth in the economy. The degree of economic growth is correlated with the generation and consumption of electricity. There is a huge potentiality for the development of number of hydel power and thermal power projects. The state is full of potentiality in respect of power generation. In spite of huge power potential, the entire NER is deficient in respect of generation and consumption of power. There is a huge potential for the development of oil, gas and energy prospects which have not been utilised to their fullest potential and large possibilities have remained unexplored due to lack of trained manpower, lack of organised efforts and a conservative mindset. All this, if properly harnessed, can bring about a radical change to the economy of the region. In the era of globalization, electricity is one of the basic inputs for achieving socio-economic development of a nation. The present per capita consumption of electricity in India is little over 400 kWh, which is much lower than that of the developed countries (five times lower as compared to world average.).

It is needless to say that economic growth of a region cannot be achieved without the growth of large or small industries and for which uninterrupted *power supply* is badly necessary. In spite of having immense potential of power generation, the State of Assam accounts for only 0.12% of total generation electricity in the country during 2003–04. The average per capita consumption of electricity in the State was 104 kWh. in 2003–05 as per Economic Survey Assam, 2005–06, which is far below the national average of 359 kWh. in the same year. Total power generation scenario in the state is not at all healthy towards the economic development. The generation has shown declining trend from 840.406 Million Unit in 2001–02 to 756.435 Million unit in 2004–05. The overall power supply position in the State during 2005–2006 was not much encouraging as the State had to witness erratic power supply during the year.

Rural electrification despite being a basic source of enlarging outlook of rural masses can also help them by enabling them to adopt modern technology in the process of production. In spite of having immense potential of power generation in the State, the performance of this sector is not encouraging. Assam accounts for only 0.12% of total generation electricity in the country during 2003–04. The average per capita consumption of electricity in the State was 104 kWh. in 2003–05 as per Economic Survey Assam, 2005–06, which is far below the national average of 359 kWh. in the same year. The situation is even serious in rural areas, as per census 2001, only 70% villages of Assam are electrified and only 16.5% rural households are electrified.

There is a regular feature of the shortage of power in the state of Assam. As per 2000–02 figure, only 16.54 per cent of rural households in Assam have been electrified which is the lowest among the states. in NER. While the highest is observed in the state of Nagaland (56.88%) followed by Manipur (52.53%). The respective percentage for the country is 43.52.

About 87 per cent of the state population lives in rural areas, that is 26,247 villages. Of these, as on March 31, 2006, only 21,586 villages have been electrified of which only 16.54 per cent of the total households in these electrified villages have electricity connection. In modern day world electrification is a key ingredient for facilitating rural economic development including alleviation of poverty, realization of socio-economic goals and overall human development. The remaining 4661 villages are still to see light of electricity. Again, 2145 unelectrified villages have been identified as remote and thus to provide 'Electricity to all' by 2012 slogan of the government is a far cry. There is no alternative but to go for non-conventional and renewable energy sources applying modern technologies. In Assam as per census 2001, only 70 p.c. villages are electrified and only 16.5 p.c. rural households are electrified. The Government of Assam has been implementing rural electrification programme in Assam through Distribution Companies. With a view to achieve electrification of all villages of Assam by 2009 and provide access to electricity to all households in line with the National Rural

Electrification Policy 2004 and Rural Electrification Policy of Government of Assam, Rural Electrification works particularly under Rajiv Gandhi Gramin Vidyutikaran Yojana (RGGVY) scheme have been carried out. Under this scheme all the census villages of Assam are proposed to be electrified by 2009. Electrification in 16 districts to be implemented by ASEB and in 7 districts by the Power Grid Corporation of India. District-wise schemes for electrification of villages have been submitted to the Government of India and approval for 13 districts has already been received.

It is encouraging to note that the Assam Energy Development Agency, the State Nodal Agency of the Ministry of the Non-conventional Energy Sources identified the potentiality of three renewable sources of energy like small hydro, biomass gasification and solar photovoltaic for electrification of remote villages. Thus the priority of harnessing non-conventional renewable sources of energy will continue for the years to come so as to carry out all the economic activities in rural areas as part of infrastructural development of the policy of globalisation.

Health is a key determinant of human capital and thereby economic growth of a region. Good health is essential to keep the labour force productive and efficient. Frequent illnesses and inadequate nutrition will have adverse impact on the incomes of households making them vulnerable. Good health not only increases productivity and earnings of an individual but also improves the overall quality of life and the socio-economic development of the general population. Malnourishment and under-nourishment can be avoided not just by poverty reduction and higher food intake but also through good health that can be brought about through improved access to sanitation and drinking water facilities.However, the public health delivery system in Assam during the past two decades has been deteriorating, more so in rural areas. Rural people of Assam face two difficulties—scarce availability of quality health services and limited affordability. In the absence of a sufficient number of qualified doctors and paramedical staff, rural inhabitants are largely left to the mercy of unqualified doctors (chemists, quacks, faith healers, etc.) who provide sub-standard services and that too, at high prices. Though the per capita revenue expenditure on health in Assam is lower compared to the average of all States, the share of SDP spent on health services in Assam is quite high, above the average of all States. While there appears to be adequate physical health infrastructure with Primary Health Centres (PHC) and hospitals, etc.

the quality of service provision is low. Poor living conditions in villages with inadequate infrastructure facilities such as electricity, roads and sanitation make it unattractive for doctors and other health workers to work in PHCs. There is also a high degree of administrative inefficiency.

Table 13.5: Rural Literacy Rate as per 2001 Population Census

	Persons	*Male*	*Female*
India	58.7	70.7	46.1
Assam	59.7	68.2	50.7
Kerala	90.0	96.6	86.7

Source: Census of India, 2001.

Education, like health, has a very significant role in accelerating the pace of socio-economic development of any region. In comparison to all India level, Assam could able to do marginally (by 1%) better in respect of rural literacy rate. The situation is even better (by more than 4%) in respect of rural female literacy rate, though rural male literacy rate in the State of Assam falls short of all India standards by a little more than 2 per cent. However, the story of literacy rate is completely different and leaves a painful impression when it is compared with that of Kerala (Table 13.5).

Rural-Urban gap in literacy rate is also a serious issue of concern in Assam. In 1991, the rural urban gap in literacy rate for the state of Assam was 30.07 per cent where as the corresponding rate for India as a whole was 28.39 per cent The gap, however, has fallen to 25.60 per cent in 2001 but it is still higher than all India standard of 21.20 per cent Again the falling rate of rural-urban disparity in literacy is also low in the State. Whereas the rural-urban literacy gap has fallen by 25.33 per cent in all India level, the rate for the State of Assam was only 14.87 per cent (Table 13.6).

Table 13.6: Rural-Urban Disparity in Literacy Rate

State/India	*1991*		*2001*		*Falling Rate in Disparity (1991–2001)*
	Rural	Urban	Rural	Urban	
Assam	49.32	79.39	59.70	85.30	14.87
India	44.69	73.08	58.70	79.50	25.33

Source: Census of India, 1991 and 2001.

Though the state government allocates huge amount of money in its budget for uplifting educational standard of the state by introducing different policies, but these policies are largely responsible for the malady. And the malady has its roots in the faulty economic policies as well. A large number of eligible children of school going age still remain out of school. The second NFHS survey indicates that 72 per cent of the population in the 6–17 age groups is attending school in Assam, which is the same as the all India average. This figure is, however, much lower than that of Kerala (91 per cent) and lower than all other North-Eastern States (80 per cent to 87 per cent). See Fig.13.3.

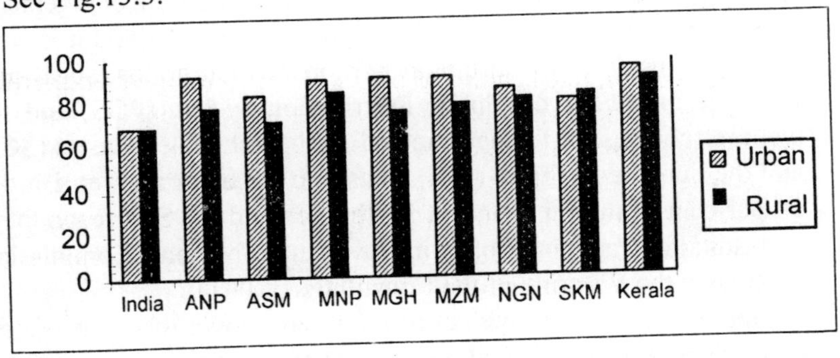

Fig. 13.3: Percentage population age 6–17 years attending school, 1998–99

The school completion rates are found to be very poor in the state of Assam in comparison to all India level. Median number of years of schooling completed among the male population age 6 and above is 4.4 compared to 8.1 for Kerala and 5.5 for all India. This low completion rate indicates high dropout rates of the students. One important reason for high dropout rate is the non-availability of educational facilities above the primary level in villages. A large percentage of the villages are still without an upper primary school. This especially accounts for a large chunk of girls dropping out after primary level. The parents are hesitant to send the girls to other villages for schooling, for fear of their security. Surveys indicate that the majority of school dropouts belong to the poorest and the least developed areas. The factors responsible for dropouts range from economic to cultural reasons. Children are pulled out of school due to economic reasons—they have to earn livelihood for their family. Gender discrimination against girl child is a major cultural issue.

The absence of women teachers in the village schools and the lack of separate toilet facilities for girls are other factors, which keep girls away from school. It is very important to tackle the problem of dropouts in order to achieve universal elementary education.

Corruption affects India at all levels of Governmental decision-making and in the distribution of state largesse. India is ranked 72nd out of 91 countries in the Corruption Perception Index, 2001, prepared by Transparency International (TI). Corruption in India not only poses a significant danger to the quality of governance, but also threatens in an accelerated manner the very foundations of its democracy and statehood. Corruption and indiscipline survive on each other's willingness to accommodate, tolerate and provide encouragement. Corruption affects governance in a significant manner and it is anti-poor. For instance, a substantial portion of food grains, sugar and kerosene meant for the Public Distribution System (PDS) and for welfare schemes for the poor, including the Scheduled Castes (SCs) and the Scheduled Tribes (STs), goes into the black market. Hardly 16 per cent of the funds meant for the STs and the SCs reach them (Consultation Paper on Probity in Governance, National Commission to Review the Working of the Constitution, 2001).

India's experience with corruption has shown that laws, rules, regulations, procedures and methods of transaction of Government business, sounds excellent, but they, cannot by themselves ensure effective and transparent administration, if the political and administrative leadership that is entrusted with their enforcement fails to do so and abuses its powers for personal gain (Sondhi, 2000). The state of Assam is not an exception to it and badly affected by corruption in all spheres of life. Perhaps the corruption at all levels is the main cause of the state's backwardness.

Besides, large scale corruption, problem of insurgency, negligence to agriculture and educational sector, environmental pollution, gender inequality, gap between rural and urban areas, consciousness of the people of the region etc. perhaps may be other constraints of economic development of the state.

Government Initiatives

Realizing the need for a focused attention to the North-east Region, the Department of Development of North-Eastern Region (DoNER) was created in September 2001 by an amendment to the Government of India's Allocation of Business Rule. The Department was formally inaugurated on 1st November, 2001. It was accorded the status of a Ministry *vide* Gazette notification of Government of India dated 27th May, 2004.

The challenge of development of the state arising from its unique situation has been accepted as a national task. Special focus has been laid on economic development of the state during various Plans and accordingly strategies have been formulated for removal of infrastructure bottlenecks, provision of basic minimum services, creating conducive environment for private investment etc. The handicap of resource-constraint has been met through special dispensation for the State and National Handloom Development Corporation will give priority in supply of hank yarn to the state to upgrade the skill of artisan, advance training programme would be organised. New emporia will be set up and financial assistance for renovation of existing emporia would be provided. The Central Silk Board will give priority to the state in implementation of its scheme. For development of markets in the state, possibilities of Export of products of the state to the neighbouring countries particularly, Bangladesh, Myanmar and Bhutan would be explored. However, different developmental schemes have been undertaken to upgrade the economic development of the state.

Besides its normal training courses for officials, elected representatives of Panchayats etc. the SIRD has been organizing regular training programmes to build the technical and managerial capacity of the rural people particularly youth, women, farmers etc. to help them to take up income generating activities in a productive and scientific manner. Through this process the institute has been making effort to facilitate the transfer of required technology for productive and sustainable management of income generating activities. The institute has been trying to give a new face to certain selected income generating activities traditionally taken up by the rural people in Assam. They are various agriculture activities, dairy farming, backyard poultry farming, pig rearing, handloom etc.

Backyard duck rearing is a traditional activity in rural Assam but, laying capacity of indigenous ducks is very low. The SIRD in association with Kerala Agriculture University introduced Chara Chemballi duck which has got a laying capacity of 200 eggs per year per duck. The institute introduced the duck in cluster of villages. Around 15000 women have been rearing ducks in SHGs after availing bank loan and other support from the institute. This effort of the institute have added value to a traditional income generating activities of Assam which in turn facilitated socio-economic upward mobility of the rural women in the clusters.

Schemes under the Ministry of Rural Development can be broadly classified into three parts: Employment Oriented Schemes, Rural Housing Scheme and Land related schemes.

Employment Oriented Schemes includes Swarnajayanti Gram Swarozgar Yojana, Sampoorna Grameen Rozgar Yojana and Jawahar Rozgar Yojana. The main aim of Swarnajayanti Gram Swarozgar Yojana *(SGSY)* scheme is to bring the poor into Self Help Groups (SHGs) through the process of social mobilization, training and capacity building along with provision of income through the process of social mobilization, training and capacity building along with provision of income generating assets. The scheme named Sampoorna Grameen Rozgar Yojana (SGRY) provides wage employment in rural areas along with the food security, creation of durable community, social and economic assets and infrastructure developments. It includes the rural poor (BPL and APL) who are in need of wage employment and are willing to take up manual or unskilled work. The programme of Jawahar Rozgar Yojana (JRY) is directed to provide wage employment to the rural poor during the lean agricultural season. It also aims to provide employment and create rural infrastructure through the Panchayati Raj Institutions (PRIs).

A number of schemes were introduced in relation to ***Rural Housing***: *Indira Awaas Yojana* (IAY) was launched with an objective to provide houses to members of S.T./S.C., free bonded labourers in the rural areas and also to non-S.T./S.C. rural poor lying below poverty line at free of cost. *Credit-cum-Subsidy Scheme for Rural Housing* (CSSRH) is introduced to help households (below the poverty line and above it) who could not be covered under Indira Awas Yojana, as either they do not fall within the range of eligibility or due to the limits imposed by the available budget. The target group covered under the scheme is rural households having an annual income of up to Rs. 32000 only. However, Below Poverty Line Rural Households, irrespective of castes, shall be given preference. *National Social Assistance Programme (NSAP)* is a social assistance programme for poor households including the aged population ensuring minimum national standards, in addition to the benefits that the States are currently providing or might provide in future. *Samagra Awaas Yojana* (SAY) aims to ensure integrated provision of shelter, sanitation and drinking water. The existing schemes of housing, drinking water and sanitation would follow the normal funding pattern. *Pradhan Mantri Gramodaya Yojana* (PMGY) scheme aims at sustainable human development at the village level. The PMGY envisages allocation of additional central assistance to the states/UTs for providing/improving the outlay of Basic Minimum Services including "Rural Shelter" in the rural areas. *Jawahar Gram Samridhi Yojana* (JGSY) which is the restructured, streamlined and comprehensive version of the erstwhile Jawahar Rozgar Yojana (JRY) has been launched to improve the quality of life of the rural poor by providing them additional gainful employment. The primary objective of JGSY is the creation of demand driven village infrastructure including durable assets to enable the rural poor to increase the opportunities for sustained employment. The secondary objective is the generation of supplementary employment for the unemployed poor in the rural areas.

Land Reforms in relation to Land Related Schemes covers the landless poor and involves restructuring agrarian relations to achieve an egalitarian social structure, elimination of exploitation in land relations; realizing the age-old goal of land to the tiller; increasing agricultural productivity and production and infusing equality in local institutions. Abolition of intermediary tenures; Tenancy reforms; Ceiling on agriculture holdings and re-distribution of surplus land; and updating and maintenance of land records are the main objectives of this programme. As a part of the wasteland development programme, *Integrated Wasteland Development Programme* (IWDP) includes checking land degradation, increasing biomass availability and putting wastelands to sustainable use. The scheme aims generation of employment in rural areas besides enhancing people's participation in the wasteland development programme sat all stages leading to equitable sharing of benefits and sustainable development.

Conclusion and Suggestion

The above analysis reveals that the rural Assam, in general, and the Rural Barak Valley, in particular still remains backward even after 60 years of independence. However, a strategy for development of rural economy and employment in the state needs with proper care and attention which may be outlined as follows:

Social sector development is most essential part of any long term strategy of rural development and reducing poverty. Efforts to reduce poverty cannot succeed unless social services like health, education and nutrition are made accessible to all levels in society.

If human resources are considered as assets, educational loans can also be grouped under the category of financial assistance. Irrigation facility if created with the help of financial assistance from bank, can improve productivity of the land where such facility is used.

However, local Government and NGOs can also play a useful role in this context. Panchayati Raj institutions came to be dominated by the socially or economically privileged sections in the local community with the consequence that the weaker groups—such as scheduled castes, scheduled tribes, and other poorer groups—were still deprived of its benefits.

Social tension is a consequence of the emerging response patterns to rural development. The major factors responsible for the deceleration of the state's economy include lack of adequate investment, low rate of capital formation, high growth rate of population, inadequate basic infrastructural facilities, weak communication linkages, perpetual flood problem, over dependence on agriculture, gross wastage of natural resources such as natural gas etc.

The growth rate in the last three Five Year Plans has been around a satisfactory 6 per cent per annum. But in case of Assam the growth rate has been much below the national figure. Special support will have to be given to achieve the targets set by the Planning Commission.

Unless the infrastructure is substantially improved, there would be only a limited prospect of horticulture and forest based products, if they are to be supplied to the rest of the nation raw and unprocessed (which, even if profitable, would not have been prudent). The same is true with floriculture and mushroom businesses. One need not over-stress that these products are either bulky or perishable in a short duration (or both). Good transportation and organized marketing system is called for Geographical conditions are again limiting factors.

It would therefore suggest starting of small-scale food processing, agro-based, horticulture-based and forest-based industries.

The growing unemployment among the educated youths has been a major area of concern for us. Therefore, the importance given to the creation of employment opportunities by giving topmost priority to the development of sectors, which have large potential for generation of employment opportunities by the Planning Commission, is very encouraging. In this vast globalizing era, the States like Assam cannot remain an isolated backwater. The large scale unemployment has resulted in serious law and order problems in the State, which needs to be addressed without any further delay.

Most of the Centrally Sponsored Schemes are funded jointly by the State Government and the Central Government. In case of rural development, the present policy of the Government of India requires 33.3 per cent State Government contribution against 75 per cent of the Central Government share in the schemes. Owing to chronic financial constraints, many state Governments have not been able to release the State Share timely. As a result, states like Assam are often made to forgo a large part of the Central Share in the scheme. In such a situation, apart from the states losing a major share of the Central fund for its rural development, this also affects the overall achievement for the Nation as a whole, since the earmarked fund remains unspent. Similar is the experience with many other Centrally Sponsored Schemes.

Rural entrepreneurship has impact on its beneficiaries with wide ranging benefits. Personnel and social benefits match the financial/ economic benefits accrued to individuals and their families. Seed production, nurseries, veterinary services practiced by the entrepreneurs has far reaching implications on the crop and animal husbandry activities of the region, through increased area, production and productivity.

Policy should be made to increase women's access to information and education so that they can equally play an active role in non-agricultural activities for which they have comparatively better chances of a fair wage or income generation.

A few appropriate forward looking policy initiatives may be suggested which would be necessary for the overall socio-economic development of the state.

The Government will have to continue to invest in social sectors like Health, Education, Rural Water Supply etc. The road connectivity is a prerequisite for development in all other sectors in the rural areas. Economic potential in rural areas can be realized, only, if we ensure rural connectivity by providing all weather roads. The power sector is important for development of both Industrial and the Agricultural sectors.

The thrust of development strategy in the village should also be to develop cottage industry in order to maximise employment. The cottage industries that could be set up are weaving, rice milling, bamboo work, pottery and handicrafts. Steps should also be taken to promote sericulture and community handloom. This can be done by making yarn available at cheaper rates, supplying of shuttle looms, and arranging for marketing of the finished products. This will generate additional income and at the same time will provide employment to the villagers. Improving food security at the household level is an issue of great importance for a backward region like the rural Assam, where thousands of poor suffer from persistent hunger and malnutrition.

There is an urgent need to take necessary steps to improve the health and hygienic infrastructure in the rural areas of Assam. The programmes relating to food security, health and pure drinking water facilities need to be implemented sincerely and honestly in different corners of the state for improving the welfare of rural households. There is need to integrate the youth into the development process in order to promote community development.

There is a strong need to shift our traditional production-oriented approach to market oriented approach. Agricultural growth need to be broad-based that can bring rural prosperity which will help in improving the quality of rural life in a sustainable manner. This requires paradigm shift in the agricultural policy to ensure food security, including nutritional security to every citizen of the region and more specifically in rural areas. The development of agriculture requires honest, sincere and efficient attention of the input and output management and policy makers. The policies for increasing agricultural production need to consider the issues related to post-harvest also in an integrated manner, which often has been a missing link.

Proper interventions should be made to encourage creation of value addition rather than mere increasing agricultural production. Food processing to capture the readymade demand in the country as well as abroad should be promoted. The tax structure for food sector should be streamlined to encourage farmers. Small and unorganized units should be organised into larger units to become global players and incentives should be given to encourage brand building and marketing. The employment policies for the rural women should be framed properly.

REFERENCES

Adelman, I. and Morris, C.T., (1973), *Economic Growth and Social Equity in Developing Countries,* Stanford University Press, Stanford.

Atkinson, A. B. (1970), *The Economics of Inequality,* Oxford University Press.

Bala, B. (1992), 'Role of Women in Agriculture—A Study of Kangra farms', Ph.D. Thesis (Unpublished) submitted to HPKV, Palampur (H.P.), pp.333

Desai, G.R. and Mahiuddin, A. (1992), 'Involving Women in Agriculture: Issues and Strategies—A Study Across Three States", *Journal of Rural Development,* NIRD, Hyderabad, Vol. II , No. 5, pp.637–651.

Dubey and Gangopadhyay, (1998), "Counting the Poor", *Sarvekshana* Analytical Report No. 1, Department of Statistics, Ministry of Planning, Statistics and Programmme Implementation, New Delhi.

Dutta, P.C. and Pradhan, B.C. (2004), 'Agricultural Development and Security of Life in North-East India' in *Food Security and Public Distribution System Today: Success and Failures* (ed.), Banerjee, Amalesh. Vedama Books (P) Ltd., New Delhi.

——(2006), 'Changing Agricultural Scenario in North-East India' in *Changing Agricultural Scenario in North-East India* (ed.) Deb, B. J. and Ray, B.D. Concept Publishing Company, New Delhi.

——(2007): "Gender Issues and Development in North-Eastern Region of India" in *Women Emancipation Focus North-East India* (ed.) Ray, A.K. and Ray, B.D. OM Publications, New Delhi.

Gengaje, R.K. and Setty, D. (1992),"A Model For Developing Agro-Enterprises Among Farm Women in Asia", *Journal of Rural Development,* NIRD, Hyderabad, Vol. 11, No.5

Ghose, A. (1993), "Social Security in an Insecure Economy", *EPW,* Nov. 6, pp. 2432–35.

Goswami, K. (2006), "Impact of Globalisation of Silk Industry in North-east India: An Assessment from Gender Perspectives":http://www.iitkgp.ac.in/facprofiles/showprofile.php? empcode= bVmVR

Hooda, I.S. (1997), "Rural Development—Some Conceptual Issues" in *Rural Development—Theory and Practice* (ed.) , Spellbound Publications, Rohtak.

Kothari, R. (1988), *State and Democracy,* Aganta Publications, New Delhi.

Lewis, A.W. (1965), *The Theory of Economic Growth,* George Allen and Unwin, London.

Myrdal, G. (1970), *The Challenge of World Poverty,* Penguin Publishers.

Martha, M. and Sen, A. (eds) (2003): *The Quality of Life,* Oxford University Press, Oxford.

Parikh, K. (1998), "Food Security—Individual and National", in Ahluwalia, I.J. and Little, I. M.D. (eds.), *India's Economic Reforms and Development: Essays for Manmohan Singh,* Oxford University Press.

Rutherford, Donald (2002) , *Routledge Dictionary of Economics,* Second Edition, (London, Rout ledge), pp. 521.

Schultz. W. (1960), "Capital Formation by Education", *Journal of Political Economy,* December, 1960.

Sharma, H.R. (2006), "Incidence of Indebtness in Rural India—A State Level Analysis", *Journal of Rural Development,* Vol. 25, (4), pp.507–536, NIRD.

Shukla, S.P. Commission (1997), *Report of the High Level Commission, Transforming the North-east-Tackling Backlogs in Basic Minimum Services and Infrastructural Needs, Part I,* Planning Commission. Government of India.

Singh, R.P. (2000), *Rural Prosperity and Agriculture—Some Emerging Issues, Rural Prosperity and Agriculture,* (ed.), National Institute of Rural Development, Hyderābad.

Sudha Rani, P. and Raju, V.T. (1991), "Participation of Women in Agricultural Operations", *Indian Journal of Extension Education,* Vol. 27, No.1 and 2, pp. 54.

Vyas, V.S. (1993), "New Economic Policy and Vulnerable Sections—Rationale for Public Interventions", *Economic and Political Weekly,* March 6.

World Bank (1986), "Poverty and Hunger—Issues and Options for Food Security in Developing countries", *World Bank Policy Study,* Washington.

Government of Assam (1999), *Economic Survey Assam, 1998–99,* Directorate of Economics and Statistics, Assam.

——(2001), *Vision Assam 2025.*

——(2001), '*Economic Survey and Annual Plans* of different years.

Government of India (2001), *Economic Survey 2000–2001,* Ministry of Finance.

——(2001), *Economic Survey*, Various Issues, Ministry of Finance.

NFHS-2, (2002), *National Family Health Survey 1998–99,* International Institute for Population Sciences, Mumbai, India.

SECTION V

Food and Agriculture

14

AGRICULTURAL DEVELOPMENT IN NAGALAND
Transition from Traditional Agriculture to Commercial Farming

B. KILANGLA JAMIR

Introduction

Raising agricultural productivity is crucial for raising income and standard of living of the rural population in Nagaland, which makes up a large fraction of the state's total population (82. 26%) and 68 per cent of the total workforce is engaged in agricultural activities in 2001. Increase in productivity and transformation of agricultural sector may thus provide other benefits to an underdeveloped economy like Nagaland by reducing rural migration, unemployment problem and strengthen the link in the development chain.

Agricultural transformation in developing economies may be described in terms of the gradual and sustained transition from subsistence to diversified and specialized production (Todaro, 2001). At the subsistence level, most output is for home consumption and a few stable food crops are the chief source of food intake. Productivity is low and only the simplest traditional method and tools are used. Capital investment is minimal, and land labours are principal factors of production. The law of diminishing returns is in operation as more labour is applied to shrinking parcels of land. With technological institutions, rigid social institutions, fragmented or non-availability of markets and infrastructure like ware housing, poor communication and transport networks between rural areas and urban centres, lack of access to institutional credit facilities and irrigation tend to inhibit the process of transaction from traditional to commercialized farming.

Despite the relative backwardness of production technologies, given the static nature of the present environment, the uncertainty that surround them, the farmers in subsistence sector do behave in a rational manner when confronted with stress or alternative opportunities.

The underdeveloped nature of the agricultural sector in Nagaland is revealed by the fact that out of a total cropped area of 3,63,420 hectare in 2003 only 17.74 per cent was irrigated mostly under terrace with a productivity of 1.79 tonne/ha (Paddy). The productivity of total crops was only 1.99 MT/ha and the cropping intensity was only 116 per cent in 2003. In Nagaland, majority of the farmers is engaged in shifting cultivation (Jhum), practicing on the hilly terrains, which is subsistence in nature, characterized by low productivity (1.33 tonne/ha paddy) using primitive tools. The major inputs are land and labour and mixed cropping pattern is being followed where the main crop is paddy because the primary concern of the farmers is meeting their family's basic food requirements. Under the system marketable surplus is negligible, yet the system has sustained the family requirements in the past.

However, in recent years there are pressures/stresses exerted upon the upland farmers in the state to increase productivity and to adopt more intensive and commercialized agricultural production system. One of the major factors that compel for the change at community level is the rapid population growth that exerts pressure on land. The state shares the highest population growth rate in the country over the last two decades (56.08% and 64.41%). Under the population pressure, the fallow period of Jhum has been reduced from 15 years and above to below 10 years, which is considered to be too short. The reduction in fallow years has reduced the soil's fertility thus reducing the productivity of the land. Moreover, under the National Forest Policy, the implementation of Jhum-plantation programme with long years of gestation period has resulted in further reduction of the Jhum cycle.

The retarded growth rate of agricultural productivity on the one hand and the increasing demand for food associated rapid population growth on the other and the growing need for additional income by the farmers in order to meet their other requirements have thus become a pressure on land. This has reduced the farmers under traditional agriculture to adapt to the changing situation by shifting towards cultivation of vegetables and cash crops. Accordingly, in Nagaland, the process of transition from pure subsistence agriculture to commercialization has been initiated in some villages in recent years by changing the cropping pattern where crops like tomatoes, potatoes, chilies, cabbages, and passion fruits are being increasingly cultivated for marketing purpose.

The success or failure of such effort of transformation in agricultural system will depends not only on the farmers' ability and skill in raising the productivity but even more on the social, commercial and institutional conditions under which he functions. If farmers have a reasonable access to credit, inputs, crop information, marketing facilities and infrastructure, there is no reason to assume that the traditional farmers will not respond to economic incentives and new opportunities that will improve their standard of living. Thus lack of innovation is not due to poor motivation or fear to change *per se* but inadequate opportunities.

To evaluate the trends of agricultural development in Nagaland the present discussion focuses on the following aspects, viz. changes in cropping pattern, growth trends of production, productivity and area and problems associated with transition from traditional to commercialization of agricultural sector.

Changes in Cropping Pattern

The cropping pattern indicates the production of are under different crops at a point of time in a region, which undergoes changes with the change in agricultural prices, technology, market demand, government policies and other related factors. It is also influenced by natural factors. The changes in cropping pattern may reflect the influence of changes in demand arising from an increase in income, population and also development of agro-based industries etc. With rising income, the demand for non-food crops may increase relatively faster and among the crops, demand may shift towards relatively superior cereals. These changes may reveal the stages of agricultural development and the nature of the economy of a region.

It is obvious that the larger the area under commercial crops, the higher will be the level of development, indicating higher specialization and commercialization of agricultural sector. Predominance of food crop is usually associated with subsistence farming. With marked improvement in farm operation a smaller area becomes sufficient to produce required food crops and thus, diverting the land area under cultivation to cultivate commercial crops (Singh and Sadhu, 1991).

In Nagaland, farmers generally produce food crops and also non-food crops of commercial crops. The major crops in the state are grouped under three broad categories as food grains, oil seeds and total commercial crops.

Table 14.1: Percentage of major crops to total cropped area in Nagaland (1961–2003)

Crop/Year	*1961*	*1971*	*1981*	*1991*	*2000*	*2003*
Food Grains	92.18	90.85	90.29	90.42	80.84	77.56
Oil Seeds	01.79	01.90	02.09	06.43	16.88	19.08
Total Comm. Crops	06.03	07.25	07.62	03.15	02.28	03.36
Total Crop	100	100	100	100	100	100

Source: Statistical Hand Books, Government of Nagaland, Kohima. 1965, 1973, 1981, 1996, 2001, 2004.

From Table 14.1, it may be observed that the food crops (cereal and pulses) predominates the cropping pattern in the state. Its relative share has however declined from 92.18 per cent in 1961 to 77.56 per cent in 2003, indicating a declining rate of 0.36 per cent per annum.

The relative share of cropped area under oil seeds (ground nuts, soyabean, sesame, sunflower, castor, rape seed, mustard and linseeds) has increased consistently and significantly from 01.79 per cent in 1061 to 19.08 in 2003, increasing at a rate of 2.44 per cent per annum. The percentage of area under commercial crops (fibres, sugar cane, potatoes, tea etc.) has increased up to 1981 with a share of 7.62 per cent; thereafter, it has declined to 2.28 in 2000 and in 2003 it increased to 3.36 per cent, exhibiting a fluctuating trend.

The increase in relative share of cropped land under non-food crops in recent years may be an indication of agricultural sector moving towards commercialization although slow and modest. The consistent shift in favour of oil seeds implies a move from low to high value crops, which might have occurred as a result of farmers' response towards changes in demand and prices. Nevertheless, the food crops still dominate the cropping pattern in the state and occupy 77 per cent of the cropped area whereas all other crops taken together accounts for only 2.44 per cent. Among the individual crops, rice being the stable food of the state, paddy accounts for 47.23 per cent of the total cropped area, followed by oil seeds (19.08 per cent) and maize (12.5 per cent).

These facts reveal that in Nagaland agriculture is still at subsistence level where the primary concern of the farmers is meeting their family food requirements. The process of commercialization has been initiated but still insignificant and slow.

Production and Productivity

For meeting the needs of the farmers' family requirement as well as to satisfy the global food requirements, any agricultural system must be capable of maintaining its productivity relatively high. Increase in yield has a greater significance for rural development as of will generate marketable surplus to earn additional income which may be invested in creating rural infrastructure and services. The trends in production and productivity of agricultural produce indicate the effort put in by the economy to meet the minimum food requirement of the people.

Table 14.2: Area, Production and Productivity

Crop	*Item*	*1961*	*1971*	*1981*	*1991*	*2001*	*2003*
Food Grains	Area	88991	91578	139655	181330	228174	248000
	Production	63530	74001	115525	210750	323570	388000
	Yield	0.71	0.8	0.82	1.16	0.14	1.56
Comm-ercial Crops	Area	7542	9218	15004	19210	10360	61100
	Production	44550	54310	152075	144550	122660	229400
	Yield	5.9	5.89	10.13	7.52	11.83	3.75
Total	Area	96533	100706	154659	200540	238534	309100
	Production	108080	128311	267600	355300	446230	617400
	Yield	1.12	1.27	1.73	1.77	1.87	1.99

Note: Area in ha. Production in tones and Yield in tones per ha.
Source: Statistical Handbooks, Govt. of Nagaland, Kohima. 1965, 1973, 1981, 1996, 2001, 2004.

The total crop area has increased by 220 per cent from 1961 to 2003, shows an annual growth rate of 5 per cent, while the yield has increased by 68 per cent only with an annual growth rate of 1.59 per cent. Therefore, the increase in total production may be due to increase in area rather than increase in yield.

The increase in area under food grains is 178.67 per cent, showing an annual growth rate of 4.15 per cent and the productivity/yield has increased consistently by 2.7 per cent per annum. Therefore, increase in yield and area combined together must have contributed to the growth of total production of food crops by 11.87 per cent per annum.

For commercial crops, the area has increased at a rate of 16.51 per cent per annum while the yield has shown a negative growth rate of –0.84 per cent per annum. Therefore, the growth in production by 2.20 per annum may be contributed by increase in area alone.

It is observed that the relationship between production and area is positive while the relationship with yield is positive but weak/ negative. In respect of total agricultural crops, the correlation coefficient value is 0.99 for production and area, while it is 0.91 with yield. Under food crops, the value of correlation coefficient is 0.98 in respect of production and area, while with yield, it is only 0.24. Under commercial crop the value of correlation coefficient is –0.08. Thus, the growth in total production is mainly due to increase in area rather than improvement in yield as the improvement in yield is determined by technological innovation and improvement in farm practices and other inputs besides natural factors. As such, the green revolution has bypassed the agriculture in the state and therefore, has no meaning to the farmers who are under subsistence agriculture.

Transition towards Commercialization

A survey was conducted by the department of Economics, Nagaland University during 2006–07 at Longkhum village, Mokokchung district, Nagaland. The village is located about 12 km. away from Mokokchung town, and situated at an altitude of 1600 m. above the sea level. It was found that farmers under traditional agriculture are responding rationally to the stress and opportunities. The Jhum cycle has reduced from 15 years and above to an average of 10–12 years, and thus cultivation of paddy on Jhum fields does not fulfil the family needs; therefore, some farmers have started to shift the Jhum land to vegetable crops cultivated for commercial purpose that give a higher income to the farmer. Thus, moving from subsistence cultivation to diversification and commercialization of shifting cultivation has been evident in the village.

Taking advantage of its proximity and easy access to the urban market of Mokokchong and the suitability of soil and climatic conditions, a few farmers have started to cultivate vegetables like tomatoes, potatoes, cabbage and chilies for commercial purpose, bringing in a significant change in a cropping pattern. In 2006 there were only 20 households engaged in the activity. Encouraged by the profitability and opportunity of earning additional income, the number of households has increased to 92 which constitute 26 per cent of the total households of the village in 2007.

The method of cultivation is almost similar to paddy cultivation, purely organic and non-mechanized and after every two years of cultivation shifts to a new plot. The average size of the farm under vegetable crops is about 1 hectare. Table 14.3, indicates the level of productivity and the relative share of cultivated area under different crops in the village.

Table 14.3: Percentage of Area and Productivity in Longkhum Village

Crop	*% area in Ha.*	*Productivity in M.T.*
Potato	26	5.92
Tomato	35	4.95
Chili	13	2.96
Cabbage	26	29.6

Source: Survey

Some Problems

Transportation and Marketing

Lack of transport facilities has impeded the transport of the produce to the market on time and other markets farther than Mokokchung town. Besides, there is no cold storage and ware housing facilities; therefore, the produce gluts in the market in the peak season which reduces the price and about 30 per cent of the produce goes waste, because these crops are highly perishable in nature which discourages the farmers to increase productivity.

Credit and Subsidy

Farmers do not have access to institutional credit and therefore depend on village money lenders. Despite the declaration of the village as 'Vegetable Village' and 'Potato Seeds Village' by the state government, no financial assistance and subsidies has been provided except distribution of seeds of inferior quality. Therefore, farmers are unable to make investment for improvement of the farm and to improve transportation system that will enable them to explore other markets.

Extension, Research and Development and Services

Due to inadequate extension services, farmers are ignorant about uses of farm residues as manure that will enhance productivity. As such, they find it impossible to cultivate the same plot for more than two successive years. Moreover, they require knowledge about controlling pests and disease management.

Also findings of research and development have not been disseminated to the farmer. Thus the system of farming is based on the traditional knowledge and crude method. Further, there is no grading and standardization of the produce.

Lack of Organization

The farming community in the village is not well organized and there is no co-ordination among them; therefore, the middlemen take undue advantage through manipulation of prices.

Conclusion

The task of transforming traditional agriculture is not simply a question of land reform or price policy. The price poly is to enhance productivity and attract an adequate share of investment resources. The secret of productivity lies in enhancing the efficiency of the agriculture system through improvements in the quality of inputs, by application of advanced knowledge and modern technology on the broad front.

Transition commercial farming is possible only if the farmers have the inputs to raise productivity and credit to purchase these inputs. Marketing facilities are equally important so as to establish the backward and forward linkages associated with the production process in the form of finance, machinery, fertilizer, seeds and so on at the input end. At the output end, the processing, manufacturing and marketing of the product need to be developed.

Expansion of communication to create outlets and market for surplus production and to maintain continuous supply of inputs is required. The present world economic scenario calls for emergence of reliable middlemen or export-import merchants acting as agents between the world and the local economies.

The problem with the transformation of traditional farming system is not the unwillingness of the farmers to accept new ideas but the public expenditure and the organization/institution of particular public services and activities to serve the agricultural sector. Agricultural research and technology suited to dry farming/local conditions have been neglected; so also the investment in people to improve human capacity in agriculture. Development of infrastructure for enhancing farm productivity is also equally important.

REFERENCES

Meier, G.M. and Rucha, J. E. (2000), *Leading Issues in Economic Development*, Oxford University Press.

Sadhu, A.N. Singh and Amarjit. (1989), *Fundamentals of Agricultural Economics*, Himalaya Publishing House.

Todaro, M.P. (2001), *Economic Development in the Third World*, Orient Longman.

15

PARTICIPATION OF WOMEN IN AGRICULTURE IN ARUNACHAL PRADESH
With Special Emphasis on West Siang District

RAM KRISHNA MANDAL

Concept of Participation

Participation is a tool to attain several distinct objectives. Once used and properly handled, the participatory approach can lead to changes in knowledge, attitudes, skills and distribution of power across individuals and community for their own development. "Differential degree" and "extent of participation" in development can be described as follows: (i) The mere use of a service; (ii) Participation through the contribution (or extraction) of resources, materials and labour; (iii) Participation through "attendance" often implying passive acceptance of decisions made by others: (iv) Participation through consultation on a particular issue; (v) involvement in the delivery of service, often as partner: (vi) Involvement as implementers of delegated powers; and (vii) Most completely participation in real decision-making at every stage—the study of feasibility, planning, implementation and evaluation" (UNICEF, 1986).

Women are an integral part of every society. The status of women in society is directly linked to social and cultural traditions, stages of economic development achieved, educational levels, attitude of the society towards women, social and religious taboos, women's own awareness, and political attainments of women in society. Such factors affect the national and also regional characteristics of the status of women. The economic status of women is determined by the role played by them in carrying on economic and non-economic activities in society. The nature and type of economic and non-economic role played by women have undergone continued transformation in accordance with the changes in socio-economic factors, education levels and technological developments and with the changing concepts regarding the extent to which women's contribution is considered desirable and necessary.

It is almost universally accepted that the woman's primary role is performed specially as a home-maker end it is for the man to provide subsistence to his family. Under certain conditions, in addition to the role of a house-keeper, women also participate sometimes in the gainful activities of the community. Thus, we find that some women work and some do not. The question—"Why does a man work"—is not a significant one because he is regarded as the natural bread earner and, therefore, he is expected to provide subsistence to his family. However, the question—"Why does a woman work"—assumes special significance when the whole range of her activities centres on household chores. Although a large number of women are engaged in household activities, they are significantly contributing to the monetary and non-monetary inputs of our national income because their works, in the context of the socio-economic setting, is generally either under-valued or not taken into account in the labour sector, in spite of fact that all their activities are productive. In this respect, the observation of Human Development Report, 1993 is worth mentioning "Women are often invisible in statistics. If women's unpaid housework were counted as productive output in national income accounts, global output would increase by 20%–30% (Human Development Report, 1993:25). In fact, the spatial variation in the level of female participation in work has started drawing greater attention since the seventies. Although sociologists and economists (Boserup, 1970; Gulati, 1975; Sundaram, 1989; Nayyar, 1989) have analyzed the conditions and factors which influence female participation in work, their studies are based on analysis of data for a state, while others relate to the country as a whole. There cannot be two opinions that the majority of women apparently work out of economic necessities; at the same time the importance of socio-cultural factors cannot be overlooked, particularly while considering the female participation in economic activities. Another interesting aspect of female participation has been its wide variation from country to country and from region to region within a country.

The position of women and their status in any society are an index of its civilization. Women are to be considered as equal partners in the process of development. But, because of centuries of exploitation and subjugation, Indian women have remained at the receiving end. In this context, in order to provide a big push, institutional support is necessary to empower Indian women in general and rural women in particular. Women empowerment demands a "Life-cycle" approach where empowerment is viewed as a process and not as an event, which challenges traditional power equations and relations. Empowerment in its simplest form means redistribution of power that challenges the male dominance. This does not, however, mean that the empowerment process adopts an antagonists approach. It is only to enable women to supplement and co-ordinate with men. Empowerment is an active process of enabling women to realize their identity, potentiality and power in all spheres of their lives (Sharma, 1992).

Our former President A.P.J. Abdul Kalam has said that empowering women was a prerequisite for creating a good nation, "when women are empowered, society with stability is assured. Empowerment of women is essential as their thoughts and their value systems lead the development of a good family, good society and ultimately a good nation". Education is a milestone for women's empowerment because it enables them to respond to opportunities, to challenge their traditional roles and to change their lives. Similar ideas were supported by the International Conference on women in 1994. It was said there that education is one of the most important means of empowering women with the knowledge, skills and self-confidence necessary to participate fully in the development process. Educating woman benefits the whole society. It has a more significant impact on poverty and development than men's education.

Social change is possible only by empowering and educating women. Jawaharlal Nehru once said, "To awaken the people, it is woman who is meant to be awakened; once she is on the move, the family moves, village moves and the nation moves". Swami Vivekananda also once said, "There is no chance for the welfare of the world unless the condition of women is improved. It is not possible for a bird to fly on one wing". Likewise no nation can flourish keeping half of its population in negligence and ignorance, as women constitute half of its human capital. A modern society cannot achieve all-round development without utilizing the talent of its women.

In the case of India in its broad regional spectrum, we find that the Southern and North-Eastern States have a higher female participation than the Northern States. This has led Boserup to conclude that the influence from West Asian culture was strong in the Northern part of India-Pakistan subcontinent and only marginal in the Southern part (Boserup, 1971:71). In fact, the Southern and North-Eastern States have a pattern more like that of South-east Asian countries. For example, according to the 1991 census, the female participation is the highest in Mizoram (43.12%) followed by Manipur (38.96%) and Arunachal Pradesh (37.49%) and it is the lowest in Punjab (14.48%). In 2001 population census, work participation rate in Arunachal Pradesh has still decreased to 36.5 per cent of the total population of the state. Thus, the variations in the level and extent of female participation in economic activity are conspicuous at each level, starting from the regional level to the district level.

In Arunachal Pradesh, the female marginal workers in 1981 census were 14,995, it fell down to only 1117 in 1991, and it went up to 41,667 in 2001. However, the female main workers have only marginally increased from 1,18,604 in 1981 to the total of 1,42,100 in 1991, and 1,89,290 in 2001 population census.

Table 15.1: Sectoral classification of female main workers of A.P. 1981–2001 (percentage)

Year	*Primary*	*Secondary*	*Tertiary*
1981	95.12	1.99	2.89
1991	89.02	1.81	9.17
2001	82.01	2.05	15.94

Sources: 1. Census of India, 1981 series—(1), Primary Census Abstract, General Population Table Part-II, (B) (i) (2) Census of India, 1991 and 2001.

Table 15.1 shows that during the 1981 Census year more than 95 per cent of the female workers were engaged in the primary sector. However, during the next census i.e., 1991, there was a significant reduction in female workers in the primary sector, and still more declined to 82.01 per cent in 2001. Thus, in Arunachal Pradesh we find that there is steady decline of work force participation rate (WPR) of females and at the same time there is significant decline of female workers in the primary sector. In this connection, the relationship between WPR of females and economic development through the "U" shaped curve (Anker, 1981:27) can be referred to. According to this theory, in the initial stages of development, the female participation rate is higher and they mainly work as family workers in the primary sector. In the second stage of development the participation rate falls due to a lack of their geographical mobility from rural to urban areas. In the third stage, the female participation rate increases particularly in the secondary and tertiary sectors because of the spread of education and change in the attitude of the people.

As per the State Forest Report, 1999 published by the Forest Survey of India, forest cover of Arunachal Pradesh is 68951sq. km. accounting for 82.21 per cent of its total geographical area. The recorded forest area of the state is 51,540 sq. km. which is about 62 per cent of its total geographical area. Thus, the state is fortunate to have such high percentage of its area under valuable forests cover against the national percentage of 23.28. Again, out of its area, 70 per cent constitutes broad and narrow valleys, 10 per cent foothills and flat areas and 20 per cent constitutes snow clad peak areas. The agricultural operations are confined to only 5 per cent of the total geographical area, out of which 62 to 65 per cent is under shifting cultivation *(jhum)*.

It is known through archaeological discoveries that in the Neolithic period around 1000 B.C., man's attitude to his environment underwent fundamental changes. It might be an accident when he took hoe from bow i.e., from hunter he became food producer. Man began to plant, cultivate and improve species of edible plants by selection. This is regarded as the first step in the transition from food gathering/hunting to food production. Among the food plants cultivated by the Neolithic people, rice, wheat, barley, millet, maize, yam and sweet potatoes provided staple food.

Almost all the tribes except the Apatanis and Khamptis in Arunachal Pradesh practise shifting cultivation. The Apatanis and

Khamptis are engaged in settled cultivation. The *jhumias* (the man who practices *jhum* cultivation is called the *jhumia*) produce all the crops, which they need. This type of cultivation is widespread among the hill dwellers of Assam, Meghalaya, Nagaland, Mizoram and Arunachal Pradesh. It is known in different areas by a variety of local names. In North-east India, it is called *Jhum*. In these wide-spread areas, there is a remarkable uniformity of the method of cultivation. It is the most primitive form of agriculture which is still in vogue in most parts of the North-Eastern Hill Region of the country. According to 2001 Census, about 80 per cent of the State's population are living in rural areas and all are directly and indirectly involved in *jhum* cultivation.

The shifting cultivation is also called slash and burn method of cultivation. It is a labour-intensive process of farming with extensive use of land. It is also claimed that slash and burn agriculture leads to deterioration of the vegetative cover on the hills: forest lands degenerate into infertile grassland and barren land space. Therefore, it is contended that this system of agriculture is unsustainable and economically impoverishing the tribal people who depended on it. The technology being primitive, the level of production and income are very low. It occupies a distinct place in the socio-economic fabric of the tribal economy of this state. The *jhumia* selects the field on the slope of the hill on rotation basis. Due to deterioration in fertility of soil the *jhumia* is compelled to shift his cultivation to another plot. He keeps the land fallow for a number of years for regeneration of forests. Again he uses the same land. That is why, this process is also called shifting cultivation. Its chief characteristics are: (i) Slash and burn operation of vegetal species; (ii) Use of human labour as chief input; (iii) Non-employment of animals; and (iv) Use of simple implements such as dibble stick, scrapper, etc. (Table 15.2).

The cycle of agricultural operation in all these areas of North-Eastern Region is marked by the following stages:

- Selecting the forested hilly track,
- Cleansing the forest tract by cutting down the jungle during December-January,
- Drying and burning of fallen shrubs/trees into ashes during February-March,

- Fencing the cleared plots,
- Worship and sacrifice,
- Dibbling and sowing of seeds for mixed cropping,
- Weeding operation,
- Watching and protecting the crops against depredation by wild animals, pests, etc.,
- Harvesting, and
- Threshing and storing.

Table 15.2: Shifting cultivation in the North East Region

State	*Annual Area under Shifting cultivation (sq.kms.)*	*Fallow Period (in years)*	*Minimum Area under Shifting cultivation one time or other (sq.kms.)*	*No. of families practicing shifting cultivation*
Arunachal Pradesh	700	3 –10	2,100	54,000
Assam	696	2–10	1,392	58,000
Manipur	900	4–7	3,600	70,000
Meghalaya	530	5–7	2,650	52,290
Mizoram	630	3–4	1,890	50,000
Nagaland	190	5–8	1,913	1,16,046
Tripura	223	5–9	1,115	43,000
Total	**3869**		**14,660**	**4,43,336**

Source: The Task Force Report on Shifting Cultivation, Ministry of Agriculture, 1983.

Table 15.3 shows the position of different states of North-East India in respect of only shifting, shifting combined with permanent, permanent and not doing any cultivation.

Agriculture is still the single largest livelihood system and occupies an important place in the economy of Arunachal Pradesh and forms a major occupation of the people of the state. According to 2001 census about 79.66% of the State's populations live in rural areas and 58.44% of the total workers are cultivators. It is not only the main source of employment, income and food, but it is also the main culture for rural families. It is seen that almost all rural women are involved in agriculture. Though women play a significant and crucial role in agriculture and allied fields, they are ignored. By and large they have remained 'invisible workers'. Because of low 'visibility' of their contributions, they are not regarded as equal partners in the developmental process. They work longer and harder than men. They also work on more tasks than men. Usually, the low income, low skilled and low productivity jobs are female specific. Almost always, labour intensive, back breaking and time consuming activities are the domain of the weaker sex (females).

Table 15.3: Shifting, Permanent and Combined Cultivation in the Tribal Society

State	*Percentage of tribal households in respect of cultivation*			
	Shifting cultivation	*Shifting combined with permanent cultivation*	*Permanent cultivation*	*Not doing any cultivation*
Arunachal Pradesh	33.50	24.20	29.60	12.70
Assam	18.60	24.00	29.50	07.70
Manipur	46.10	24.50	15.40	04.10
Meghalaya	15.40	38.20	21.60	14.80
Tripura	12.10	11.60	53.20	23.10

Source: Patnaik, 1984.

Household and community roles among the Arunachalee Tribes are also sharply gendered. Men and boys may hunt and fish, but good production and preparation is the women's responsibility. Men will perform certain specific tasks like slashing the trees for *jhuming* or using the plough for settled cultivation. Traditionally only men handled the spade to prepare the fields. But this seems to be changing as men withdraw from farming operations. The author saw many women in the fields using spades. Generally, tasks which require more physical strength are undertaken by men such as cleaning of jungle for *jhum* cultivation, setting fire to it before the seed is sown, collection of house-building materials from jungle etc. But the success of agricultural operation depends upon women as they are the ones who carry out most of the work like sowing, weeding, harvesting etc. There is no division of labour as such between married and unmarried women.

Geographical Area of the Study

The West Siang District extends over an area of 12,006 sq. km. approximately in the central region of Arunachal Pradesh bounded by Tibet (China) in the north, Assam in the south, Upper Siang District and East Siang District in the East, and Upper Subansiri District and Lower Subansiri District in the West. Its topography is mainly mountainous inter-spread with gentle slopes and low-lying valleys kissing the plains of Assam. The altitude of this district varies from 200 m. to 1890 m. above the sea level. West Siang District comprises five sub-divisions and twenty circles with headquarters at Galo.

Of all tribal groups of West Siang District, the Galo ranks first in population and are predominant at Galo, Basar, Tirbin, Liromoba, Darak, Kaying and Likabali circles and sub-division-wise they are predominant in Galo, Basar and Yomcha sub-divisions. Therefore, our study is confined only to Galo women.

Agricultural Work of Galos

The main occupation of the Galos is agriculture both *jhum* and wet rice cultivation. In *jhum* cultivation, which is also called 'slash and burn' method of cultivation, several crops like paddy, maize, millet, chilli, bean, pumpkin, banana, sugarcane etc. are grown. Of late, people find it more reliable and assured production, to adopt wet rice cultivation Nevertheless, the *jhum* is still very popular. Because of its multiple cropping pattern, there is lesser chance of crop failure in *jhum* and always serves as support in the lean period. That is why; the people are still in the stage of *jhum* cultivation with a dibble. The whole area is a network of hills, on the slopes of which, the Galos have their agricultural fields. Some of the fields are even at a height of 4,000 to 5,000 feet. After the selection of sites for cultivation, the trees in the fields are felled, generally in the month of February and the whole area is cleared of grasses and creepers. These cut trees are left in the field for nearly a month to dry and by March, they are fired. Efforts are made to see that the whole field is burnt together. The Galo area has a heavy and continuous rainfall, March is generally a dry month having clear sun shine. After the fire is out, the products of this *jhum* fire are utilized in a number of ways. The ashes are left strewn all over the field, which serve as manure. The un-burnt or charred wood is utilized in three different ways: the big and massive logs are used for their indigenous methods of contour-logging, which, to some extent, checks the soil erosion; the thicker sticks are used for fencing the field; and finally, the smaller ones are used as fuel, which are carried everyday by women in their conical baskets, hung on the back, while returning from the field. At the time of felling the trees, cleaning the jungle, setting fire and fencing the fields, efforts are made to see that all the villagers do their respective work together, as these occupations are considered the responsibility of the whole village. Care, however, is taken to ensure that no *hilok* trees are cut, as these trees are believed to be the abodes of spirits. If, however, their cutting is essential, as it often becomes so, due to their abundance in the jungle, offerings of fowls and eggs are made to the spirits, so that they may not get annoyed and cause damage to the crops. *Pute Sidi*, another spirit, believed to reside on the trees in the jungle, is also propitiated with sacrifices.

A major portion of their time is devoted to agricultural activities, which demand a great deal of labour and hard work. Co-operation has its inherent social and psychological advantages. During the work, they feel that one is for all and all for one. Big plots, cleared in this way, contain a number of smaller plots, individually owned by different families. The individual families take care of their own plots. Only the fencing is jointly made, as it caters to the common interest of all the plot-holders. But an individual has every right, guaranteed by social sanctions, to requisition the help of his co-villagers for sowing or harvesting his plot, in case he falls short of the required hands and in return, he has to entertain those, who participate in such activities, in a feast.

Crops

Together with paddy and maize is also sown in the same field. Maize is sown in separate holes and millet is strewn all over the field. Maize, however, is sown in three different ways; firstly, it is sown separately in the month of January and February; it is also sown in the same field with paddy or a little after the paddy has been sown; and finally, it is sown in an altogether separate field, depending upon the condition and the quality of the soil, in the months of June and July. Brinjal, mustard, Chilli and Giyi (Brassica species) seeds are also sown at that time. The latter, however, is not utilized for extracting oil, but only the leaves are taken as vegetable. All these crops are sown together, and thrive almost at the same time. This mixed cultivation meets three major needs: food from paddy and maize; drink from millet; and vegetables from brinjal, mustard, chilli and giyi.

The corn is ripe by September-October, and then starts the harvesting. The time of harvesting may vary according to the time of felling the trees, burning them and sowing seeds. These are dependent on the rains and the time varies from area to area. Harvesting implements are conspicuous. In the harvesting of paddy, the long conical basket is suspended from the shoulders on the back. Ears of paddy are picked out by hand and put in it. When the basket is full of ears of paddy, it is brought to the house made in the agricultural field and collected on the bamboo made mat. Some paddy ears are taken separately on the mat and pressured by feet frequently changing their position till the paddy is separated from the ears. After the harvest is over, the grains are brought to the village and stored in the granary.

Keeping in view the importance of this sector the State Government has always given priority to various agricultural programmes in development plans for attaining self sufficiency in food grains. But the progress/improvement in this sector has not been up to the expectation. The main reasons for this are its topography which is a hilly one, predominance of shifting cultivation, lack of irrigation facilities, lack of technical know-how etc. However, efforts are being made to dissuade the people from shifting cultivation and induce them to take up permanent cultivation, where possible, and proper utilization of available cultivable land. In the beginning, the people showed a tenacious attachment to their indigenous methods of cultivation but, with the gradual propagation of the idea through the villages, some amount of success has been achieved. But the nature of land does not provide scope for bringing about permanent cultivation on a large scale, so that it can completely replace shifting cultivation. In the areas, where there is no scope for plough cultivation, terracing of the *jhum* fields with provision for irrigation by tapping the hill streams has been done. People, as a whole, still show a tendency to cling to their own traditional methods, having socio-religious sanctions.

Objective and Hypotheses

The objective of the study was to investigate the work participation of Galo women in agriculture in West Siang District of Arunachal Pradesh.

In the background of the above consideration and the objective, the research study proposed to examine the following hypotheses during the course of the study:

(i) In subsistent tribal economies, the division of labour is more demographic in nature, i.e., based on age and sex parameters.

(ii) A large part of the work performed by the male in general and female folk in particular are confined to land resources particularly agriculture and forest. The extent of availability of these resources for livelihood as well as for commercial purposes likely to determine the variation in the nature and pattern of work.

Methodology and Data Source

It is said that social science research is an enquiry or investigation, which has clearly defined parameters. It is a system of critical, controlled and empirical enquiry. There are three approaches of social science research, which the researchers are to follow in the field of research i.e., qualitative, quantitative and action research. The researcher has adopted the quantitative as well as qualitative approach in the present study. But the quantitative approach of research goes with the experimental research and survey studies.

Moreover, the selection of method of research depends upon the nature of the problem in hand. The plan of works and the procedures of this study were formulated eventually through a format questionnaire-*cum*-interview schedule related to the predefined factors considered for observation. We selected five different villages in a circle in such a way that each village was chosen more or less equidistantly to each other. From each village of that circle 10 women were randomly sampled and interviewed for the collection of the requisite data in such a way that 3 were from the age group of (15–25) years, 4 from the age group of (25–35) years and 3 from the age group of (35–45) years. We gave more weightage to respondents of age group (25–35) years because they suited our objectives more accurately. Respondents of age groups (15–25) years are more advanced and those of age group (35–45) years or above are traditional; that is why, both were given less weightage for our study. In this way 10 × 5=50 Galo women were selected from each circle. In the West Siang District, seven circles out of twenty circles where Galo are predominant were selected. In this way 50 × 7=350 Galo women were interviewed.

The inclusion of villages under study was subject to distance from the district head quarters, mode of communication and concentration of people. The women were randomly sampled and interviewed for the collection of the requisite data. This study was based on both primary and secondary data. While secondary data had been collected from different reports and journals, primary data had been collected through personal investigation with the help of structured questionnaire and participation method. Samples had been selected through random sampling technique without replacement.

Field Survey

The field survey was conducted in the month of January 2007 only in some selected villages in the district of West Siang, where the Galo people are more in number. The report has been presented in Table 15.4.

Table 15.4 shows that there is difference in perception according to age composition among the little age (15–25), middle age (25–35) and old age (35–45) groups. None of the respondents was below 15 years or above 45 years of age. The women between the age group of (15–45) years generally remain very active in agricultural work. The highest number of respondents (54.3%) belonged to the age group of (35–45) years engaging in the agricultural activities regularly. The lowest number of respondents (0.95%) also belonged to the age group of (35–45) never taking part in agricultural activities. The respondents who worked regularly in agricultural field were 19% in the age group of (15–25) years, 41.4% in the age group of (25–35) years and 54.3% in the age group of (35–45) years. The respondents who engage frequently in the agricultural activities were 33.3% in the age group of (15–25) years, 30.7% in the age group of (25–35) years and 23.8%

in the age group of (35–45) years while engagement in this respect occasionally were 37% in the age group of (15–25) years, 25.7% in the age group of (25–35) years and 20.9% in the age group of (35–45) years.

Table 15.4: Distribution of Work Participation in Agriculture among the Women at different Age Group

Area under survey	*Age group*	*Res-pondent*	*Agricultural Activities*			
			Regu-larly	*Freq-uently*	*Occasi-onally*	*Never*
West Siang	15–25	105 (100)	20 (19)	35 (33.3)	39 (37)	11 (10.4)
	25–35	140 (100)	58 (41.4)	43 (30.7)	36 (25.7)	3 (2.1)
	35–45	105 (100)	57 (54.3)	25 (23.8)	22 (20.9)	1 (0.95)
Total		**350**	**135 (38.57)**	**103 (29.42)**	**97 (27.71)**	**15 (4.28)**

Note: Figures in parenthesis indicate percentage.

If we want to see the respondents who worked never in the agricultural fields, we got the lowest percentage i.e., 0.95% in the age group of (35–45) years, highest percentage i.e., 10.4% in the age group of (15–25) years and 2.1% in the age group of (25–35) years. As overall observations, we saw that 38.57% women were engaged in agricultural activities regularly, 29.42% women were engaged frequently and 27.71% were engaged occasionally of all the three age groups. But 4.28% of women were never engaged in agricultural activities.

Findings

The percentage of women engaged regularly in agricultural activities was increasing with the increase in age groups and those were decreasing with the decrease in the age groups in the district. As explanation we can say that the lower age groups are diverting themselves from the agricultural activities with the impact of globalization and development of education in the state. It was also seen that the women who occasionally or never worked in agricultural field were mostly living in the urban and semi urban areas engaged in government jobs or in private business leading very busy lives. This study, however, focused on the point that the Galo women of the study area enjoyed lower status than men despite their hard work in household and agricultural fields.

In addition to the work at home, the rural women played an important role particularly in agricultural production which was the main occupation of the villagers. Most of them were directly or indirectly engaged in agricultural activities. A few of the village women were doing salaried jobs like clerks, school teachers etc.

Conclusion and Way for Development

Men dominate women, but women also have ways of getting things done according to their desires and wishes. Indian women present a paradoxical picture for the interpreter of Indian society. The view is that the Indian women are disadvantaged and discriminated against behavioural reality, while her participation in the highest political and social spheres is another undeniable reality.

Efforts should be made so that cognitive empowerment of women can carry her to self-confidence and self-reliance, i.e., psychological empowerment which can lead to further social action or economic activity that stimulates political and economic empowerment. Different academic strategies and other plans are drawn out for this purpose. But training and education for empowerment of women in the state result in individual empowerment and social transformation whereby, women have more control over their lives and more roles in the changing society to eliminate or reduce gender bias and discrimination.

To maintain the proper quantitative balance between various economic activities is one of the principal functions of the economic system which should operate to give equal freedom of choice to men and women. Women play not only a supplementary role but their role in economic development is vital, positive and essential.

Development will set momentum when all are part of it, when it is generated by all the segments, when all contribute their potential best and when all share its benefits optimally. Development will be promoted with the integration of women, and will be constrained with the neglect of women. Development requires the effective participation of all, tribal, non-tribal, men and women. Effective participation will be possible only with increasing awareness, promotion of efficiency and skill, last but not the least, by the change in attitude and outlook.

The need for school going age girls to assist in economic activities such as agriculture and cattle grazing, household chores and child care prevent them form utilizing educational facilities. Incentives offered have been inadequate to meet the cost of education of girls of disadvantaged families. Families give priority to the education of boys as social norms tend to ascribe an exclusively domestic role for girls with their future circumscribed by early marriage and child-bearing and rearing.

Education is one of the most crucial factors that allow women to compete as equals in the professional world and to earn an income of their own. A certain amount of fund should be earmarked for women's education in every state budget and proper utilization of this fund should be done effectively.

In this regard, educated girls have an important role to play in terms of creating motivation for girls' education in the community by dispelling the fears that educated girls marry outside. To cope with the present situation boys also must go ahead in the line of education and consequently the community's awareness about girls' education and attitude towards culture-specific roles of girls will change. From the above study it can be said that the participation of female labour in Arunachal economy is quite high and they are mainly employed in the primary sector of the economy. However, as economic development takes place and female literacy rate increases, the female workers withdraw themselves from the primary sector because of their newly earned status through literacy. As a result, there is a drastic fall in the work participation rate of females in all the districts of Arunachal Pradesh in 1991. Thus, the "U" shaped pattern as proposed by the various social scientists in relation to economic development and work participation of females has been portrayed beautifully in Arunachal Pradesh. The overall effect of literacy in work participation of females is also found to be negative. As the literacy rate increases, the female workers withdraw themselves from the primary sector. But they are not getting suitable employment opportunities in the secondary and the tertiary sectors, except for the government jobs, particularly in urban areas. However, the job absorption capacity in the Government services is also limited.

Suggestions

- Women should play first a vital role in decision making with their male counterparts in their homes,
- Contemporary women should assert themselves as decision-maker in all state bodies, church, socio-cultural institutions, NGOs and organized bodies,
- The educational system has to play an important role in this direction, as it is the only medium through which the image of a girl-child as second class citizen can be removed. Mass media too has a very important role to play for bringing out a total revolution in social attitudes and public opinion. The existing institutions should be de-institutionalized and they should be reconstituted on the basis of gender equality. Female editors should replace male editors on their own rights,
- With development and change in the world on all fronts, like the economy, culture, politics, trade, industry, calls for education for women are heard everywhere. To cope up with the global change, tribal women require infrastructural facilities, mobility, new mechanized training, and socio-economic contact etc. For that they require support of the financial institutions, government, NGOs, proper qualitative educational facilities and training etc., and
- The government should encourage entrepreneurs, specially the local people, and provide training facilities to produce more skilled men and women. Efforts should be made by the government for improving the techniques of production. Design is very important in the handloom industry. A research design centre should be established in the state for revival and revitalization of local arts and crafts and to conduct research on scientific line with an aim to preserve the local arts and crafts without losing their originality.

Acknowledgements

This paper is a part of a UGC sponsored minor research project completed in 2007. The author is grateful to the UGC.

REFERENCES

Alam. K. (1987) "The Changing Role of Women in the Rural Economy of Assam", Conference Volume of the Indian Economic Association. Seventieth Annual Conference, Jaipur.

Anker, Richard. (1981), "Demographic change and the Role of Women" in Richard, Anker (ed): *Role of Women in Developing Countries,* I.L.O. Publications, Geneva, p. 27.

Behera. M.C. and Roy. N.C. (1997), (eds) *Trends in Agrarian Structure in the Hills of North-east India.* Commonwealth Publications New Delhi.

Bhorali.D. (1998), (eds) *Economic Development of the North-Eastern Region,* Spectrum Publications , Guwahati.

Bhuyan, B.C. (1993), (ed), *The Tribal women,* Omsons Publications, New Delhi.

Bora, M.M. and Bhattacharya, A. (1996), "Raising the status of Plain Tribes Women through Income Generating Training" in Medhi, K. (ed): *Status of Women and Social Change,* Women's Studies Research Centre, Gauhati University, Guwahati, pp. 102–03.

Bora. D.K., Duarah. D.K. and Paul. B. (1997), *Impact of Urbanization in Arunachal Pradesh,* Director of Research, Government of Arunachal Pradesh, Itanagar.

Bose. M.L. (1997), *History of Arunachal Pradesh,* Concept Publishing Company, New Delhi.

Boserup, Ester (1970), *Women's Role in Economic Development,* George Allen and Unwin, p.71.

Chetana, K. (1986), *Social and Economic Dimensions of Women's Development,* Discovery Publishing House, New Delhi, pp. 6–9.

Chowdhury, J.N. (1982), *Arunachal Panorama,* Directorate of Research, Arunachal Pradesh, Shillong.

Das. G. (1995) *History of Arunahcal Pradesh in Transition,* Vikas Publishing House Pvt. Ltd., New Delhi.

Das Lipi, *et al.* (2006), "Decent work and Empowerment of Women in Agriculture", *Kurukshetra,* Vol. 54, No. 7, May, pp. 21–22.

Duarah, D.K. (1998), *A Handbook of Arunachal Pradesh,* M/s Frontier Publisher and Distributor, Itanagar, p. 28.

Directorate of Information and Public Relations (1968), *NEFA: The Land and the People,* NEFA Administration, Shillong, p.14.

Dutta. S. (1997), (ed) *Studies in the History, Economy and Culture of Arunachal Pradesh,* Himalayan Publications, Itanagar.

Dutta, C, S. (1994): *Arunachal Pradesh District Gazetteers, East Siang and West Siang Districts,* Government of Arunachal Pradesh.

Gulati Leela (1975), "Female work participation, A study of inter-state differences," *Economic and Political Weekly,* January.

Jagdish. P. (1987), "Women in the Labour Force : A Case Study of Bihar", Conference Volume of the Indian Economic Association, Seventieth Annual Conference, Jaipur.

Goswami, A.K. (October 1996), "Women in the vision of Kalidasa" in Medhi, K. (ed), *Status of Women and Social Change,* Women's Studies Research Centre, Gauhati University, Guwahati, pp. 54–55.

Mandal, R.K. (2005), *Arunachal Economy: Socio-Economic Transformation,* Champion Publisher and Distributor, Itanagar, p. 41.

——— (2005), "Literacy in Arunachal Pradesh: Trends, Features and Growth", an article submitted to Rajiv Gandhi University, Rono Hill, Itanagar.

Mibang, T. (1994), *Social Change in Arunachal Pradesh,* Omsons Publications, New Delhi.

Mishra. K. (1991), *Women in a Tribal Community : A case Study of Arunachal Pradesh,* Vikash Publishing House, New Delhi.

Nandal, Santosh (2005), "Political Empowerment of Indian Women at Local Level—Key of Social and Economic Development", *Journal of Global Economy,* Vol.I, No.4, Oct-Dec, Mumbai, pp. 243–246.

Motiram (2006), "Scheduled Castes' Education in India; Issues and Challenges", *University News,* March 27 April 02, Vol. 44, No. 13, pp. 1–5.

Pandey. B.B. (1993), *The Buguns : A Tribe in Transition,* Himalayan Publications, Itanagar.

Srivastava, L.R.N. (1962), *The Gallongs,* Directorate of Research, Govt. of Arunachal Pradesh, Itanagar, p.8.

Sundaram, I.S. (2006), "Women Empowerment: Basic Issues," *Southern Economist,* April 1 and 15, Vol. 44, No. 23 and 24, p.8.

Vashistha, K.C. and Malik, S. (2002), "Some strategic Efforts Towards the Empowerment of women", *University News,* February 4–10, Vol. 40, No. 5, p. 16.

Verma, B.M. (1981), *Rural Leadership in a Welfare Society,* Manthan Publication, New Delhi, p. 61

Wahan, P. and Venatadasappa, T. (1998), "Female Labour Force Participation in Karnataka", *Indian Journal of Labour Economics.*

16

BAMBOO FLOWERING AND IT'S IMPACT ON SOCIO-ECONOMIC LIFE OF TRIBAL PEOPLE IN MIZORAM

R.K.P.G. SINGHA; L.H. CHHUANAWMA and BHARTENDU SINGH

Introduction

India enjoys the largest bamboo resource in the world with 125 species, belonging to 23 genera which spread over an area of over 10 million hectares. In other words, it covers about 13 per cent of the total forest area of the country. In the North-east region of India, bamboo covers approximately 28 per cent of the forest area. Out of about 58 species available in the NE region, one specie, viz. *Melocanna baccifera*, also known as *Muli Bamboo* (locally known as *Mautak*), flowers once in about 48 years. The present flowering is due after 2004 in the NE region over an area of about 18,000 sq. km. The states identified were include Tripura, Manipur, and Meghalaya, Assam with Mizoram as epicenter.

Bamboo flowering or *Mautam* in local language, is a buzz word now-a-days in Mizoram. It is also a matter of great concern because it is related with socio-economic life of tribal people in this region. Bamboo flowering has great significance in socio-economic life of Mizo people due its bad impact on their life in the past. It is not the first time to witness the event of bamboo flowering in Mizoram. The impact on the tribal economy of bamboo flowering are a memorable events as it brought famine in the past. It is an established fact that the famine called *Mautam* ravages the Mizoram hills once every 40 to 50 years as the rats multiply by millions and devastate the standing crop, remaining nothing for the farmers. The last time which struck by *Mautam* in Mizo hills were in 1965–66. It is also an established part of the Mizo oral tradition that there is a relationship between bamboo flowering and famine due to increase in rat population. From time immemorial many beliefs are also associated with bamboo flowering. In general, bamboo flowering is considered as a bad omen (John and Nadgaura, 2002). Moreover not much work has been undertaken to unravel the mystery of the *Mautam* but Mizos know from their past experiences that if it comes, there will be a disastrous situation in the region. It is reported that bamboo flowering has already started and resulted in massive increase in rodent population and affected 42343 Mizo families and confronting hardship due to destruction of their crops by rodent, wild boars and birds because of the result of the bamboo flowering.

In this paper an attempt has been made to study the impact on the socio-economic life of Mizo people brought about by bamboo flowering. The paper also tried to highlight the preventive measure taken by the government to tackle the situation. The paper is mainly based on various government reports, daily news paper, journals and personal experiences from the fields of affected areas.

Review of the Literature

India has the largest bamboo resource in the world with 125 species of bamboo belonging to 23 genera and spread over an area of 10.03 million hectares or 12.8 per cent of the total forest area. In the North east alone, there are about 58 species covering 28 per cent of the forest area (Dhar, 2003).

According to Peter Foster (2004), *Mautam* (in Mizo term, *Mau* means bamboo and *Tam* means death) is the name given to the cyclic ecological phenomenon that occurs every 48 years, in the India's North-eastern state of Mizoram, which covers around thirty per cent of wild bamboo forests. During this period, *Melocanna baccifera* (locally known as *Mautak*), a species of bamboo in the state flowers, which is invariably followed by a subsequent plague of bandicoot rats whose actions cause devastating famine.

In NE India and Bangladesh *Melocanna baccifera* (*M. baccifera)* and *Bambusa tulda* (*B. tulda)* both have life cycles of 48 years. These two species do not flower together at the same time: *B. tulda* flowers 18 years after *M. baccifera*. The famines caused by the flowering of *M. baccifera* are known as the *"Mautam"* famines. These occurred in Mizoram in 1815, 1863, 1911 and 1959. The flowering of *Bambusa tulda* causes the "Thingtam" famine, and these occurred in 1785, 1833, 1881, 1929 and 1977. *Mautam* famines are more severe because the fruits of *M. baccifera* are much larger and can support larger populations of rats." *Melocanna Baccifera,* locally known as '*Mautak*', comprises over 90 per cent of the bamboo population in Mizoram (Maraland_net, 2006).

According to K. Sangthuama, the FCS and CA Minister, "We are not going to prevent bamboo from flowering nor are we trying to prevent the resultant rodent proliferation, we can't because it is natural. But we are trying to make sure that we have enough stock of rice for the *Mautam* period. As the state's allotment of rice does not meet our demand, we are asking for funds under Bamboo Flowering and Famine Combat Scheme (BAFFACOS) for procurement of additional 30,000 quintals of rice per month for three months. The procurement will be made through the Open Market Sales Scheme and Rs. 8.55 crore will be required".

The State Government is trying to combat the situation. According to the staff reporter of *Newslink,* under the Bamboo Flowering and Famine Combat Scheme (BAFFACOS), the department had spent Rs. 90 lakhs for the repair of 59 godowns in remote parts of the state during 2004–05. In the following financial year 2005–06, the department spent another Rs. 228 lakh of BAFFACOS funds for repairing 40 godowns, 39 staff quarters and godown approach roads. Now that godowns have been repaired, may be to withstand possible rodent attack, the department had earmarked Rs. 180 lakhs for 20,000 quintals of rice in addition to the normal state quota for the current financial year

In past, the famine (*Mautam*) has changed the social and political scenario of the state. Nearly 50 years ago, the Assam Government did not take any serious action when the famine came in Mizo hills (when Mizoram was a part of Assam), thousands of angry Mizos took up weapons to fight what they felt was an indifferent Government. But now Mizoram is a state by itself, no longer part of Assam and the Mizo National Front (MNF) was born of the *Mautam*—is in power. Chief Minister Zoramthanga confirmed the Government was happy to pay an Indian rupee to everyone who kills a rat and collects its tail (Bhaumik, 2002).

According to James Lalsiamliana, assistant plant protection officer in the state agriculture department, "Dulte and surrounding villages in Champhai district had been hit hard by a sudden spurt in the rat population. Bhupui or late harvest paddy is being attacked by rats in many places in Champhai district along the Mizoram-Myanmar border including North Eastern parts of the state bordering Manipur." Thentlang villagers in Serchhip district also reported that many *jhum* fields were pillaged by the rodents.

Government's Initiative

Bamboo flowering in Mizoram is a natural phenomenon and it occurs from time to time generally after every interval of 40–50 years which is already stated above. Bamboo flowering as such cannot be stopped in any way but the consequences of such flowering is a matter of great concern and brings famine due to large scale growth of rodent population which devastate the paddy crop which has witnessed in the past in this region. It is very interesting to note that about 40 years ago Mizoram's current Chief Minister Zoramthanga joined the Mizo National Famine Front to conduct relief for his hungry tribesmen during the Mautam. When his leader Laldenga dropped the word Famine from the title and the Mizo National Front went underground to fight India, Mr. Zoramthanga followed him to the jungles. Mr. Laldenga signed an accord with Delhi in 1986 and returned to normal life but Mr. Zoramthanga followed him on the road to power. Mr. Laldenga is no more now and Mr. Zoramthanga is the Chief Minister of Mizoram. At present also bamboo flowering has been started since 2004 and there is a fear that food shortage may occur if proper measure is not taken by the present Government well in time as the rodent population already started to damage the standing crop and Mizoram is not sufficient in rice production. Mizoram has to import rice and other essential commodities from outside state. It is worth mentioning that Mizoram is an undeveloped state comparing to other states of our country. There is no any big industry and only small scale industries are found. Many of these industries are sick units due to various known and unknown reasons. So, there is no any alternative source of income due to backwardness of this region.

Moreover, there is no any flat land and being a hilly state, agriculture is the main occupation of the state. *Jhum* or shifting cultivation has been practicing in Mizoram since time immemorial. A large population depend on jhum cultivation and it is not self-sufficient to feed the entire population and the state has to import from outside. Because of this on going situation due to bamboo flowering and many types of crisis may occur such as political, social, economic, law and order problem and so and so forth.

From various sources it is learnt that as bamboo flowering started in various places of Mizoram and there has been massive increase in rodent population and caused destruction of crops. It has affected 42342 Mizo families. Chief Minister, Zoramthanga stated in Assembly that above stated families have started facing hardship due to destruction of their crops by rodents, wild boars and birds, which multiplied because of the bamboo flowering. The Mizoram Government has sanctioned funds to help these families under Food for work programme. In a study it is found that by the month of February and March 2006, a gregarious flowering is observed in the following places:

Table 16.1: Places affected by Bamboo flowering in Mizoram

SL. No.	*Name of Places*	*District Name*
1.	Khawhai to Saitual	Champhai
2.	Baktawng to Chhingchhip	Serchhip
3.	Bilkhawthlir	Kolasib
4.	Paikhai	Aizawl
5.	Eastern part of Kolasib	Kolasib
6.	Dawn to Haulawng	Lunglei
7.	Sekhan to Bukpui	Kolasib

Source: James Lalsiamliana, 2006.

The Initiative taken by the Government may be Discussed in Little Detail as hereunder

The birth of BAFFACOS

The first concrete step taken by the Mizo National Front government's response to the Mautam could be traced to a meeting called the 'State's preparation for impending gregarious bamboo flowering—2006 and 2007 in Mizoram' held at the chamber of the Chief Minister Mr. Zoramthanga at Aizawl on August 13, 2004 under the chairmanship of the Chief Minister. The main agenda of the meeting was: 'to chalk out suitable and comprehensive plan and strategy for the possible catastrophic events'. The meeting was attended by Ministers, Chief Secretary, Commissioners and Secretaries and Heads of Departments. Some of the notable decisions made in this meeting were:

Formulation of a scheme called Bamboo Flowering and Famine Combat Scheme (BAFFACOS) to tackle the Mautam menace. This was the most important decision taken in this meeting. For, it was through this Scheme that almost all, but not all, the schemes and projects that the State Government devised to deal with the *Mautam* menace are to be implemented. To tackle the Mautam, a plan known as Comprehensive State Action Plan covering five years (2004–05 to 2008–09) would be drawn up by various departments of the State Government. This Plan would be submitted to the Union Government for getting funds.

BAFFACOS Action Plan

The Working Croup has prepared a Comprehensive Action Plan on BAFFACOS for a period of five years (2004–2009) with a total proposed outlay of Rs. 566.55 crore. The Comprehensive Action Plan of BUFFACOS was submitted to the Planning Commission of India in October 2004 for approval and sanction of the fund.

Initially (2004–05), thirteen departments of the State Government were covered under BAFFACOS. Two more departments were covered in 2005–06, taking the total to 15; but in 2006–07 there were only eleven departments and in 2007–08 just four departments besides the Rural Development Department (the nodal department) were left under the scheme.

In 2004–05, the thirteen Departments were: Health and Family Welfare, Rural Development, Revenue, Food and Civil Supplies, Agriculture, Horticulture, Animal Husbandry and Veterinary, Sericulture, Industries, Fisheries, Soil and Water Conservation, Information and Public Relations, Environment and Forest. Two more departments—Public Works and Local Administration were added in 2005–06, taking the total to 15. Four departments such as LAD, PWD, LR & S, Fisheries, and S & WC were excluded in 2006–07. In 2007–08, only four departments, viz. Horticulture, E & F, PWD and RD continue to be implement schemes and projects of the BAFFACOS.

Salient Features of BAFFACOS

BAFFACOS aims at meeting challenges posed by the dreaded *Mautam*. The state is meant both "to prevent and combat the *Mautam* phenomenon". The salient features of this scheme are as follows:

(a) Survey of Bamboo flowering areas,
(b) Survey of rodent incidences and their population,
(c) Publicity, awareness campaign and training,
(d) Eradication by local rat-traps,
(e) Purchase of rodenticides and free distribution to needy families,
(f) To offer facilities to *Jhum* farmers to shift to other occupations like, life-stock rearing, Horticulture, Fisheries, Cottage Industries, Sericulture, etc.,
(g) Bamboo extraction and enumeration, rodent control, regeneration of flowered areas through Farm control and Departmental Bamboo Plantation and Research aspects, development, etc. from the Environment and Forest Department,
(h) Land reforms,
(i) Construction of link roads,
(j) Animal diseases combat,
(k) Generating awareness regarding rodent-borne human diseases and treatment,
(l) To sensitize all concerned regarding socio- economic impact of epidemic prone, rodent-borne diseases,
(m) Documenting health related events to be utilized in effective planning for Bamboo flowering in future, and
(n) Conducting surveillance on rodents, insects, dogs and human beings.

Funds

A whopping Rs. 1,8085.20 lakhs or Rs.180.85 crores have been allotted between 2001–03 and 2007–08 for combating the Mautam. While a major chunk of funds (Rs. 12500.00 lakhs or 55.31 %) is being used/allotted for implementing various projects and schemes under the BAFFACOS, a smaller amount of money (Rs. 5585.20 lakhs or 44.68 %) is being used/allotted outside of the specific scheme of the BAFFACOS during the same period. The state has not generated any resource for funding schemes intended to tackle the Mautam. Some of the funds come directly to the state from the Twelfth Finance Commission, some by way of one time Additional Central Assistance, Normal Central Assistance, the Department of Development of the North-eastern Region (DONER), etc.

Table 16.2: Funds utilized/allotted to combat the Mautam (2001–2008)

Years	*Rupees in lakhs*	*Sources of funds*	*Remarks*
2001–2003	20.28	ACA	already spent
2003–2004	3104.32	DONER	already spent
2004–2005	2000.00	ACA	already spent
2005–2006	4300.00	ACA/TFC/MEF	already spent
2006–2007	4032.00	ACA/TFC/MEF	already spent
2007–2008	4628.60	NCA/TFC/MEF/MOA	on-going
Total amount:	**1, 8085.20 lakhs or 180.85 crores**		

ACA=One time Additional Central Assistance, DONER=Department of Development of North-Eastern Region, TFC=Twelfth Finance Commission, MEF=Ministry of Environment and Forest (Government of India), NCA=Normal Central Assistance, MOA=Ministry of Agriculture (GOI)
Source: Compiled from various Government reports.

Implementation of BAFFACOS

The various schemes implemented by the Government to fight against the *Mautam* can be divided into two categories—those under the umbrella of BAFFACOS and those outside the BAFFACOS ('non-BAFFACOS schemes'). So far, Rs. 9000.00 lakhs (66.88 % of the total expenditure) was spent on the BAFFACOS while Rs. 4456.60 lakhs (33.12 % of the total expenditure) was spent on 'non-BAFFACOS' projects. This means that a total of Rs. 13456.60 lakhs have already been spent on various schemes (both BAFFACOS and non-BAFFACOS) to fight the *Mautam.* As of June 2007, a staggering Rs. 6000.00 lakhs has already spent before the money has actually been received from the Central Government. The State Government, therefore, had to pool its scarce resources from elsewhere in order to implement the BAFFACOS schemes.

It must be noted here that as far as implementation of schemes devised to tackle the *Mautam* is concerned, our focus is on the BAFFACOS. However, implementation of the non-BAFFACOS schemes may also be stated in a few words.

The Environment and Forest Department was the first department in the state that took steps well in advance to combat the impending *Mautam.* During 2001–2003 the E&FD of the State Government spent Rs. 20.28 lakhs on plantation of bamboos. During 2005–05 and 2007–08, under a Centrally Sponsored Scheme for "Management of Gregarious Flowering of *Muli* Bamboos in the North-East" (launched in the eight North East states), the Department of E&F has also been implementing schemes such as plantation of bamboos, construction of link roads, making of ropeways, etc. For these CSS, the department spent Rs. 1596.35 lakhs. Rs.865.45 lakhs the department receives in 2007–08 from the Union Ministry of Agriculture under the National Bamboo Mission is being utilized for bamboo plantation and related works. Rs. 3104.32 received from the DONER during 2003–2007 was used by the state Public Works Department for construction of bamboo link roads.

BAFFACOS was launched in the financial year of 2004–05 in the state with much fanfare and publicity. The Scheme is to last for five years till 2008–09.

Achievement reports of the Health and Family Welfare Department in implementation of BAFFACOS during 2004–05

1. For strengthening laboratory, and for prevention, field and laboratory diagnosis and treatment of rodents borne diseases the followings has been purchased:

    (a) Medicines worth Rs. 15,42,796,
    (b) Laboratory reagents worth Rs. 2,57,110, and

(c) Equipments like B.P. instruments, Stethoscope, Thermometer, Hot air oven, Bio-safety cabinet, Video camera, Still camera, Computer P4 with printer, Laptop computer, Photocopier, Refrigerator, Trinocular microscope with Fluorescent attachment, Centrifuge, Weighing balance, Water Distillation Plant, Autoclave, Bacteriological Incubator, Rodent Trap, Emergency lamp, Malathione (Insecticides) and Tissue culture anti-rabies vaccine worth Rs. 22,53,176.

2. For the establishment of State and District BAFFACOS Cell and for operational costs the following has been purchased;

   (a) Office furniture worth Rs. 3,83,906, and
   (b) Stationery items worth Rs. 6,44,800.

3. Public awareness so as to prevent from rodent borne diseases has been made through documentary film, hoarding, leaflets, poster, electronic media, newspaper, magazine, NGOs, community leaders and workshop. Rs. 23,50,000 has been expended for these purposes.
4. For overall supervision, monitoring of project implementation and for fieldwork, rodent and carnivore surveillance etc. two vehicles have been hired. For this purpose Rs. 4,20,000 has been expended.
5. Border area survey has been undertaken and the expenditure for this purpose is Rs. 3,00,000.
6. In the prevention, diagnosis, management and control of rodent borne diseases training of core team and various health staff has been given and Rs. 10,00,000 is expended.
7. Field studies have been undertaken to areas of recent plague outbreak at Surat, Himachal Pradesh and Uttarakhand. Rs. 3,19,530 has been expended.
8. POL for hired vehicles worth Rs. 2,99,154 have been purchased.
9. Other operational costs—Rs. 1,36,990.
10. Officers' Training TE—Rs. 79,734.

Total expenditure so far spent comes to Rs. 99,87,196.00. But it is not yet over, it will continue for few years more and the Government will require more money to tackle the situation in an effective manner in near future also.

As already stated above, initially (2004–05), thirteen departments of the State Government were covered under BAFFACOS. Two more departments were covered in 2005–06, taking the total to 15; but in 2006–07 there were only eleven departments and in 2007–08 just four departments besides the Rural Development Department (the nodal department) were left under the scheme. In allocation of funds, emphasis was given to departments considered more ideally suited to deal with the rural poor and farmers most likely to be affected by the *Mautam.* Those departments are: Horticulture, Agriculture, Animal Husbandry, Environment and Forests, Industries, Public Works Department, Food and Civil Supplies.

Assessment

It is true that it is somewhat too early to assess the impact of the various BAFFACOS schemes being implemented on the lives of the people (especially of the poor) and the economy of the state because the scheme is not yet wound up. And a proper assessment of a subject must precede an in-depth study of the subject in question, but this is not done in this case. This being said, from whatever limited data and materials available at hand, a humble attempt is made here to assess the BAFFACOS.

A small section of the people including the rural poor certainly has benefited from implementation of the BAFFACOS, and certainly lots of money came into Mizoram through the schemes. However, considering the sheer amount of money involved in the scheme, and the noble intention of the scheme—that is to ameliorate sufferings of the people due to the *Mautam* and to improve economic conditions of the rural poor, one is tempted to have a critical look at the whole issue of the state's response to the *Mautam* with reference to the BAFFACOS.

After three years of implementation of the scheme, since 2004–05, there is no visible positive impact on the lives of people affected or likely to be affected by the *Mautam.* Mr. A. Raja, the Union

Minister of Environment and Forests, Government of India, in his letter dated March 14, 2006 addressed to the Chief Minister of Mizoram observed that "Although a number of early initiatives were taken by the State of Mizoram, but results are not clearly visible".

There are several reasons for this, such as:

The State Government seemed to have started the scheme too late. When it realized the impending calamity, there was a mad rush to prepare plans to combat the coming famine. The entire State Comprehensive Action Plan for BAFFACOS at an estimated cost of Rs. 566.55 covering five years (2004–05 to 2008–09) was completed within about just two months, between second half of August 2004 and October 2004. In fact, various departments were directed to complete their respective Action Plans within one month (August 14, 2004–September 15, 2004, exactly 32 days). Much of the Plans had to be made per force from the comforts of the office without taking into consideration ground realities.

And since all the schemes have been executed by the State Government departments, there is simply no scope for participation of the rural poor or for enhancing his purchasing power that is needed perhaps more than anything else.

There seems to be a lack of good intent as well. In 2004–05, the Revenue Department 'carried out' land reforms. It spent Rs. 150.00 lakhs surveying 120 villages. But no surplus land was found, no land ceiling fixed, no tenancy rights were talked about. The most it did was issuing periodic *'patta'* or ownership to a farmer that was available even before. The only difference was that this time farmers were grouped to cultivate similar crops (perhaps to suit the interests of big companies that have been signed up to buy produce in large quantities from such farm lands).

It is not that the ruling class in the state is unaware of the gravity of the problem and the danger that the *Mautam* could bring in. For the Chief Minister Mr. Zoramthanga said as much in his letter dated August 11, 2006 to the Union Minister of Rural Development: "The last *Mautam* occurred during 1958–60, the results of which were disastrously many. Most notable of all was the formation of an NGO called the Mizoram Famine Front to combat the scourge of the famine and to provide succors to the famine stricken people on the State *(sic).* Ultimately the efforts of the front took a political turn leading to the birth of a political party called the Mizoram *(sic)* National Front (MNF) (and the rest is history) which is currently in power". That a young and fresh graduate in English Literature (Honours course) from college Zoramthanga was driven, as it were, by the *Mautam* into the jungle in 1966 to spend another twenty long years carrying guns is today at the helms in Mizoram seemingly oblivious of the dangerous terrains Mizoram is yet heading into is an irony, to say the least.

Present Scenario

At this juncture various reports are coming from various corners relating to bamboo flowering in Mizoram and have resulted in the increase of rodent population. At the same time in many districts large scale damages of crops are also seen. It has estimate that 15453 hectare of cropped land has already been affected. It is also estimated that massive rat population would affect 80 per cent of the crop next year. The expected yield for the rice crop in 2006 was 26279 tonnes, but the actual yield was only 13658 tonnes. The loss of crops in various districts estimated between 40 per cent and 80 per cent. Among the various districts it is found that Kolasib is the worst affected and crop loss is estimated over 80.17 per cent which is quite high in this district.

The State Government demanded financial aid of Rs.35.62 crore to implement food for—work programme for the affected farmers in the state. At present there are 205528 families that hold food ration cards in the state. It is reported that the State Government has spent more than Rs. 62 crore of the Rs. 67.7 crore relief fund provided by the centre in 2006. The Government also demanded to the centre to release Rs. 69.7 crore set apart for the state this year, and another Rs. 38.2 crore to help the affected farmers. It is also stated that the rodents which feed on the flowers have destroyed half the rice crop this year. Crops like maize, brinjals, bananas and passion fruits have been widely damaged apart from rice crop which matter of great concern.

Conclusion

It can be concluded that bamboo flowering has a significant impact on the socio-economic-political life of tribal people of Mizoram. It was witnessed in the past and the consequences of such event created social turmoil in Mizoram particularly though bamboo flowering also occurs in other parts of North-eastern states but the impact is not as devastating as it happened in Mizoram. There has been very limited work in this field to assess the various aspects related to bamboo flowering and also to know the actual impact of bamboo flowering on the tribal economy of Mizoram. It is right time on the part of researchers, individuals, government as well as social organizations of international, national and regional level to study the menace of bamboo flowering and its consequences so that there should not be any further famine in this region. The occurrence of such event may be converted into overall economic benefit of the people of this region as bamboo is considered as the green gold which can be utilized in various industrial and other household purposes to benefit the affected farmers. The outcome of the work can be utilized to frame various policies by the government and public at large to tackle the ongoing situation. It should be converted so called bad omen to good omen and the people of this region should not fear about this, rather people should accept the reality of such situation in distant future to come.

REFERENCES

BBC (News) World Edition, 4 December, 2002.

Bhaumik, Subir (2002). Rat boom sparks India hunger alert, *BBC News,* December 4, 2002.

Deccan Herald, Sunday May 30, 2004.

Dhar, Aarti (2003). When flowering spells famine, *The Hindu,* October 26, 2003.

Foster, Peter (2004), "Bamboo threatens to bring Indian famine", news.telegraph.co.uk, Oct. 14, 2004.

Haukhum Hauzel, Principal Secretary to the Government of Mizoram: General guidelines in preparing Action Plans under BAFFACOS. No. G.12013/4/2004–SPB Government of Mizoram, Planning and Programme Implementation Department (State Planning Board), Aizawl, the 3rd September 2004.

Jhon, C.K. and Nadgauda, R.S., Bamboo flowering and Famine, *Current Science,* Vol.82. No.3, 10 February 2002.

Lalnunmawia, F., Disaster Management for the impending crisis due to gregarious flowering of bamboo in NE India, *Science Vision,* Vol. 5, No. 3, 2005.

Lalsiamliana, James, *Mautam—Present Scenario vis-à-vis Government Perspective,* Documentary paper of The Symposium on Bamboo flowering and its consequences, held on 3rd October, 2006 (World Habitat Day) held at Auditorium, Pachhunga University College, Aizawl, Mizoram.

Maraland_net, Mautam famine hits Eastern Mizoram, maraland.net, November 3, 2006.

Minutes of the meeting of Working Group on Bamboo Flowering and Famine Combat Scheme under the chairmanship of Chief Secretary, Government of Mizoram, Aizawl, on September 2, 2007.

Planning and Programme Implementation Department, Government of Mizoram: Achievement Reports on Bamboo Flowering and Famine Combat Scheme (BAFFACOS) during 2004–05 and 2005–06.

Staff Reporter, *Newslink,* "No more starvation in Mautam famine", February 28, 2007.

Various issues of News Magazine, *the North-east Sun.*

Various issues of the *Mizoram Post,* the Daily local News Paper.

Various issues of the News Magazine, the *North-east Window.*

Various issues of the *Times of India,* News paper.

Wikipedia, the encyclopedia.

17

TRANSITION OF AGRICULTURE IN THE HILL VILLAGES OF NORTH-EAST INDIA
A Micro Study

KOMOL SINGHA and SAJU MATHEW

I

India may be aspiring to industrial self-sufficiency. Even if world trading arrangements could be so designed as to promote the industrial exports of the less-developed countries, the ability of a country to industrialize is dependent in the first place on the production of a surplus from agriculture to feed an increasing proportion of non-agricultural workers and to purchase imports which are urgently needed. There is no evidence that a country can accelerate its rate of economic growth from non-agricultural activity when it is overshadowed by a large agricultural sector which is pre-occupied with self-subsistence production (Haswell, 1967:1). Agriculture continues to be the main stay of the tribal hill villages of North-east India. However, despite the obvious favourable agro-climatic conditions, various factors, some of which are unique to the region have been responsible for the arrested development and lack of agricultural growth of a sustained and widespread kind. Over and above the usual marketing and credit problems and lack of working capital, there is very little diversification in occupations and very few inputs are made to increase the productivity of land. The economy is of a subsistence kind and cultivation in these tribal villages is mainly for self-consumption. The development of an agrarian economy is possible only when diversification of crops and technology is adopted according to time and situation (Singh 2007), and '*Farm-to-Market*'

(The World Bank in India, November 2006: 3) links are created. The '*Buraku*' community in a pine-covered hill village 'Nike' in Japan (Beardsley, *et al.* 1959: 3) is founded on the requirements of intensive agricultural technology and agrarian economy, which were dominant through centuries of Japanese history. For Radwan and Lee (1986:2), *Horizontal and Vertical Expansion* of agriculture could develop Egyptian villages. According to the recent district-wise data compiled by Indicus Analytics, farm output in Nagaland's eight districts out of eleven has grown at double-digit rates over 2000–05 whereas the all India average was only 2.6. This is primarily due to a shift in crop patterns (*Yojana,* December 2007). For example, total transformation of the people's economy was seen in Latin America due to the introduction of sugar cane by leaving aside rice and maize cultivation (Gudeman, 1978).

The objective of this paper is two fold. In the first place, this paper tries to highlight some of the glaring issues in initializing agricultural growth and some unique challenges in creating marketable surplus. Secondly, the paper is a modest attempt at finding some possible solutions to these challenges. This paper is primarily centred on the results of a primary field survey of 202 sample households out of 432 households in Maram Khullen (Table 17.1), a typical hill tribal village in Manipur carried out in October 2006. The survey was conducted through a structured questionnaire scheduled to obtain the data required for the purpose of the study. In preparing this paper, the study goes little beyond the quantitative analysis of the field survey results. It covers wide range of other primary and secondary data to analyse the dynamics of agrarian change in the village over the last few years. Personal interviews with the villagers were also taken as one of the main methodologies of the study.

After a brief introduction and statement of objectives of the study in the present chapter (Part I), the Part II gives a brief analysis of the agrarian system of the village and the potentials of the agriculture in this village. Part III deals with the arguments of the data collected and the observations made. This chapter further discusses the problems faced by the village and the possibilities in creating marketable surplus. And finally, Part IV tries to give some ways and means to overcome the difficulties in creating marketable surplus in the hill villages.

Table 17.1: Main Occupational Structure in Maram Khullen

Main Occupation	*Total population*	*Per cent*
Cultivation*	736	31
Salaried	141	6
Self-employed	64	2.7
Working in private firm	95	4
Student	976	41
Jobless	364	15.3
Total	**2376**	**100**

* Out of 432 households in the village, 428 are engaged in agriculture (99.07 per cent).

Source: Survey.

II

The Marams, particularly of Maram Khullen are no longer nomads; hunting for food and shifting cultivation have been discarded long ago. They are now settled agriculturists. Agriculture is the main occupation and rice is the main crop of this village. 99.07 per cent households in the village are living on agriculture, but only 31 per cent of the population is engaged in it directly as primary occupation. At present, shifting cultivation (*Jhum*) is practically being disowned in this village and other hill areas also, particularly in Manipur. There are probably three factors for not practicing shifting cultivation in Maram Khullen. *First,* as population increases and because of the constant urbanization process, there is no virgin forest available for Jhum cultivation. *Second*, it is not only a primitive and labour intensive method, but also inconvenient for cash crop cultivation. *Third*, Maram Khullen has sufficient inherited land for settled cultivation (Table 17.2).

Table 17.2 : Secondary Occupational Structure in Maram Khullen

Secondary occupation of the family	*Total population*	*Per cent*
Cultivation	73	3.07
Weaving	385	16.21
Teaching	56	2.35
Business	9	0.37
Others (including jobless, students and children)	1838	77.42

Source: Survey.

In the case of land use system, this village is more or less same as other tribal villages in the state. Nevertheless, there are some unique features as regards to land use system of this village. Land ownership system of this village can be classified into four categories: (1) *Common village land.* (2) *Clan land.* (3) *Morung land*[1]. (4) *Individual land.* In this village, as in almost every other hill villages of the North-east, particularly in Manipur, there is no standard measure of land. People own inherited land which they cannot sell to other tribes or villages. The land has been individually appropriated in terms of *Alupak* in Maram Khullen. An *Alupak* is a plot of land in one particular area owned by a family. Regardless of the size of the land, it should be continuous and in a single stretch, not overlapping with an *Alupak* of some other family. Hence, an *Alupak* can be a small plot of land or it can also be a large plot of land. If a parent has two sons, the plot is to be divided equally into two smaller plots; each of the plots is also called an *Alupak.* Table 17.3 shows the size of agricultural land holdings in terms of *Alupak* in Maram Khullen.

Table 17.3: Size of Agricultural land holding in Maram Khullen (in terms of Alupak)

Size of land	*No. of household*	*Per cent (of the total no. of households)*
Landless family	13	3
1 only	90	21
2 only	188	43.5
3 only	111	25.6
4 only	30	7

Source: Survey.

1. The common village land includes those areas which are too far for cultivation—forest land, cattle grazing land, places for worship, play ground, public entertainment place, land reserved for public purposes etc. The village authority takes care of these lands and these are used for the welfare of the village. This common land/property is neither inheritable nor transferable nor can it be sold to other village or tribe. There is one provision for addition to village land, if there is any disputed land of an individual with other tribe or village which he cannot settle by himself, the land is normally handed to the village authority. The village authority fights for it and the land becomes village property.

2. The clan land belongs to a particular clan and is passed on from one generation to the next. It has got a very specific significance as the clan always extends a helping hand to the needy and provides a portion of it if one of its members is in desperate need of it. The clan also gives land to immigrants on the condition that the immigrant agrees to become one of them. The clan also generously helps divorced women or widows if they decide to live with them and remain faithful.

3. Morung land includes woodlands from where firewood is gathered for common use. During every alternate year, the land is utilized for certain vegetables either for commercial or for domestic use. It is not transferable to any of the members or to an outsider. Occasionally fire wood is cut for commercial purposes for Morung fund. At times, this land is cultivated by the members of the Morung for common purposes.

4. Individual land includes forestland, Jhum land (not in practice in the village now), wet-rice field, grazing ground and large grassland for hunting purposes. The land is well demarcated by stones, hill range, rivulets etc. This is normally inherited permanent property. All these lands are held individually and are inheritable as well as transferable to other members. No restriction is made, nor is any tax imposed on the community by the land owner for keeping animals on a particular land meant for grazing purposes. The forest and grass lands which are too far for cultivation or are yet to be cultivated are reserved for future cultivation. These can also be utilized for hunting or trapping animals. A portion of the meat (usually half of it) of any animal killed in these forests by traps is given to the land owner as tax. However, no tax is levied on animals killed individually with a spear or gun since the act signifies bravery on the part of the hunter.

In the study of village agriculture, soil type, ownership system and variability of rainfall influence the cropping pattern and agricultural practices. Two key features of agriculture in Maram Khullen are: the predominance of ***wet-rice cultivation*** and the practice of ***intercropping system***. They follow only wet-rice cultivation during monsoon, and vegetables and horticultural crops are cultivated mainly for self-consumption through intercropping system. In intercropping, several crops are grown together with a certain number of rows of one crop followed by a number of rows of the next crop and so on, in a definite ratio (Taylor and Adelman, 1996: 69).

Cropped area of this village can be divided broadly into *four* categories:

1. *Fertile and sedimentary soil on the bank of the Barak River*: It is about 10–12 km from the village and it is the farthest land for cultivation of Maram Khullen. This land serves as a rice bowl to the entire village. It is exclusively used for wet rice cultivation and almost all the people of this village live on this land.
2. *Terrace cultivation on the less steep hill slopes*: This land is also exclusively used for wet rice cultivation. This land is prepared in a step like manner so as to preserve runoff water from the upper hill slopes.
3. *Land on the very steep hill slopes*: This agricultural land is nearest to the village. It is basically used for intercropping purposes. This land is not used for rice cultivation because its steepness does not allow for preservation of runoff water/ rain water. Vegetables like potato, tomato, cabbage, beans, chili, maize, cucumber, coriander and squash are cultivated on this land and it is also mainly for self-consumption.
4. *The fertile soil on the hill plateau*: This land is used mainly for cash crops like potato, beans, ginger, etc. This land is owned by the clans in the village. Potato for commercial purposes is mainly produced from this land.

Rice has been grown by the cultivators of this village since time immemorial and it accounts for more than 80 per cent of the total cropped area. Seeding is done at the onset of pre-monsoon rain in the month of March. It is done in a separate higher area and not in the cultivable land. The area for seeding is dug by spade after which the soil is burnt with the help of fire-wood and dry leaves. After waiting for 2–3 days to let the fire die out completely, sowing of seeds is carried out. Transplantation starts in the month of June and is followed by weeding from around the last week of July till August. Harvesting season starts from the month of October and, sometimes from November depending on the weather condition.

The method of cultivation adopted is still very crude. The whole area for cultivation is dug by spade in the dry season before the arrival of rain. First round of ploughing takes place when monsoon starts with the help of buffaloes. Second and final round of ploughing is done after a week of first round ploughing and it is followed by transplantation. Weeding is done manually. Harvesting is done with the help of sickle. Threshing is done by cane/bamboo thresher in the field itself on account of the distance between the field and the village. After threshing, the straw is left in the field itself because there is not much use of it in the village.

In case of wet land/rain—fed rice cultivation on the hill slope terrace fields, only spade is used for cultivation. Since these plots are prepared in small-size step fashion on the hill slopes in order to preserve water catchments, it is not possible for the plough to move freely there. Likewise, other crops on the steep hill slopes are cultivated with the help of spade and dibbers only.

The economy of Maram Khullen is basically of a self-subsistence kind. Farmers cultivate mainly for self-consumption, and the surplus if there is any, is sold in the local market. In recent years, cash crop cultivation has commenced but it has not been on a large scale. Main cash crops in the village are potato, ginger, passion fruit etc. Potato for market purposes is cultivated in a particular place called *Ragong*[2] which is a clan land. This place is about 3–4 km from the village in the North-west direction and is very fertile and suitable for potato cultivation. Potato plantation starts in the month of February-March and harvested in the month of July-August. If it is for self-consumption, it is harvested in the month of September-October. However, if it is for commercial production, harvesting is done in the month of July-August when the water-content of the potato is very high which is actually profitable for the farmers. A potato farmer can earn approximately Rs. 40,000 annually on an average with the traditional method of cultivation at the existing rate of Rs. 6–8 per kg.

Ginger is also another important cash crop of Maram Khullen. It is planted in the month of April and harvested in the month of January. Ginger stems and leaves are widely used in Manipur and if the cultivation is for stem and leaves only, it is harvested in the month of December. They are sold either in the local market or in Imphal.

Ginger cultivation is also can be carried out on a large scale that they can supply to the bigger markets outside the state.

Other Kharif crops are sown one after another during June-July months and sowing continues till August. Squash (*Biscoti* in Maram) is abundantly available in Maram. It grows wildly without any maintenance. It grows on the roadside, in the barren land, in the bush, creeping practically everywhere in Maram Khullen. The market price of squash is Rs. 3–5 per kg. Similarly, pumpkin grows abundantly everywhere. It is mainly used as a fodder for pigs in the village.

Maize is also one of the most important crops in the hill villages of North-east and cultivation of maize does not require much maintenance and cost. Moreover, the soil of this region is very conducive for its cultivation. In Maram Khullen, every household cultivates it for self-consumption and no family cultivates it for selling in the market. Cabbage is another abundantly grown vegetable in this village. The type of cabbage found in this village and neighbouring villages is very different from the cabbage available elsewhere in the valley. It is of a bigger variety (tree type) and this too, the farmers cultivate mainly for self-consumption.

The Rabi crops like mustard, coriander, tomato, etc. are sown in the months of September and October in the steep hill slope areas. Most intercropping activities are done with these crops. Marketable surplus, if any, is generated from these crops (other than potato and passion fruit). Another peculiar crop in the village is the Tree Tomato[3], which is a lesser known vegetable in the hill villages of the North-east. It is very popular and commonly used by the Marams. Locally known as *Athingti*, the fruit is used as a tomato substitute in various preparations. It grows abundantly in Maram Khullen. It bears fruit when it is about 1½ to 2 years old and continues to be productive for at least 7–8 years. The average yield of a tree is 10–15 kg. of fruit annually and it is harvested throughout the year.

Among the horticulture crops, passion fruit and guava are grown abundantly in Maram Khullen. Passion fruit is one of the crops which have immense export potential. Though it is native to Brazil, it is found in many parts of North-east India, particularly in the hill areas of Manipur, Nagaland and Mizoram. The ripe fruit can be eaten fresh or the juice, after its extraction is used for preparing squash. Its tender leaves are also used as vegetable by the Marams. In Maram Khullen, passion fruit is cultivated in the mid hills to high hills. It thrives best under cool and humid climate, free from extreme cold and heat (very suitable in Maram Khullen's climate). Passion fruit is very much suited to soils having high organic matter content and soils which are well-grained. It grows best in sandy loam to clayey loam soil. It is a very productive fruit and the total yield ranges from 10–12 tonnes per hectare annually. Harvesting period starts from the month of May and continues till December. It is sold in the local market as fresh fruit or is sent to the Exotic Juice Ltd. at Mao Gate, a border town of Manipur, where the processing is done. After processing, it is sent for packaging to Bangalore for the drink brand 'Passip'. Cultivation of this fruit is taken up on a large scale by the NGO, called International Fund for Agricultural Development (IFAD). Maram has sufficient clan land and other areas which are not properly utilized for cultivation. IFAD gives loans to the co-operative farmers for cultivation of passion fruit and after harvesting the fruit is again taken back by the former for processing at Exotic Juice Ltd. It is a type of *Contract Farming*[4] we come across in other parts of the country.

III

Unlike in a nomadic life, development does not signify only sufficient food production and shelter. It must be beyond food, shelter and clothing. The problem with Maram Khullen, as in most other hill villages of the North-east is that despite the vast potential for good agricultural production, the village continues to be poor and there is a seeming contentment among the cultivators with whatever little they produce. It is a sort of Backward Sloping Supply Curve (Boeke, 1953). The motivation to produce more than the subsistence level is missing altogether. They do not consider agriculture as an avenue. This sector is highly neglected and undermined by the people in the villages. Almost all the families/households in the village (Maram Khullen) are engaged in agriculture (99.07%), but only 31 per cent of the population in the village engages directly in this sector as a primary occupation. Despite immense potentials in the village, this sector becomes a profession by chance, but still it is the last resort when they cannot find better avenues like, government jobs or any other easy money minting occupations.

An analysis of the data reveals some interesting facts:

- One important characteristic of the tribal people in the hill villages is that they are not very acquisitive in nature. The people are more guided by social standing and social values rather than narrow considerations of profit and loss or acquiring more assets. They have a laidback attitude which conditions them into feeling contented with the little they produce for self-consumption.
- There is no practice of double-cropping in Maram Khullen. As mentioned earlier, this is because of the lack of irrigation facilities and secondly, because of the superstition that double-cropping would bring bad luck to the village. Consumption of fertilizer in agriculture is very negligible or even zero.
- Market failure is one of the most important features in the hill tribal villages. Their agricultural produces are mainly used for self-consumption. If there is any surplus, it is sold at the village market, which has limited demand of the produces.
- Credit and physical infrastructural facility is very much limited. Farmers are unaware of the low interest credit facilities. And the agro-infrastructure is very limited in the hill villages.

As far as the tribal village market is concerned, it can be referred to as *place markets*, where buyers and sellers meet face to face. The term 'market' as in the modern market does not refer to a condition of mutual knowledge of buyers and sellers and the price situation (Ramamani, 1988: 165). Ultimately, it is only opportunities for assured and remunerative marketing that will determine the economic viability of farming, both as a way of life and as means of livelihood. The hill villages, because of their being land-locked regions, have little provision for marketing the surplus produce in bigger markets in the plains. This is rather unfortunate because there are many food crops that grow abundantly in Maram Khullen. For instance, crops like pumpkin, squash, guava etc. are found growing wildly almost everywhere. These are sold at a good price in the market. However, because of high transportation costs, there is little incentive to produce these crops solely for marketing purpose. Sometimes, the local traders do go to the markets in Imphal but these are few and far in between. The transport fare more than offsets the profit the traders would get. There are no purchasing agents or marketing societies to act as middlemen or intermediaries. Hence, most of the produce is sold to the people within the village itself. And because of market failure, there is no difference between the prices of the food crops in the local market and the bigger markets in the plains.

There are no institutionalized credit agencies to advance loans and other credit to the local cultivators and, even if there are, the villagers are mostly unaware of them. As part of the exercise to avail loans and credit to the cultivators in Maram Khullen, IFAD started some initiatives in 2004 but this somehow could never take off. Cultivators need appropriate institutional support to enhance their agricultural competitiveness. Institutional support to confer on small farm cultivators, the power and the economy of scale is vital to enhance the productivity and profitability of small farms.

The implements used in cultivation are mechanically very simple. They are mainly made from raw materials collected from the forest. Almost all the peasants use traditional tools like Wooden Plough, Sickle, Hoe, Thresher, Spade, Dao, Yoke, Dibber, Leveller, etc. All the implements except the Spade and Dao are locally available. The iron or steel-tipped instruments are purchased from the market.

Maram Khullen has sufficient agricultural produce to feed the population. The average land holding in the village is 0.4 per cent *Alupak* (Table 17.3). Only thirteen families in the village (*i.e.* 3%) are landless and thirty of them (7%) have 4 *Alupak* each. Average annual income of a family in the village is Rs. 42,970 which is quite low in an agrarian economy and the average family size in the village is 5.5. The per Capita Income (PCI at current price) is Rs. 7,812.80 only. But the food crops produced in the village are self-sufficient and there is no possibility of starvation or farmers' suicide as in other part of the country. So, some sort of non-monetised sector is involved in the village. But the development of an agrarian economy is impossible unless and until its produces are made marketable surplus. Development of an economy goes beyond sufficient food production. Cash crop cultivation is still not popular in the village because people here are not commercially oriented and they do not consider agriculture as an occupation of choice. This idea was also highlighted in the study of an agrarian village in Egypt by Petra Weyland (1993), in which many educated young people take up Government jobs which secure for them a minimum monetary income. Though 99.07 per cent of the households are engaged directly or indirectly in agriculture, only 3 per cent of the population in Maram Khullen considers agriculture as an occupation by choice or by compulsion (Table 17.1).

Here arises a question for us is, despite all these potentials for developing the agricultural sector, why cannot this village produce marketable surplus? The answer is very simple and the situation is more or less same in other hill villages of North East India as well. Market failure or market imperfection is one of the stumbling blocks in developing the agricultural sector in the hill villages. During the harvesting season, the vegetable/horticulture crops are hanging and creeping everywhere in the village. Nobody is there to buy it because everybody is having the same crops in their own garden. And on the other hand, the quantity is not big enough so that they can export them outside the village or the national market regularly. Secondly, even if the productivity of land is high, they cannot produce marketable surplus because of the low level of technology, infrastructure and the lack of credit facilities.

IV

In the preceding part we have discussed the opportunities of marketable surplus, which is the pre-condition for developing an agrarian economy. For harnessing the opportunities discussed above, we have identified *three* policies which suit the environment of hill economy particularly in Maram Khullen.

The first and foremost policy for materializing the opportunities available in Maram Khullen is ***Production by Masses*** (Swaminathan, 2006). It means cultivation of the productive crop which suits the soil of the region by many farmers at the same time. It helps in capturing market at the economies of scale. As the cultivators do not produce much more than the subsistence level, the total produce is meager and is unable to cater to the market demand. However, if all (or many) cultivators start producing the abundantly growing food crops at the same time in larger quantities, then a constant supply of the produce can be made which will ensure a good profit. Hence, priority should be given to the 'production by masses' category of farming. For this to become a reality, the involvement of the entire community is a must. Priority should be given to mitigation of the problems faced by the cultivators in marketing their small surplus produce. Marketing becomes economically viable only when a constant supply of the produce can be created. Hence, the *production by masses* type of farming assumes greater significance in these hill tribal villages. When the cultivators start producing a particular crop simultaneously, the advantage due to economies of scale can be realized. If everybody in the village (Maram Khullen) produces the productive crops like potato, passion fruit, squash etc. at the same time, they can create a bigger market supply. On the other hand, production by masses creates economies of scale due to the indivisibility of basic infrastructures or by curtailing transport cost (Table 17.4).

Table 17.4: Approx. cropped area of the village in Maram Khullen

(in per cent)

Food crop	Per cent	Cash crop	Per cent
Rice	50	Potato	10
Vegetables	20	Passion fruit	6
Other crops	9	Ginger	5

Source: Survey.

Secondly, ***Contract Farming***[5] is also equally important for the development of agriculture in the hill villages particularly in Maram Khullen. It signifies a firm or an investor taking the whole responsibilities of investment and marketing of the produce. This arrangement gives security to the poor farmers as regards crop failure, market failures etc. Since the cultivators, on their own do not produce surplus goods because of the inhibiting transportation and marketing costs, a pre-production arrangement for sale between the farmers and private firms, processing units, etc., can be made. This type of agribusiness model in the lines of 'contract farming' would be beneficial to the cultivators in the matter of access to adequate or timely credit, good quality inputs, new technology, employment generation, separation of production and marketing risks, better farm practices, etc. The essence of such an arrangement is the commitment of the cultivator to provide an agricultural commodity of a certain type, at a time and a price, and in the quantity required by a known and committed buyer. Here, the farmer would grow the contractor's crop on his land, harvest and deliver to the contractor a quantum of the produce, based upon anticipated yield and contracted acreage. This would be at a pre-agreed price and the contractor assumes all the risks of marketing the produce. But it needs sincerity on the part of farmers in supplying quality, quantity and timely delivery. Perhaps this may be the reason why the Passion fruit farm funded by IFAD is not improving in Maram Khullen (Table 17.5).

Table 17.5: Percentage of area under the cultivation of different crops

(in approx.)

Food Crops		Cash crops	
Rice	70	Potato	30
Maize	10	Passion fruit	10
Other Vegetables	10	Ginger	10
Others	10	Others (self-consumption)	50
Total	**100**	**Total**	**100**

Source: Survey.

If cultivators are sincere enough, this kind of arrangement is one of the best means to create marketable surplus particularly in Maram Khullen. Contract Farming System is successfully working in many parts of the country. By entering in to contract farming with '*Pepsico*' in Punjab, the average yield of the contract farmers is 25–50 per cent higher than the state average, while their per hectare income is reported to be 40 per cent higher than that of other farmers. Normally, poor farmers in the village do not accept any new policy or method easily because they do not want to take risk. So, the contract farming system takes care of the risk taking part of the poor farmers.

Thirdly, the ***expansion of technology*** (Beardsley, Hall and Ward, 1959; Radwan and Lee, 1986) is also one of the most essential components in developing the agricultural sector. It is nothing but a ***vertical expansion*** (*op. cit.*), which means increasing productivity of land under the cultivation through technical progress. It deals with the impact of technology and agro-infrastructure in developing agriculture. The superstitious belief of the tribal villagers as regards the practice of double-cropping should be removed by educating the villagers about its benefits. Also, methods of improving soil health through integrated nutrient supply by using fertilizers have to be encouraged. The quantum of agricultural output in the village (Maram Khullen) can be multiplied several timeby applying new improved seeds and other mechanical methods including double cropping system. The vast paddy field is free right after harvesting till the next monsoon arrives. Only one tractor is there in the village and it is absolutely free in the off season (during winter). So, there are number of ways to create marketable surplus from this sector in this village.

There is no dearth of credit advancing agencies for the cultivators but most of the villagers are not aware of them. The few who are aware and avail themselves of loans through these agencies have the tendency of misusing the credit or not repaying it in time. This discourages the financing institutions from providing necessary credit and other financial assistance to the cultivators. The villagers should be made aware of the various credit advancing agencies and the need for repaying the loans in time.

Without a positive economic environment, agricultural growth is impossible. The challenges found in the North-East are, in many ways different those prevalent in other parts of the country. The strategic models or Road Map towards developing the agricultural sector should be region-specific. Agriculture in the hill villages of North-East with its unique problems needs a comprehensive Road Map in order to tap its vast potential. The failure to chart out a North-East-specific agricultural policy has led to the arrested development of agriculture in the hill tribal villages of this region and the perpetuation of poverty in general.

NOTES

1. It means Bachelor's dormitory, built by any of the *well-to-do* family in the village, generally in a clan. It is a tradition for Maram Khullen that clan chief has to build a Morung and it is a pride for them. In the Morung, there is a fire place in the middle of the house squired by four logs of wood used as seats. There are two long beds on both sides of the fire place made of

single plank or wood. It can accommodate minimum of 13 to 16 persons and is always open for male members. Fire wood is provided by the Morung owner. But *now-a-days* it is used very occasionally during the feast in the village. 'Morung land' also signifies a land owned by members of a particular Morung of a clan. Here it is to be noted that a clan may have four or five Morungs depending on the number of people of a clan. Greater the number of people in the clan more is the number of Morungs.

2. It is the name of a plateau owned by clans used mainly for commercial potato cultivation.
3. It is of medium height (3–5.5 m), half-woody, fast growing and shallow rooted. The long-stalked pendant fruit is borne singly or in clusters of 3–12, is smooth, egg-shaped and pointed at both sides. Its botanical name is *Cyphomandra betacea sendt.*
4. For more detail idea, please refer to Sunil Phougat's article "Contract Farming", *Yojana,* September 2006, pp. 47-48.
5. For more detail idea, please refer to Sunil Phougat's article "Contract Farming", *Yojana,* September 2006, pp. 47-48.

REFERENCES

Edward, Taylor J. and Adelman Irma (1996): *Village Economies,* Cambridge University Press.

Gudeman, Stephen (2004): *The Demise of a Rural Economy: From Subsistence to Capitalism in a Latin American Village,* Routledge and Kegan Paul, London.

Haswell, M.R. (1967): *Economics of Development in Village India,* Rouledge and Kegan Paul.

Ramamani V.S. (1988): *Tribal Economy: Problems and Prospects,* Chugh Publication, Allahabad.

Radwan Samir and Lee Eddy (1986): *Agrarian Change in Egypt: An Anatomy of Rural Poverty,* Croom Helm, USA.

Singh, Priyoranjan Ch. (2007): "Development of Hill Tribal Villages in NE" a National Seminar paper presented in SJC, Kohima on 14–15 September.

Yojana, August and September 2006 issues; Ministry of Information and Broadcasting, Government of India, New Delhi.

INDEX